Lecture Notes
in Business Information Processing 265

More information about this series at http://www.springer.com/series/7911

Paloma Díaz · Narjès Bellamine Ben Saoud
Julie Dugdale · Chihab Hanachi (Eds.)

Information Systems for Crisis Response and Management in Mediterranean Countries

Third International Conference, ISCRAM-med 2016
Madrid, Spain, October 26–28, 2016
Proceedings

 Springer

Editors

Paloma Díaz
Universidad Carlos III de Madrid
Madrid
Spain

Narjès Bellamine Ben Saoud
ENSI
Maounba University
Tunis
Tunisia

Julie Dugdale
LIG
University of Grenoble
St Martin d'Heres
France

Chihab Hanachi
University of Toulouse Capitole
Toulouse
France

ISSN 1865-1348   ISSN 1865-1356   (electronic)
Lecture Notes in Business Information Processing
ISBN 978-3-319-47092-4   ISBN 978-3-319-47093-1   (eBook)
DOI 10.1007/978-3-319-47093-1

Library of Congress Control Number: 2016954266

This Springer imprint is published by Springer Nature
The registered company is Springer International Publishing AG
The registered company address is: Gewerbestrasse 11, 6330 Cham, Switzerland

Preface

Welcome to the proceedings of ISCRAM-MED 2016, which was held at Universidad Carlos III of Madrid. The conference chairs along with a huge group of devoted and hard-working colleagues, including the program chairs, the Steering Committee members, the Program Committee members, and of course the local organizers, put all their effort to make this third edition a successful event for ideas sharing and networking.

Information systems and technologies can play a key role in crisis management to support preparation, response, mitigation, and recovery processes. Many different technologies can be used to improve decision making and taking, from intelligent systems to social and ubiquitous computing, GIS, games and gamification, and virtual and augmented reality. However, solutions have to be envisaged as sociotechnical systems where the human capabilities, expectations, and goals, both individual and collective, have to be taken into account. Technology is not enough to guarantee a better management process and, therefore, the International Conference on Information Systems for Crisis Response and Management in Mediterranean Countries focuses not only on engineering technologies but also on their application and on the reflective practice from which we can learn how to successfully integrate these technologies in real crisis.

After two editions celebrated in Toulouse (France) in 2014 and Tunis (Tunisia) in 2015, the third event took place in Madrid during October 26–28, 2016, organized by the Interactive Systems Group –DEI Lab of Universidad Carlos III de Madrid (dei.inf. uc3m.es). This conference is an ISCRAM (iscram.org) event organized in Mediterranean countries, alternating between the north and the south of the Mediterranean Sea. In recent years, many crises have taken place around the Mediterranean Sea and there are some common threats in the area that are worth being analyzed in a global way at a Mediterranean level rather than as isolated phenomena. In addition, our shared roots and history as well as common geopolitical issues led to solidarity among people and cross-country interventions. In this context, the conference becomes the perfect forum to exchange and share information and knowledge about these crises, since it provides an opportunity to address and discuss new trends and challenges among academic researchers, practitioners, and policy makers.

In this edition, we received contributions from Algeria, Australia, Austria, Cyprus France, Germany, Greece, Ireland, Italy, Lebanon, Morocco, Poland, Spain, Sweden, Tunisia, and the UK. Thanks to our program chairs, Ignacio Aedo and Giuliana Vitiello, and the 37 members of the international Program Committee who took care of the peer-review process, we were able to collect three reviews for full papers and at least two for shorter contributions. At the end of this strict review process, 30 papers were accepted in different categories with an acceptance rate of 33.3 % for full papers. Accepted papers, short paper, posters, and demos cover a wide range of cases illustrating the use of technologies like visualization, gamification, sentiment analysis, mobile computing, crowdsourcing and collective computation, security, social networks, or simulation and modeling. These contributions deal with different aspects of crisis management, including sense making, decision taking, coordination, civic engagement and participation, preparation, and response. The variety of topics and perspectives made the conference program richer and more attractive not only for the academic researchers but also for practitioners.

We also had two outstanding invited speakers representing both academia and other organizations to broaden our perspectives on crisis management. On the one hand, Dr. Anxo Sánchez from the Interdisciplinary Group in Complex Systems (GISC, www.gisc.es) talked about how to derive knowledge about social interaction and human behavior, a topic that could inspire our works on citizen participation or inter- and intra-agency coordination among others. On the other hand, Mr. Nuno Nunes from the International Organization for Migration talked about the role of this organization in Mediterranean crisis and the use of IOM's Displacement Tracking Matrix (DTM), a system to track and monitor displacement and population mobility.

We would like to thank again all the organizers, chairs, reviewers, invited speakers, our sponsor Universidad Carlos III of Madrid, and the participants who made this event possible.

Enjoy this book that collects the contributions of this year as we enjoyed preparing it and spread the word among other communities and researchers to make this community even stronger. Improving our capacity to react and recover from crisis is a common effort in which we can all contribute and there are still many areas and open issues to explore. Let's start working together for ISCRAM-MED 2017!

September 2016

Paloma Díaz
Narjès Bellamine Ben Saoud
Julie Dugdale
Chihab Hanachi

Organization

Conference Co-chairs

Paloma Diaz	Universidad Carlos III de Madrid, Spain
Narjés Bellamine Ben Saoud	Ecole Nationale des Sciences de l'Informatique, Tunisia
Chihab Hanachi	University Toulouse 1, IRIT Laboratory, France
Julie Dugdale	Université Pierre Mendés Franc, France

Program Co-chairs

Ignacio Aedo	Universidad Carlos III de Madrid, Spain
Giuliana Vitiello	University of Salerno, Italy

Steering Committee

Chihab Hanachi	University Toulouse 1, IRIT Laboratory, France
Frédérick Benaben	Ecole des Mines Albi Carmaux, France
François Charoy	University of Lorraine, France
Narjés Bellamine Ben Saoud	Ecole Nationale des Sciences de l'Informatique, Tunisia
Julie Dugdale	Université Pierre Mendés Franc, France
Tina Comes	University of Agder, Norway
Victor Amadeo Banuls Silvera	Pablo de Olavide University, Spain

Proceedings Co-editors

Paloma Diaz	Universidad Carlos III de Madrid, Spain
Narjés Bellamine Ben Saoud	Ecole Nationale des Sciences de l'Informatique, Tunisia
Chihab Hanachi	University Toulouse 1, IRIT Laboratory, France
Julie Dugdale	Université Pierre Mendés Franc, France

Local Organization Committee

Teresa Onorati	Universidad Carlos III de Madrid, Spain
Telmo Zarraonandía	Universidad Carlos III de Madrid, Spain
Andri Ioannou	Cyprus University of Technology

Marco Romano   Universidad Carlos III de Madrid, Spain
Andrea Bellucci   Universidad Carlos III de Madrid, Spain
Vaso Constantinou   Cyprus University of Technology

Web and Media Committee

Teresa Onorati   Universidad Carlos III de Madrid, Spain
Pablo Acuña   Guud.tv, Spain
Gabriel Montero   Universidad Carlos III de Madrid, Spain

Program Committee

Carole Adam   LIG CNRS UMR 5217 - UJF, France
Ignacio Aedo   Universidad Carlos III de Madrid, Spain
Fred Amblard   IRIT – University Toulouse 1 Capitole, France
Eric Andonoff   IRIT – University Toulouse 1 Capitole, France
Baghdad Atmani   Computer Science Laboratory of Oran (LIO),
                              Oran 1 University, Algeria
Elise Beck   Université Joseph Fourier, France
Narjes Bellamine   ISI and Laboratoire RIADI/ENSI
Lamjed Ben Said   ISG Tunis, Tunisia
José Hilario Canós   Universidad Politécnica de Valencia, Spain
François Charoy   Université de Lorraine – LORIA – Inria, France
Malika Charrad   High Institute of Computer Science ISIMED,
                              Gabes University, Tunisia
Chantal Cherifi   Lyon 2 University, DISP Laboratory, France
Hocine Cherifi   University of Burgundy, France
Tina Comes   UiA, Norway
Monica Divitini   IDI-NTNU, Norway
Ioannis Dokas   DUTH, Greece
Julie Dugdale   LIG, France
Paloma Díaz   Universidad Carlos III de Madrid, Spain
Shady Elbassuoni   American University of Beirut, Lebanon
Mohammed Erradi   ENSIAS Rabat, Morocco
Daniela Fogli   Università di Brescia, Italy
Benoit Gaudou   UMR 5505 CNRS, IRIT, Université de Toulouse,
                              France
Chihab Hanachi   University Toulouse 1, France
Muhammad Imran   Qatar Computing Research Institute, Qatar
Elyes Lamine   Université de Toulouse, ISIS, Mines d'Albi, France
Fiona McNeill   Heriot Watt University, UK
Teresa Onorati   Universidad Carlos III de Madrid, Spain
Francois Pinet   Cemagref, France
Robert Power   CSIRO, Australia
Marco Romano   Universidad Carlos III de Madrid, Spain
Monica Sebillo   Università di Salerno, Italy

Abstracts of Invited Talks

Working Together: An Experimental Approach to Understand Collaborative and Prosocial Behavior

Angel Sánchez[1,2,3]

[1] Grupo Interdisciplinar de Sistemas Complejos, Departamento de Matemáticas,
Universidad Carlos III de Madrid, 28911, Leganés, Madrid, Spain
[2] Institute UC3M-BS of Financial Big Data,
Universidad Carlos III de Madrid, Madrid, Spain
[3] Institute for Biocomputation and Physics of Complex Systems (BIFI),
University of Zaragoza, 50018, Zaragoza, Spain
anxo@math.uc3m.es

Abstract. An accurate knowledge of the interactions between people is key to agent-based models of human behavior in different contexts, and in particular for simulations of emergency and crisis management. We discuss here how information on human interactions can be obtained from behavioral experiments and how different social aspects affect responses in situations involving cooperation towards a common goal.

Keywords: Generosity · Expectations · Cooperation · Social dilemmas · Experimental evidence · Computational social science

The computational study of social phenomena has been focused on the emergence of all sorts of collective phenomena and behaviours from among individual systems in interaction, including segregation, cooperation, reciprocity, social norms, and institutions [1]. Recent developments include data driven simulations, carried out to compare with, understand, and if possible predict real-life phenomena. In particular, data arising from ICT-based sensing frameworks is having a stronger impact here than in other areas, since the knowledge of the underlying social interaction gained from sensors is crucial from many points of view. However, while careful analysis of data should yield intuitions on human interactions and decision-making, it is often the case that different sets of data or even different analysis of the same data may lead to incompatible proposals. Experimental work specifically designed to discriminate between alternatives is then needed to choose among them.

In this talk, I will discuss how knowledge on interactions among people, able to drive simulations of many socially relevant issues, including crisis and emergency management, can be gained through carefully designed experiments. I will present examples of several social factors affecting collaborative or cooperative work from diverse viewpoints. Thus, I will consider the following:

- Collaboration in groups when people can choose their partners using information about their past behavior [2] and the effect of actors being able to fake their own behavior [3].
- Collaboration among people involved in a hierarchical structure when the benefits of working together depend on the respective ranks [4].
- Collaboration in different social dilemmas, where choosing to help others may or may not lead to benefits for self, allowing to characterize human behavior in a few 'phenotypes' [5].
- Collaboration in groups where, starting from an inhomogeneous distribution of wealth, a common goal must be achieved, in a manner very similar to climate change mitigation [6].

In closing, I will sketch how the observed behaviors can be then used in agent-based models and a few further lines for research in this direction.

References

1. Conte, R., Gilbert, N., Cioff-Revilla, C., Deffuant, G., Kertesz, J., Loreto, V., Moat, S., Nadal, J.-P., Sánchez, A., Nowak, A., Flache, A., San Miguel, M., Helbing, D.: Manifesto of computational social science. Eur. Phys. J. Spec. Top. **214**, 325–346 (2012)
2. Cuesta, J.A., Gracia-Lázaro, C., Ferrer, A., Moreno, Y., Sánchez, A.: Reputation drives cooperative behaviour and network formation in human groups. Sci. Rep. **5**, 78–43 (2015)
3. Antonioni, A., Tomassini, M., Sánchez, A.: Cooperation survives and cheating pays in a dynamic network structure with unreliable reputation. Sci. Rep. **6**, 27–160 (2016)
4. Cronin, K.A., Acheson, D.J., Hernández, P., Sánchez, A.: Hierarchy is detrimental for human cooperation. Sci. Rep. **5**, 18–634 (2015)
5. Poncela-Casasnovas, J., Gutiérrez-Roig, M., Gracia-Lázaro, C., Vicens, J., Gómez-Gardeñes, J., Perelló, J., Moreno, Y., Duch, J., Sánchez, A.: Humans display a reduced set of consistent behavioral phenotypes in dyadic games. Science Advances (2016, in press)
6. Gutiérrez-Roig, M., Gracia-Lázaro, C., Vicens, J., Bueno, N., Gómez-Gardeñes, J., Perelló, J., Moreno, Y., Duch, J., Sánchez, A.: Poorer people contribute more to climate change mitigation (2016, Preprint)

The Role of the International Organization for Migration in the Mediterranean Crisis

Nuno Nunes

Cluster Coordinator
Camp Coordination and Camp Management Team (CCCM),
Preparedness and Response Division (PRD),
International Organization for Migration (IOM),
Geneva, Switzerland
nnunes@iom.int

Abstract. Mr. Nunes will explain the IOM's role in in the Mediterranean crisis; specifically, the use of the IOM's Displacement Tracking Matrix (DTM). During his speech, Mr. Nunes will give an introduction to the DTM, provide examples of its application and approaches in the Mediterranean crisis, and finally, share results and ways to move forward.

The Displacement Tracking Matrix (DTM) is a system to track and monitor displacement and population mobility. It is designed to regularly and systematically capture, process and disseminate information to provide a better understanding of population mobility, whether on site or en route. This information provides knowledge on the movement, locations, vulnerabilities and needs of displaced populations throughout the course of a crisis[1].

Using the years of experience of DTM implementation worldwide, IOM established the Flow Monitoring System (FMS) in 2015 to gather and disseminate more qualitative information on populations moving through the Mediterranean. This system uses data captured from flow monitoring points in Greece, the Former Yugoslav Republic of Macedonia, Serbia, Hungary, Slovenia, Libya, and other transit countries to create weekly flows compilations that are used to analyze trends across the region. Information is gathered about migrants' profiles, including age, sex, areas of origin, levels of education, key transit points on their route, cost of journey, motives and intentions. This allows IOM to tailor relevant programming to the specific needs in the different locations.

So far in 2016, the DTM's FMS has tracked 248,418[2] arrivals in the Mediterranean, mostly coming from Afghanistan and Syria. However, the system allows us to go beyond the numbers and identify specific needs for the moving populations. Mr. Nunes will provide up to date information and give specific examples on how the FMS helped uncover specific needs of displaced populations arriving in Mediterranean countries.

Data and information is registered through many actors. The data on arrivals is registered then collated by IOM through consulting with ministries of interior, coast guards, police forces, and other relevant national authorities. The survey is

---

[1] http://migration.iom.int/europe/ - http://www.globaldtm.info.

[2] http://dtmodk.iom.int/docs/Europe%20Med%20Migration%20Response_Sitrep%2025%20-%2014%20July.pdf.

collected through primary data collection conducted by IOM staff in strategic transit locations along the routes. Respondents to the survey voluntarily complete a 16-item questionnaire that helps provide more in-depth, qualitative data.

In addition to this, IOM has been actively implementing other DTM components inside the countries where most of the migrants are coming from. These include tracking internal mobility of population affected by crisis in Iraq, Syria, Afghanistan, Pakistan, Lake Chad (Nigeria, Niger, Chad, and Cameroon), Yemen, Somalia, Ethiopia, Libya, Sudan, and others. This provides another layer of information of internal dynamic of population mobility in countries of origin. Some regional and cross regional analysis are currently ongoing to bring comprehensive insights out of these many layers of information.

The DTM's FMS along the routes and in-country DTM implementations have been significant in providing important information that helps uncover the needs of populations moving through the Mediterranean; however, the next step is to ensure this information is turned into action. IOM must do its best to ensure this information not only gets shared timely with the right actors, but that they are able to interpret it correctly to do evidence-based programming to address the identified needs of migrants, from their points of origin and along the routes of their journey.

Contents

Information and Knowledge Management

Collaboration and Coordination

Social Computing

Issues in Humanitarian Crisis

Mobile Apps for Citizens

Emergency Management and Smart Cities: Civic Engagement Through Gamification

Marco Romano[✉], Paloma Díaz, and Ignacio Aedo

Information Technology Department, Universidad Carlos III de Madrid, Madrid, Spain
{mromano,pdp}@inf.uc3m.es, aedo@ia.uc3m.es

Abstract. Nowadays, an increasing amount of cities tend to improve their community life applying smart city principles. The basic idea is to connect citizens to each other, to services, infrastructures and political and non-political organizations to take advantage of a continuous collective collaboration. In this context, the Emergency Management (EM) process becomes a critical aspect. It can exploit the citizens and organizations collaboration to reduce the risks of emergencies and the response time, to act more efficiently and with a better awareness. In this paper, we describe the redesign of an Emergency Notification (EN) application that is part of a set of applications aimed at providing citizens and organizations with easy and immediate means to cooperate. The redesign is based on Gamification and the Self-Determination Theory (SDT) principles in order to improve the user experience and foster the civic participation. The new gamified design was evaluated through an exploratory focus group involving common citizens and practitioners.

Keywords: Gamification · Civic engagement · Emergency system · Mobile device · Smart City

1 Introduction

In the last decade European Union and national governments have allocated funds to promote research in the area of the "Smart City". There is no standard definition of what a Smart City is. In this work we assume the following definition [10, 11].

A city exploiting IT services to connect people to each other, to city services, infrastructures and organizations with the goal to create a common conscience or knowledge that can improve the community life of the same city.

Emergency Management (EM) [12] is a crucial area that can take advantage of the Smart City approach. EM can significantly improve citizens' quality of life, not only helping them during a crisis, but also through an adequate monitoring activity to prevent damages and victims [7]. One of the most critical aspects of EM is Emergency Notification (EN) that is concerned with how to get updated and accurate information from the very first stages of the event and how to notify affected people [19]. In order to support this activity, EN systems have been developed with the aim at improving the performance and the efficiency of such activities. As explained in [8], a possible approach to achieve this is by counting on the collaboration of citizens that are directly

© Springer International Publishing AG 2016
P. Diaz et al. (Eds.): ISCRAM-med 2016, LNBIP 265, pp. 3–14, 2016.
DOI: 10.1007/978-3-319-47093-1_1

involved into the crisis acting as human sensors. In this way, it is possible to take advantage of the so called citizen journalism referring to the common practice of sharing different kinds of messages from anywhere and at any moment of the everyday life. Citizens can share their knowledge and their social capabilities to create a knowledge base supporting the whole community during or before a crisis.

For this to be possible, civic engagement becomes a factor of paramount importance in the Smart City context. One of the strategies explored during the last years to improve the engagement of citizens is to apply game elements or what is known as Gamification [1].

In this paper we present the redesign of an EM mobile application [9] aimed at improving both the quality and the speed of the communication between citizens and EM organizations. The aim of the redesign is to incorporate game elements into the application in order to foster the civic participation in the EM process. The new design is expressed as a paper prototype that was evaluated through a focus group with real stakeholders to investigate the possible acceptance of the new design and the usefulness of the game elements.

The rest of this paper is structured as follows: Section 2 introduces the reader to the underlying concepts of the gamification and of the civic engagement. In Sect. 3 we present the new gamified design. Section 4 describes the focus group activities that we used to evaluate the design. Finally, in the last section some conclusions are given.

2   Gamification and Civic Engagement

Gamification is commonly referred to as the use of game-elements in non-game contexts [6]. The goal is to foster the usage of a system or the users' participation by motivating them with engaging techniques. The term Gamification was used for the very first time by Nick Pelling in 2002 [1]. Werbach and Hunter in [2] describe how gamification techniques have been used successfully in several contexts, including education [3], medical applications [4], and ecommerce platforms as eBay or Amazon. In all these cases the gamification techniques managed to increase the use of tools by offering a funnier and more enjoyable user experience.

Nowadays, the gamification principles are also applied in the Smart City domain. Indeed, their capability to engage users with a system is exploited to promote citizen participation into the political and administrative decisions of their own city in platforms like *Community PlanIt*, *MindMixer* and *Love Your City!*

Community PlanIt (communityplanit.org) allows citizens to participate in missions proposed by the local government for which they earn virtual coins that can be invested to support real projects of their city. *Mysidewalk* (www2.mysidewalk.com), currently used in Fort Worth in Texas, allows local organizations or governments to send information to people living in a concrete area to get quick feedback and make better decisions supported by the interested community. The citizens are rewarded with points that can be used to buy some small goods such as water bottles. *Love Your City!* [5] is an interactive mobile platform aimed at involving neighbors to live and care for the neighborhood together. Users can participate in missions or spontaneously send comments or other information about their neighborhood. Users have different roles and levels that allow to assign different missions and responsibilities. Finally, the system presents some typical aspects of videogames that are: limited time to accomplish a mission, statistics about time and points and user profile customization.

These examples show how game principles can be readily applied to civic contexts. They are used to mainly incentivize people to support, influence and improve public decisions. This is made possible through a collaboration process among citizens and specific organizations. EM process can benefit from such paradigm since the civic participation to the emergency decisions and the continuous collaboration among the different phases of the process are considered crucial [16, 17].

The main reason to use gamification is to increase motivation. It is possible to distinguish between intrinsic and extrinsic motivation. Being intrinsically motivated means to be motivated because one's believes in the underlying values of something or because one finds it interesting and enjoyable. Being extrinsically motivated means to expect something in return for what one does such as a prize, a reward or money [18]. According to the Self-Determination Theory (SDT) [13], human beings are inherently proactive, with a strong internal desire for growth, and the basic human necessities that promote motivation fall into three categories: *Competence*, *Relatedness* and *Autonomy*. *Competence* means to learn to deal effectively with the external environment as for example solving difficult missions, developing artistic abilities or other competencies. *Relatedness* is about social connections such as interacting or competing with friends, family and others. Finally, *Autonomy* represents the innate need to control of one's life and to perform actions in harmony with one's values.

In the next section we describe the redesign of an EM application considering game elements as intrinsic motivators to foster the civic participation in EM.

3   Paper Prototype

In this section we present the gamification redesign of an EN application presented in [9]. The original application is aimed at connecting citizens with EM organizations to improve and enrich their communication. Figure 1 shows the original interface design of the application that was created through a participatory design process involving real EM practitioners working in IT companies with extensive experience in developing emergency systems, the Police Department of Valencia and the Civil Protection of Madrid. The application allows users to quickly collect multimedia content that is sent to EM organizations. The user profile is preregistered into the system and the user position is retrieved on the go and displayed. Photos and videos previously taken in a certain period of time (e.g., few minutes before) are preloaded into the application considering that they are probably related with the particular circumstance being reported so it is probable that users would add them to the notification.

Fig. 1. The original user interface of the EN application

In order to enhance the user experience and to foster the civic engagement, the application was redesigned using gamification principles. The gamification process is based on the inclusion of game elements such as missions, ranking, points and levels.

During the redesign process some new functionalities and screens were added. In particular, we added the following new screens:

1. *Control center allows user to access all the new views*
2. *Mission control allows users to select and control missions prepared by EM organizations*
3. *Training room allows users to select a training course*
4. *Personal achievements visualizes the list of the user's achievements*
5. *Ranking provides a comparative list of achievements obtained by different categories of users.*

The users follow the rules of a typical videogame; they can get points for sending EM notifications, for accomplishing missions and for attending training courses. Missions and training have a required access level; points allow users to progress up a level. We chose a classic list of game levels described in Table 1. The levels classification is inspired by classical videogames levels classification and more in particular by the famous videogame Rocket League[1].

Figure 2a shows the home of the application. In particular, users can go through the "Emergency Notification" icon to send a traditional notification to the EM organizations.

---

[1] www.rocketleaguegame.com.

Table 1. Citizen level in the gamified notification system.

Level	Points
Rookie	0–99
Semi-pro	100–199
Pro	200–299
Veteran	300–399
Expert	400–499
Master	500–599
Legend	>600

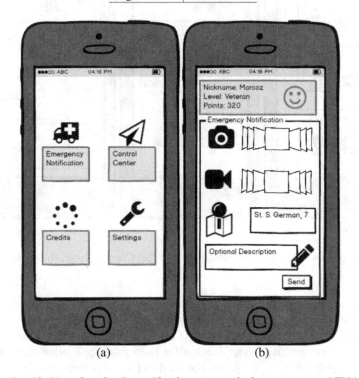

(a)   (b)

Fig. 2. Gamified interface for the notification system: the home screen and EN interface

In Fig. 2b, the app allows users to collect data and send the notification. The screen is the same of the original application but includes details of the user as usually done in a videogame (nickname, avatar, level and points).

Figure 3a shows the "Control Center" that is the kernel of the gamified design. Through this screen, users can access to the list of the missions (Fig. 3b), the list of the training courses (Fig. 3c), the personal achievements (Fig. 4b) and the users ranking (Fig. 4c). Each mission or training requires a minimum access level and has a determinate number of reward points. The status can be *open* when a user can still enroll in, *close* if it is already terminated or *in progress* when the user is enrolled in but the mission/ training is not still accomplished. The mission can be any activity considered adequate by one of the EM organizations using the system. Starting from previous work [14, 15] aimed at identifying possible forms of citizens' participation during an emergency, we developed the following feasible missions: *Quarter exploration, Malfunctioning, First Aid, Volunteer Request.*

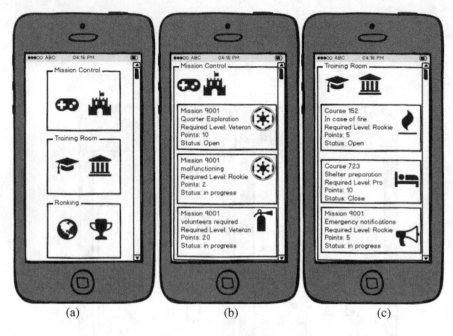

(a)   (b)   (c)

Fig. 3. The main new screens of the gamified design: (a) Control center, (b) Mission control, (c) Training room

The mission *Quarter exploration* asks citizens to explore their neighborhood and collect data as photos, video, positions and notes about possible dangerous situations such as unstable trees after a storm. Figure 4a shows an example of the *Quarter exploration* using the basic notification application. On the top the application shows the time consumed during the mission, the points obtained so far and percentage of the explored district area. *Malfunctioning* is about concrete structures or urban fabric that can be monitored by a citizen such as the status of manholes, sidewalks or lamppost painting. *Firs Aid* is about helping somebody in a not extremely critical situation. Finally, *Volunteer Request* is about recruiting people to face or mitigate a crisis situation.

As for the training courses, users can attend courses about any subjects considered useful by EM organizations to face or get ready for an emergency. Examples of courses can be about what to do in case of a specific emergency, first aid, how to stay in a shelter, how to prepare a correct EM notification, etc.

Missions and trainings on the one hand try to activate the motivational category of *Autonomy* and *Competence*. Regarding the *Autonomy* citizens can manage independently missions and courses. They can choose on the basis of their personal preferences and ethical motivations. Regarding the *Competence*, users can develop their personal

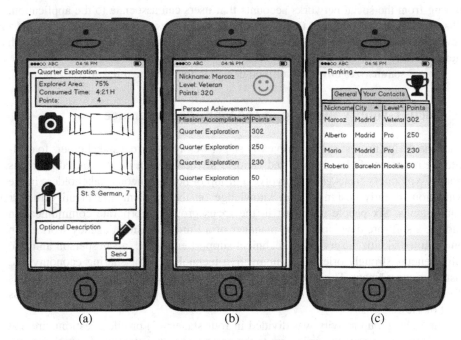

Fig. 4. (a) Represents a mission in progress, (b) shows the user achievements in terms of points and missions accomplished, (c) presents a comparison with other users' achievements

competences by getting experience with missions and learning through the trainings. Their progresses are reflected by points and levels and are always visible to them.

Finally, the Personal achievements and the Ranking screens provides information about the users. Information is about the personal achievements (Fig. 4b) such as the missions accomplished with the associated gained points, the current level and points or can be about the user ranking (Fig. 4c).

Table 2. A summary of the three SDT areas and how they are stimulated by the new design.

SDT area	Rationale
Relatedness	Players can compare their results with other players, in particular they can see the general ranking or the ranking of their social network contacts
Autonomy	Each player can select any mission or course as far as she has the required level. The final goal is to be useful for the society by participating actively in the EM process sending emergency notifications and being prepared to respond to a crisis
Competence	Players can use the training room to learn how to act in emergency situations, how to improve the preparation or they can learn just by acting in a mission. User competences are reflected by means of points and levels

Here the users can compare their progress with a general ranking of people who use the application or with the progress of their contacts. The contact list can be generated starting from the social networks accounts that users can associate to the application. This functionality is included to deal with the *Relatedness* intrinsic motivator with a view to stimulate user engagement by comparing and sharing their progresses with friends, family or other social connections.

Table 2 summarizes how the gamified design stimulates the three areas of the SDT.

4 Focus Group Validation of the Gamified Interface

Since the design process is still in an early stage, we involved real stakeholders to evaluate the inclusion of gamification and validate the new design in an exploratory focus group. Exploratory focus groups involve a group of heterogeneous stakeholders in the evaluation of early design to gain knowledge on the problem and identify further requirements. Six people took part in the focus group: a corporate communication student, a software developer (SD) manager of a European Union agency working in innovation and citizen services, a technical support employee, a salesperson and two entrepreneurs strongly oriented to innovative technologies for sharing economy and customer engagement. The heterogeneity of profiles allows us to have different points of view covering both the technical and non-technical perspective as well as a business point of view.

The focus group activity was divided in four stages: (1) profile questionnaire and personal presentation (2) introduction to the prototype and context (3) discussion about the prototype (4) discussion about extrinsic motivators.

In the first stage, participants were required to fill out a questionnaire about their profile whose results are summarized in Table 3. They were asked about their profession, age, their game habits and their knowledge about gamification. Four participants reported to have at least a basic knowledge about what gamification is, but just one of the entrepreneurs effectively use it in his engagement activities. In general, both video games and traditional games were rarely played by participants though they recognized that the game logic is often integrated in many of the applications and web sites they use.

Table 3. The profiles of participants in the focus group.

ID	Age		Video Games	Type	Traditional Games	Times	Gamification Knowledge
1	24–34	Student	Once a year	xBox	Once a year	Table games, cards	Yes
2	35–45	Salesperson	Never	/	Never	/	No
3	35–45	Technical support	Never	/	Never	/	No
4	24–34	Entrepreneurs	Once a month	Smartphone	Once a year	Table games, cards	Yes
5	35–45	SD manager	Every day	Smartphone, PC	Once a month	Chess, cards	Yes
6	24–34	Entrepreneurs	Once a month	Console	Once a month	/	Yes

At the beginning of the second stage, participants were introduced to the EM context and to the prototype. Then, they were left free to explore the paper prototype and make questions about it. In the last stage, they were asked to express their opinions about the prototype and in particular about the integrated game elements. The focus group followed a semi structured list of questions conducted by the leader who had the responsibility to cover all the questions, examine in depth some not considered aspects and get all the participants to talk and completely explain their opinion. Some of the most interesting opinions are reported below.

The salesperson, who is the oldest participant, was perplexed about the idea of including game elements into crucial systems. In her own words, *"Speaking of game elements applied to crucial applications makes less serious what is supposed to be an ethical obligation"*. Anyway she added that for youngest people probably the idea can be useful to encourage them to care more about the community.

Another participant, who is a software developer manager, stated that at very beginning had the same opinion about the usage of game elements in serious contexts. Then, after studying the design, he found it really useful and engaging interacting with the game elements. In particular, he considers really stimulating the possibility to learn what in his opinion is more useful for himself and to select missions with a real impact on the society. Moreover, speaking of levels and points he said *"the mechanism based on levels looks persuasive and useful to deal just with those things you are able to do"*.

In general, the idea to have game elements integrated into an EN application was well received by the participants who considered the application stimulating. One of the participants said *"the application seems to be able to create a stronger community by stimulating people to improve oneself and act for the common good"*.

For all the participants the geographical component seems to play an interesting role. Indeed, all of them agreed with one of the participants' affirmation: *"I would feel directly involved if the mission were close to my place"*. One of them supported this affirmation explaining *"you always think that somebody else will take care of an emergency happened far from you but when you see that it is near to your community you feel immediately involved"*. For such reason the design should give more emphasis on this aspect to improve civic engagement.

Starting from the considerations regarding the civic participation to emergencies happen near to the one's community, the focus group leader tried to move the discussion on how to improve the civic participation when a crisis is far. A mission scenario was provided to the group: *a volunteer enrolment for supporting a community affected by an earthquake and located five-hours far by train.*

For the sake of clarity, the distance is considered an important information; the participants had to focus on a place enough far from them but still reachable in a one-day trip. This is to avoid obstacles apart from the motivational ones. The subject was not easy for the group, but a participant's suggestion was supported by all: *"The mission should indicate the number of people needed and how many users are responding. If I saw just a few people enrolled in a critical situation I would be ethically stimulated to give my help"*. Therefore, we understand that is important to provide more details about the participants to a mission. After all, allowing people to relate oneself with the others is exactly an intrinsic motivator.

Other considerations were about the "training room". It is supposed to be a place where a user can learn something without pressure, where and when (s)he prefers. It appeared useful to the group but in case of emergency the participants agree that would be better to have a different section where they can access to immediate information as "first aid". This section could present also a message system to ask for an online help.

Finally, regarding the opportunity to add some extrinsic motivators, the leader asked the participants about possible rewards for their participation. In particular, the questions were (a) *Would you like to exchange your points for small goods such as water or milk bottles?* (b) *Would you convert your achieved points in votes to orient your city decisions?* (c) *Would you appreciate to receive formal written certificates attesting your expertise and your participation to missions and/or trainings?* Nobody liked the idea to exchange points with goods, one explained "*Doing good for your community to receive something in exchange seems to be not ethic at all*". This remarks that rewarding users with physical can be useless or even deleterious. On the other hand, regarding the chance to influence their own city choices through their civic participation the group demonstrated a strong appreciation. "*Having more weight in the political decisions of my own city is really stimulating*". Respecting before, the participants demonstrated to appreciate more a social reward than a physical prize. Contrarily to the reaction to the second question, the group was almost indifferent to the possibility to receive formal certificates: "*Receiving certificates can be something appropriate but not really stimulating*". A suggestion considered interesting by the whole group was "*The certification can be useful and motivating if they can be used in public contests or to get enrolled in an emergency organization*". Again in this case, it is clear that connecting the usage of the application to a social reward can be strongly stimulating.

The result of this focus group suggests that the new gamified design has the potentiality to foster the civic engagement by making the system interesting and enjoyable. The possibility to freely decide to learn specific topics or to participate to real missions in harmony with one's values looks adequate and stimulating. Moreover, the participants demonstrated that the choice to recognize the one's growth through levels and points, as it happens in classical videogames, hits the nail on the head. Another interesting finding is about the motivator of the *Relatedness*. It looks a strong motivator with still unexploited potentialities. While, the comparison between users' achievements is considered really stimulating, we can even more drag users into the system by sewing this motivator into the different application steps. For example, by allowing a user to see what the others are doing, who is participating to a mission and how much benefit their participation is generating for the activity purpose.

It is also interesting to see the rewards that our participants consider adequate as extrinsic motivators. Physical goods are considered non-ethical, formal eulogies adequate but a few interesting, while having more influence on the political decisions of their community or some advantages in public contests are strong stimulators.

5   Conclusions

In this paper we investigated the opportunity to integrate game elements into an existing EN application. The aim is to improve the user experience by activating some intrinsic motivators described by the SDT in order to foster a continuous civic engagement during the whole EM process. The new design is presented in form of a paper prototype and include the typical elements of videogames such as points, levels, missions, consumed time, and user profile. The prototype was discussed and evaluated with 6 participants of a focus group. As a result, we can state that the new design might be able to foster the civic engagement effectively.

Some other interesting considerations are about the way to reward citizens for their participation. Rewarding them with physical objects looks to be ethically incorrect and deleterious. Contrary, civic recognition and the opportunity to influence their community choices are considered as good motivators.

As future work, we plan to implement the gamified design taking into account the suggestions of the focus group. Moreover, we also plan to evaluate the new prototype both in terms of usability and user experience involving different groups of real stakeholders including teen agers and people with little technology familiarity and working strictly with real EM organizations. This will allow us to prove the preliminary results obtained so far, obtain additional suggestions and motivations, and to lay the foundation of the civic engagement in the EM domain.

Acknowledgments.   This work is supported by the project emerCien grant funded by the Spanish Ministry of Economy and Competitivity (TIN2012-09687).

References

1. Pelling, N.: The (short) prehistory of gamification. Funding Startups (& Other Impossibilities), Haettu, p. 7 (2013)
2. Werbach, K., Hunter, D.: For The Win: How Game Thinking Can Revolutionize Your Business. Wharton Digital Press, Boston (2012). ISBN 1613630239
3. Kapp, K., Blair, L., Mesch, R.: The Gamification of Learning and Instruction: Game-Based Methods and Strategies for Training and Education. Wiley, New York (2012)
4. McCallum, S.: Gamification and serious games for personalized health. Stud. Health Technol. Inf. **177**, 85–96 (2012)
5. Stembert, N., Mulder, I.J.: Love your city! an interactive platform empowering citizens to turn the public domain into a participatory domain. In: International Conference Using ICT, Social Media and Mobile Technologies to Foster Self-organisation in Urban and Neighbourhood Governance, Delft, The Netherlands, (2013)
6. Deterding, S., Dixon, D., Khaled, R., Nacke, L.: From game design elements to gamefulness: defining gamification. In: Proceedings of the 15th International Academic MindTrek Conference: Envisioning Future Media Environments, pp. 9–15. ACM (2011)
7. Schöning, J., Rohs, M., Krüger, A., Stasch, C.: Improving the communication of spatial information in crisis response by combining paper maps and mobile devices. In: Löffler, J., Klann, M. (eds.) Mobile Response. LNCS, vol. 5424, pp. 57–65. Springer, Heidelberg (2009)

8. Goodchild, M.F.: Citizens as sensors: the world of volunteered geography. GeoJournal **69**(4), 211–221 (2007)
9. Romano, M., Onorati, T., Aedo, I., Diaz, P.: Designing mobile applications for emergency response: citizens acting as human sensors. Sensors **16**(3), 406 (2016)
10. Washburn, D., Sindhu, U., Balaouras, S., Dines, R.A., Hayes, N.M., Nelson, L.E.: Helping CIOs Understand "Smart City" Initiatives: Defining the Smart City, Its Drivers, and the Role of the CIO. Forrester Research, Inc., Cambridge (2010)
11. Nam, T., Pardo, T.A.: Conceptualizing smart city with dimensions of technology, people, and institutions. In: Proceedings of the 12th Annual International Digital Government Research Conference: Digital Government Innovation in Challenging Times (dg.o 2011), pp. 282–291. ACM, New York (2011)
12. Drabek, T.: Emergency Management: Principles and Practice for Local Government, p. xvii. International City Management Association, Washington, D.C. (1991)
13. Ryan, R.M., Deci, E.L.: Self-determination theory and the facilitation of intrinsic motivation, social development, and well-being. Am. Psychol. **55**(1), 68 (2000)
14. Romano, M., Onorati, T., Díaz, P., Aedo, I.: Improving emergency response: citizens performing actions. In: ISCRAM 2014 Conference Proceedings – 11th International Conference on Information Systems for Crisis Response and Management, pp. 170–174 (2014)
15. Díaz, P., Aedo, I., Romano, M., Onorati, T.: Supporting citizens 2.0 in disasters response. In: Proceedings of Conference on Methodologies, Technologies and Tools enabling e-Government MeTTeG, pp. 1–10 (2013)
16. Dynes, R.R.: Social capital dealing with community emergencies. Homeland Secur. Aff. **2**(2) (2006)
17. Aldrich, D.P.: The power of people: social capital's role in recovery from the 1995 Kobe earthquake. Nat. Hazards **56**, 595–611 (2011)
18. Malone, T.W.: Toward a theory of intrinsically motivating instruction. Cogn. Sci. **5**(4), 333–369 (1981)
19. Malizia, A., Onorati, T., Díaz, P., Aedo, I., Astorga-Paliza, F.: SEMA4A: an ontology for emergency notification systems accessibility. Expert Syst. Appl. **37**(4), 3380–3391 (2010)

Improving First Aid Skills: How Local Conceptions of Risk Influence User Engagement with the First Aid App in Israel and Malta

Susan Anson[✉], Maurice Said, Hayley Watson, and Kush Wadhwa

Trilateral Research Ltd., London, UK
{Susan.Anson,Maurice.Said,Hayley.Watson,
Kush.Wadhwa}@trilateralresearch.com

Abstract. First Aid Apps enable the public to learn skills that could save their lives and increase their resilience. A comparative review of the adoption of the First Aid App by Red Cross National Societies revealed context specific factors influencing local app engagement. Drawing on these differences, this paper compares engagement in response to critical events in Israel and Malta. Whilst Malta has been consistently ranked as the second most natural disaster risk free nation, Israel has been plagued by a variety of ongoing conflict related crises. This paper discusses local attitudes to risk and their influence on community engagement with the app. The evidence indicates that local conceptions of risk not only influence app engagement but also the motivations for adopting the app, the development of the app and the ability to retain the public's interest in the app.

Keywords: First aid app · User engagement · Risk

1 Introduction

The increased use of smartphones and tablet computers has resulted in mobile technology and its associated software applications (i.e., apps) becoming part of our daily lives [1]. Health related apps enable users to access a vast amount of information anywhere and at any time that could potentially save their lives. One such example is the First Aid App, adopted across the Red Cross Red Crescent (RCRC) network. The First Aid App enables users to learn or refresh first aid skills or disaster countermeasures before and during an emergency [2]. While the First Aid App is available in 76 countries, the rates of adoption vary from as few as three users in Cameroon to 249, 974 users in Mexico [3]. This paper examines how local conceptions of risk have potentially influenced these rates of adoption and app engagement in two Mediterranean countries with contrasting risk profiles; Israel and Malta. The results here are intended to provoke discussion and questions for future research into possible relations between risk and the increased use of first aid apps.

© Springer International Publishing AG 2016
P. Diaz et al. (Eds.): ISCRAM-med 2016, LNBIP 265, pp. 15–21, 2016.
DOI: 10.1007/978-3-319-47093-1_2

2   First Aid Apps

The increasing use of smartphones and related apps globally provides a medium for spreading health related information to a wider audience. There are many different health apps available for this purpose. For instance, in March 2013, mobile phone users could choose from approximately 97,000 health related apps [4]. Research highlights how the use of first aid and CPR (Cardiopulmonary resuscitation) apps by either laypeople or health care professionals, significantly improves the performance of lifesaving skills in an emergency [5]. However, research by Thygerson et al. found that not all First Aid Apps provide equal value [5]. Based on an analysis of 65 free and paid-for First Aid Apps available on iTunes, the study found mixed levels of adherence to first aid guidelines, with the majority of guidelines not being adhered to by at least 50 % of the apps analysed. For instance, of the 65 apps analysed, only 32.3 % adhered to the guidelines for performing a head-to-toe check for injuries. Thus, whilst there are a wide range of First Aid Apps for the public to choose from, attention should be placed on apps developed by recognised first aid providers that adhere to first aid guidelines.

Whilst the authors are not aware of any research that specifically examines the influences on users' adoption of and engagement with First Aid Apps, studies have recently begun investigating the factors influencing the adoption of health apps. For instance, based on the Technology Acceptance Model (TAM) II, Cho et al. investigated how health consciousness (individual interest in and awareness of one's own health), health information orientation (the extent to which an individual seeks information from different sources), eHealth literacy (the ability to engage with and apply health information from electronic sources), Internet health information use efficacy (the cognitive ability to search for health information using the Internet), and subjective norm (social influence) influence perceived usefulness and the perceived ease of use in relation to adopting health apps [4]. The study found that the perceived usefulness of health apps was strongly related to health consciousness and subjective norms. Furthermore, the perceived ease of using health apps was significantly influenced by Internet health information efficacy. Whilst the study by Cho et al. provides an understanding of the different factors influencing the adoption of health apps, there is a dearth of research on the factors influencing the adoption and use of First Aid Apps. Against this backdrop, this paper examines how local conceptions of risk influence the use of and engagement with the First Aid App in two Mediterranean countries, Israel and Malta.

3   Methodology

Following the release of First Aid Apps by the American Red Cross and the British Red Cross, the Global Disaster Preparedness Centre (GDPC) launched the Universal App Program in May 2013 in order to expand the availability of the app into new countries [6]. The research that this paper is based on involved a comparative study of the development, rollout and marketing of the First Aid App across nine countries. Semi-structured interviews were conducted with Red Cross members involved in the development and rollout of the app in each of the countries [13]. The interviews were accompanied by desk based research into the Red Cross national societies involved and, demographic and technological data about the countries being investigated. Google Analytics was also utilised to monitor user engagement with the app and comments boards on Google Play and iTunes were consulted to record users' views of the app. The two countries focused on in this paper have very different levels of risk and we seek to explore what the app may reveal about local attitudes to risk. As the app adoption rates vary significantly, with Malta having 4,504 users compared to 124,775 First Aid App users in Israel [3], the GDPC commissioned a cross-country comparative analysis to understand the potential impact of the host organisation in encouraging the use of the app and, specific factors influencing local user engagement with the app. Semi-structured interviews were conducted with five members of the Malta Red Cross and two members of the Magen David Adom (MDA - the equivalent of the Red Cross in Israel).

The desk based research analysed the risks faced by each country by collecting data from the EM-DAT website, the international disaster database, as well as each organisation's website and news reports. Google Analytics data was examined for different time periods, including: the first six months of the app's life, six months of comparable app activity between June and November 2015, the entire life of the app, and following two critical events that occurred in each country. The first six months of the app's life were selected in order to compare National Societies' marketing strategies and user engagement in the initial weeks following the launch. The final six months leading up to November 2015 served to compare changes in user engagement since the launch of the app, whilst the period following critical events served to observe fluctuations in user engagement and to determine whether critical events were impacting on engagement with the app.

4   Local Conceptions of Risk

The analysis of primary and secondary data offered insights into the significance of the First Aid App in countering risks, and illustrated how the app was adapted to suit each community. The comparison between Malta and Israel provided particularly interesting insights into how two Mediterranean countries with very different levels of risk adapted the app to their needs and points to some local perceptions of risk in each country. Whilst the relations between conceptions of risk and app adoption may be made solely on each country's risk profiles, the data collected through interviews and the analysis of Google Analytics data adds another level of depth to the analysis. Specifically, interviewees indicated that monitoring of user engagement with the app allowed them to connect with members of their own communities and learn from them (see examples further in this section). The interviews also provided the basis for questions that could drive further research, such as: In what ways do mobile applications foster communication between first responders and the general public? To what extent and how, does the organisation's reputation affect communication? One example of the latter is the increased engagement between Malta Red Cross personnel and 'beachgoers' discussing the app's features during lifeguarding duties.

Interviews revealed that Israel does not have serious natural disasters, but suffers from severe security threats related to terrorism and armed conflict (interviewees referred to stabbings and missile attacks in particular). According to interviewees, these types of attacks are considered to be the third most significant threat to people's lives. The most pertinent and widespread risks were considered to be road accidents and domestic accidents. According to EM-DAT, the most severe natural disaster in the last 20 years was a forest fire that killed 44 people. Casualties were also attributed to floods (18), a pandemic (12), and storms (27) [7]. Although Israel suffers from a variety of risks, particularly conflict related, interviewees revealed that few emergency services exist. According to one interviewee, MDA is the only official emergency service for Israel. The latter suggests that people's ability to help themselves is key here. The MDA are concerned with the provision of first aid and first aid training, including providing first aid instruction for the volunteer program that they operate. They maintain storage of blood, plasma and their by-products and are involved in the transportation of patients, doctors, nurses and other medical staff. In addition, they also deal with the evacuation of those wounded or killed in road accidents [8]. A key motivation for MDA in adopting the app was to give users a sense of safety and security, i.e., in the event of an emergency to have information readily available to them at any time (even without any connectivity). Another key motivation for introducing the First Aid App in Israel was to reach out to young people, to provide them with something "cool". Furthermore, MDA wanted to use the app for marketing purposes. Increasing their marketing capability would also ensure that a wider audience would learn about first aid, as well as the emergency services provided by MDA.

Some similar observations were noted in the case of Malta, although the local context and level of risk was considerably different. According to the 2014 UN 'World Risk Report', Malta was classified as the second safest country in the world and the second country least susceptible to natural disasters [9]. Crime in Malta is also very low, with the most pertinent risks being: poor condition of roads and erratic driving, flooding during winter torrential rains and, in summer, the risk of jellyfish bites [10]. More recent risks, focused around the coastal areas, are the strong sea currents that have resulted in a number of drownings, as well as spinal injuries from recreational diving in coastal zones [11, 12]. Members of the Malta Red Cross stated that the app would aid the organisation in spreading awareness of first aid. Since a major part of the organisation's activities is focused on the provision of first aid instruction and training, they also hoped that the app would act as a refresher for those who had already taken a first aid course and, would provide them with an ever available source of information that would give them the confidence to provide first aid assistance in the event of an emergency. In fact, Red Cross members cited lack of confidence as one of the main reasons for people not providing first aid assistance in emergencies, out of a fear of 'getting it wrong' or 'being sued'. One interviewee's impression was that locals deemed preparedness to be somebody else's responsibility, such as nurses or paramedics, but never their own. Another interviewee stated that people are not aware of what to do in an emergency situation. In response to these diverging levels and perceptions of risk, the app took on very different formats following development in each of these country contexts. In Israel, MDA specifically developed guidelines for dealing with knife attacks and what to do in the event of air attacks. The most popular first aid topic accessed by users was 'bleeding', which is indicative of people's perceptions of risk whether this is in dealing with particularly devastating road accidents, or knife attacks or the result of civil conflict. The Malta Red Cross on the other hand, developed a section of the app that dealt with beach-related incidents such as how to deal with jellyfish stings and the risks of sunburn and, removed much of the section on dealing with natural disasters.

5 Risk Based App Engagement

Earlier in this paper we highlighted some of the perceptions of risk that were brought to our attention by Red Cross members in Malta and Israel (MDA). In the case of Malta, the level of risk to hazards and large-scale critical events was deemed to be non-existent. Rather, risk for Malta Red Cross members in this context, was represented by a perceived general apathy to emergency situations and a lack of involvement by laypeople in providing assistance in emergencies. Red Cross members asserted that people were likely to rely on others to help them rather than help themselves. Conversely, perceptions of risk in Israel centred around the frequent and real threat of violence and conflict. The appeal of the app among members of the general public was also its ability to deliver notifications on developing emergencies. For example, following the spate of stabbings in late 2015, the app was immediately updated with information on what to do in the case of such an emergency.

To further illustrate how events influence user engagement with the app and what they reveal about risk, research was conducted into user engagement with the app during and after critical national events. On October 8th 2015, seven civilians and one soldier were wounded in four different stabbings across Israel. The attacks were carried out by Palestinians in what were the first of a string of attacks on Israelis using "everyday" objects like knives and cars which, due to their ubiquity and everyday use, are readily available and raise little suspicion [14]. The data revealed an overall surge in user engagement with the app in the days following the stabbings, with a particularly high increase on the day after the stabbings with a surge of 244 % (+4406) of users. Given that the most popular first aid topic on this day was bleeding, it is safe to assume that the event had a credible impact on user engagement. The three most popular topics on the day were: bleeding (3,882 views), stabbing victim (3,814 views) and burns (1,922 views). The MDA stated that one of the main motivations for adopting the app was to give people a sense of safety and security. Given that the random and widespread attacks using 'everyday objects' could have been geared at targeting people's sense of security, the overwhelming increase in user engagement with the app during and following the incident, suggests that the app may well have succeeded in providing a source of security in a time of uncertainty.

Conversely, in the case of Malta the event of national significance was a choking incident, given the absence of high risk events plaguing the island state. On 22 September 2015, a 57-year-old woman choked to death while having lunch in a packed restaurant. Neither the staff nor any other diners were able to properly assist her. Her brother released a public appeal for catering staff to be trained in basic first aid and the news story caused a stir in the local community with a surge in newspaper reports on the importance of first aid [15]. Two Malta RC interviewees stated that such incidents tended to increase public awareness and interest in first aid, but this interest was short-lived. In fact, a similar incident had taken place in 2001, where a 20-year-old had also choked to death in a packed restaurant. Despite appeals then for catering staff to learn basic first aid, no action had been taken and the incident was quickly forgotten. Interviewees used these examples to explain small surges in interest in the First Aid App, as well as to demonstrate the lack of preparedness of the local community. Data illustrated that there was a notable increase in user engagement in the days following the choking incident, where user engagement on the two days following the incident was more than double the 30-day average following the event (40 users as opposed to the monthly average of 14.8), and the most popular first aid topic was 'choking'. This is probably due to newspaper articles in the national newspapers during these two days that highlighted the importance of first aid and, where commentators actively referred to the First Aid App.

In these two case studies we have illustrated that although the levels of risk are very different in each country, some common threads may be drawn between them. In both cases the increased user engagement with the app suggests that users turn to the app to give themselves a sense of security; knowledge of first aid is perceived as a means to countering risk. However, whilst choking may be seen as an incident that may be prepared for and averted through basic first aid, the level of safety in Maltese day to day life suggests a reluctance to learn or apply such skills and points towards dependency on emergency services. As Malta Red Cross members alluded to, the real risk is a general apathy towards first aid and preparedness. The situation seems to be reversed in the case of Israel, where risk is governed by unpredictability and frequency and thus, a necessity to be self-reliant or to be able to help others. The latter comes across in the MDA's insistence on targeting younger people in what may be interpreted as an attempt to instil basic first aid skills from a young age, as well as in the regular and immediate updating of first aid information available on the app.

6   Conclusion

This paper has examined how local conceptions of risk influence local engagement with the First Aid App in Israel and Malta. It has shown how conceptions of risk in Israel and Malta not only influence engagement with the app but also the motivations for adopting the app, the development of the app and the ability to retain the public's interest in the app.

Further research with users is required to understand how different types of critical events impact upon the use of and engagement with the First Aid App. This information could be used to support Red Cross Red Crescent National Societies in developing app content and additional features (e.g., warning notifications), and in promoting the app before, during, and following critical events.

Acknowledgements. We would like to thank the Global Disaster Preparedness Center (GDPC) for commissioning the research project, and the project partners (Fraunhofer Institute for Open

Communication Systems, Utah State University and the Asian Disaster Preparedness Center) for their support in conducting the research. In addition, we would like to thank the interviewees for their participation.

References

1. van Velsen, L., Beaujean, D.J., van Gemert-Pijnen, J.E.: Why mobile health app overload drives us crazy, and how to restore the sanity. BMC Med. Inf. Decis. Making **13**(1), 1 (2013)
2. American Red Cross. http://www.redcross.org/news/article/Universal-First-Aid-App-Brings-Livesaving-Information-to-Millions
3. Global Disaster Preparedness Center. http://preparecenter.org/activities/universal-app-program
4. Cho, J., Quinan, M.M., Park, D., Noh, G.-Y.: Determinants of adoption of smartphone health apps among college students. Am. J. Health Behav. **38**(6), 860–870 (2014)
5. Thygerson, S.M., West, J.H., Rassbach, A.R., Thygerson, A.L.: iPhone apps for first aid: a content analysis. J. Consum. Health Internet **16**(2), 213–225 (2012)
6. Global Disaster Preparedness Center. https://preparecenter.org/sites/default/files/universal_app_program_faqs.pdf
7. EM-DAT. http://www.emdat.be/country_profile/index.html
8. Mdais. https://www.mdais.org/en/
9. United Nations University – Institute for Environment and Human Security, Work Risk Report 2014. Report, Alliance Development Works (2014)
10. Gov.uk. https://www.gov.uk/foreign-travel-advice/malta/safety-and-security
11. Times of Malta. http://www.timesofmalta.com/articles/view/20130908/local/Majority-of-drownings-in-Malta-are-foreign-men.485203
12. Malta Today. http://www.maltatoday.com.mt/news/national/41703/lifeguards_assist_three_with_spinal_injuries_in_comino#.VmBfYr9VUYW
13. Trilateral Research Ltd., Fraunhofer Institute for Open Communication Systems, Asian Disaster Preparedness Center and Utah State University, Comparative review of the First Aid App, report (2016)
14. Haaretz. http://www.haaretz.com/israel-news/1.679439
15. Times of Malta. http://www.timesofmalta.com/articles/view/20150924/local/updated-appeal-after-woman-dies-choking-on-piece-of-meat-restaurant.585576

Scenario-Based Evaluation of 112 Application "Pomoc"

Anna Stachowicz[1(✉)], Marcin Przybyszewski[1], Jan Zych[2],
Patrycja Młynarek[1], and Rafał Renk[3]

[1] ITTI Sp. z o.o., Poznań, Poland
{astachowicz,mprzybysz,pmlynarek}@itti.com.pl
[2] Faculty of Social Sciences, University JKU in Kielce, Kielce, Poland
janzych@cyberman.com.pl
[3] Adam Mickiewicz University, Poznań, Poland
rafal.renk@amu.edu.pl

Abstract. In this paper evaluation of 112 application "Pomoc" ("Help" in English) is presented. Application provides functionalities of calling European emergency number 112 with automatically sending GPS-based (General Positioning System) location of calling person. Evaluation was realized in the form of scenario-based table-top exercise, where experts from the area of emergency and crisis management could observe potential benefits of using application "Pomoc" in simulated trains crash. Application has been developed during the EU 7th Framework Programme project SOTERIA, which deals with On-line and Mobile Communications for Emergencies (http://soteria.i112.eu/). Paper presents also possibilities and benefits, which were discussed during the exercise, of using social media in crisis and emergency situations. Application "Pomoc" is currently in prototype version, not integrated with 112 system yet.

Keywords: Mobile application · Emergency management · Emergency calls · 112 calls · Geo-location · Social media

1 Introduction

Together with the pervasive and still growing use of smartphones, use of mobile apps is more and more popular. These mobile apps are related to every area of life – from games and apps used for fun, through the education, sport and lifestyle apps to the news and lifesaving applications. These last, are applied to the emergency and crisis management response in many, different ways. There are applications specially designed for crisis management purposes – such as warning apps or 112/911 apps. However, there are also solutions with the wider use, which can be applied in rescue actions, like navigation services, simple weather or flashlight apps. Such mobile apps like Whatsapp or social media apps can be used for communication, when other communication means fail, but Wi-Fi hot spots are available. On the other hand, some applications like 112 or warning apps or even maps may work without Internet connection. Although variety of mobile apps existed, there are still some places for new developments and improvements. To fill the gap of lack of mobile app enabling calling emergency number 112, with the sending GPS-based location in the same time in Polish 112 system – application

© Springer International Publishing AG 2016
P. Diaz et al. (Eds.): ISCRAM-med 2016, LNBIP 265, pp. 22–29, 2016.
DOI: 10.1007/978-3-319-47093-1_3

"Pomoc" ("Help" in English) has been developed. This application has been created during the project SOTERIA and it is already introduced in [1]. Thus, just as a short remainder – application provides two main functionalities in case of emergency – supports the communication with PSAPs (Public-Safety Answering Points) by calling emergency number 112 and delivers GPS-based location. Additionally, user can introduce information about her/himself – such as name, age, gender as well as ICE (In Case of Emergency) number and information about any disease, allergy, needed medications, that can be further helpful in rescue action. There are two parts of application, i.e. mobile app for citizens and prototype version of desktop application for PSOs (Public Safety Organizations). Currently, they are not integrated with Polish 112 emergency call system yet. First evaluation of the solution is presented in [1]. Here, second evaluation of the application is described. It was realized during the Campaigns of experimentation in the SOTERIA project, where application "Pomoc" has been presented in scenario-based exercise with representatives of PSOs experts. Because of the fact, that project SOTERIA deals with on-line and mobile communications for emergency, during the exercise also aspects of using social media for emergency response have been analyzed. This paper is mainly focused on evaluation of application "Pomoc", however general conclusions and recommendations regarding the use of social media in emergency response are also presented. Research questions to be answers are:

1. How much useful mobile apps and social media generally and in particular emergency scenario would be, what information is the most desirable by PSOs and what information should be shared with citizens?
2. What improvements to the app "Pomoc" are recommended by PSOs?
3. What steps should be taken to integrate mobile apps and social media use to the current emergency and crisis response?

2 Rationale and Related Works

According to the Eurobarometer studies [2], 63 % of EU citizens access the Internet every day, in which 61 % users access the Internet via a smartphone, and 30 % via tablet. Nevertheless, Eurobarometer studies about the data protection [3] proves that more than half of citizens (55 %) is very or fairly concerned about the recording of their everyday activities via mobile phone or use of mobile applications (listening in on calls, geo-location). Surveys conducted in the project EmerGent[1] showed that overall 87 % of surveyed citizens use smartphone [4]. From the perspective of application "Pomoc", it is interesting because among 1034 respondents across Europe, 306 of them were from Poland. Moreover, 16 % of citizens have downloaded a smartphone application that could help in a disaster or emergency (including e.g. warning apps, weather apps or emergency call apps). On the other hand, this study revealed that awareness of such applications as Twitter Alerts[2] or Facebook Safety Check[3] is very low, only 32 % and

---

[1] EU FP7 project EmerGent: http://www.fp7-emergent.eu/.
[2] https://twitter.com/fema/alerts.
[3] https://www.facebook.com/about/safetycheck/.

4 % of regular users of these social media respectively know mentioned apps [4]. Considering location - c.a. 25 % of citizens share their personal location information during emergency[4]. All studies presented above show that there is a huge potential to online and mobile solutions for emergency to be used by citizens. However, they also highlight the need of education and advertisement of such apps as well as the need of ensuring privacy and security of the solutions to be accepted by the users. Mobile apps related to crisis and emergency management can be of different kind. Staring from preparation and warning apps - American Red Cross offers the whole range of mobile apps for citizens, relevant to different emergencies[5]. In Poland, there is official waring app called RSO[6] (Regionalny System Ostrzegania – Regional waring system in English), providing both – current warnings as well as tutorials – how to act in case of particular crisis or emergency. RSO app has been downloaded more than 100 000 times, so there is a potential for mobile apps for emergency in Poland. There are also mobile apps, which engage citizens in providing information, location, photos and videos [5] or performing specific actions [6]. Other group of apps very useful in emergency and crisis response are those providing information about location. It can be in the form of navigation services, like Google Maps or MapsMe[7] (used by refugees in the recent immigration crisis, because it does not require Internet connection [7]) and apps enabling user to send her/his location to friends (GPS, find me![8], TuJestem – Polish app – "I am here"[9]). Finally, there are 112 mobile apps enabling user to call local emergency services, they have been summarized shortly in [1]. However, there is no official 112 app in Poland and only typical 112 app will call directly emergency center (it cannot be realized by apps of other types). Thus, unavailability of such app in Poland and the fact that other social media-based mobile apps do not offer full capabilities ensured by "Pomoc", were the main rationale for developing this application. Additionally, 112 apps are popular to some extend in other countries [1], which proves the right direction to provide similar app in Poland.

3 Methodology and Scenario

In order to evaluate application "Pomoc" – workshop with experts from the area of crisis and emergency management was organized. It took place on May 17, 2016 at the Adam Mickiewicz University in Poznań, Poland, attended by five representatives of different public safety organizations, like fire brigade, army, crisis management structures and public security and safety sciences. Their experience in the field ranges from 6 to 30 years, both from operational personnel and management staff. The workshop was the part of the SOTERIA project Campaigns of experimentation, where solutions offered

---

[4] Citizens attitude towards Social Media (Infographic): http://www.fp7-emergent.eu/publications/.
[5] http://www.redcross.org/get-help/prepare-for-emergencies/mobile-apps.
[6] https://play.google.com/store/apps/details?id=pl.tvp.komunikaty&hl=en.
[7] Application MapsMe, http://maps.me/en/home.
[8] https://play.google.com/store/apps/details?id=gpsfindme.benamati.it&hl=en.
[9] http://tujestem.eu/.

by the project are exercised. Thus, during the workshop application "Pomoc", together with the aspects of the use of social media were presented in the scenario of hypothetical emergency. Participants had opportunity to familiarize with the solutions, their functionalities and in which way they can support public safety organizations during response actions, as well as recognize their limitations. The use of mobile apps and social media was the subject of discussion and analysis.

After discussions participants filled in the questionnaire, however, it was treated as experts' opinions (due to small number of participants). Therefore, in this article only qualitative results are presented, not quantitative data.

The workshop was carried out on the basis of the hypothetical scenario of two trains crash and derail. It was a simulation experiment with so-called "operating skip", where following parts of the scenario and response actions were presented at particular moments, not in the real time. The accident involved passenger train and freight train, carrying ammonia. As a result of accident there was a high amount of injured (out of 350 passengers) and there was ammonia leakage. A nearby road was impassable. Accident has been visualized in the system currently used by Polish PSOs, with the highlights in which rescue actions and how SOTERIA solutions could be used. Regarding application "Pomoc" the following problems that can be solved by application have been discussed:

- Emergency event notification via:
  - the emergency number 112 or other emergency numbers in Poland
  - mobile applications such as "Pomoc"
- issues of precise location of victims:
  - sufficiency of current methods
  - usefulness of apps "Pomoc"
- helping people with specific illnesses, first aid.

Regarding the use of social media (by PSOs and citizens), the following advantages were presented (supported by the scenario):

- providing relevant information in the form of photos, videos
- providing additional channel of communication
- easy way of informing the public about: the current situation, unpassable road and alterative roads, how to prevent ammonia poisoning, how to act in case of being injured or poisoned, progress in reuse action.

4   Results and Discussion

During discussion with experts, valuable feedback about the application "Pomoc" and the use of social media was received. Discussion was navigated by the research questions, thus, according to them results will be presented.

1. How much useful mobile apps and social media generally and in particular emergency scenario would be, what information is the most desirable by PSOs and what information should be shared with citizens?

Starting from the evaluation of application "Pomoc", experts found it useful in case of emergency, because fast location of the event is still one of the problems in emergency response. Considering the use of social media – currently, Polish public safety organizations generally do not use social media for the purposes of crisis and emergency response. There is no regulation in this matter. Social media are mostly used to disseminate information or warnings to citizens, as it is done e.g. via Facebook page of Crisis Management Center in Poznań[10] or Twitter account of the Government Centre for Security[11]. As the most desirable information received from citizens during emergency – PSOs indicated location, photos and description of the event. Videos from the scene were not considered to be critical. These results are applicable both to "Pomoc" and to the use of social media. It is interesting in comparison with EmerGent project studies, where PSOs indicated situation updates (73 %) as the most important, then photos (67 %), public mood (62 %), videos (59 %) and specific information (56 %) [8]. Within the studies presented in this paper - PSOs claimed that they would rather prefer to receive information from citizens via specific mobile app, than via existing Facebook or Twitter app. Apps approved and managed by national authorities would be independent from external owners and management. However, using also existing social media to send warnings would widen the range of audience. Having in mind scenario presented during the experiment – PSOs listed the most important information that could be distributed to citizens:

- information about location and the scale of emergency event
- information about closed roads and alternative roads
- information about response action
- warnings about consequences of the event, like e.g. danger of ammonia poisoning.

It is worth to mention that in Poland, information coming from social media maybe is not used so much by PSOs, but is very much used by media. One TV station manages special portal called Contact24[12], where citizens can send photos and videos, thus, in case of emergency, accident or disaster – information, photos and videos are broadcasted to the public through this portal very quickly. Asked about the trust to information coming from social media – experts would trust mostly the information coming from the trusted users. The following, expected benefits from using app "Pomoc" and social media were discussed:

- decrease the time to response and time to locate incident and victims
- reduce volume of calls on emergency number
- increase situational awareness
- improve resource planning
- increase public trust and confidence and public engagement.

PSOs were positive that in all these aspects using social media and emergency-related apps would be helpful to some extent. However, emergency events are those for which

---

[10] https://www.facebook.com/czkpoznan/?fref=ts.
[11] https://twitter.com/RCB_RP.
[12] http://kontakt24.tvn24.pl/.

public safety organizations are trained and prepared, so the use of social media as additional source of information would be more useful in not typical, unpredicted events. Moreover, during the short-term response, PSOs would not have much time to analyze additional data. During emergency, dispatcher will try to get as much important information as possible from the first person, who calls.

2. What improvements to the app "Pomoc" are recommended by PSOs?

In order to guide further developments – possible improvements of the application "Pomoc" have been discussed. One of the valuable propositions was to facilitate people, who cannot speak (due to injury or disabled people) by sending predefined fixed alert to emergency center together with geo-location. Moreover, there was suggestion to separate all functions, i.e. to enable a call and send information about the user when GPS signal is not available, secondly to enable send GPS location through SMS when mobile network signal is too poor to make a call. These suggestions are specific to "Pomoc". PSOs are concerned about ensuring the privacy of location and communication. They recommended that different levels of privacy should be provided, which the user can change at any time. These privacy-related issues are applicable both to "Pomoc" and other tools. Additionally, experts would appreciate emergency-related solutions to be already installed in the phone, as an app or as a special button. Such a feature is provided in Samsung's phone, at least Galaxy S5 – called Safety Assistance[13]. By pressing Power button 3 times it enables user to send Help Messages to introduced beforehand user's Primary Contacts (like family or friends). Popularization of similar capabilities would help in rescue operations.

3. What steps should be taken to integrate mobile apps and social media use to the current emergency and crisis response?

As one of the most important aspects experts indicated that discussed solutions should be properly and widely advertised to be used by citizens. This confirmed previous validation of the application, that educational campaign should be done [1]. Interesting idea was to add advertising of app or tutorial to some well-known and popular game or tutorial of emergency notification in the form of game, to get the interest of young people. Young people have been addressed because in experts' opinion – they do not consider danger and possibility of emergency. Generally, many people do not follow any recommendations how to prepare for crisis, disaster or emergency, before something happens. Thus, Polish specialists suggested to have well defined dissemination strategy to convince people to use such applications. From the other hand – trainings for PSOs and especially to emergency dispatchers would be also needed. The use of such apps should follow legal regulations and be unified in all regions. Additionally, reliability and accuracy of the solutions as well as its regular updates are very important and determine application success.

---

[13] http://www.androidcentral.com/how-use-safety-assistance-features-galaxy-s5.

5   Conclusions and Further Works

In this paper – scenario-based evaluation of application "Pomoc" has been presented. Experts in the field of crisis and emergency response discussed the issues related to the use of mobile apps as well as aspects of the use of information coming from social media. PSOs appreciated the idea of application "Pomoc", but indicated that it still requires further developments. PSOs expressed their concerns as well as recommendations how to improve the application. They suggested separating functionalities of calling and sending location, which applies specifically to "Pomoc". There were also recommendations, that apply to all emergency-related apps, such as ensuring different levels of privacy and integration of such solutions already with the smartphones. In order to use mobile apps and social media in the real response actions - appropriate legal regulations and guidelines should be specified. Finally, since currently Polish PSOs do not use discussed solutions - wide educational and dissemination campaign to familiarize both citizens and PSOs with the solutions and their benefits should be conducted. Further works regarding application "Pomoc" will follow experts' recommendations, starting from technical improvements and then focusing on approaching local authorities to talk about possible integration with 112 emergency system. Limitation of the research presented in this paper is small number of experts participated in the workshop, providing only qualitative results. Thus, additional talks with PSOs as well as with groups of citizens are planned in the near future as the next stages of SOTERIA project Campaigns of experimentation. These will provide also the perspective of non-experts users and will increase the number of respondents. Moreover, another types of scenarios and the form of workshop will be considered to investigate how these aspects can influence obtained results.

Acknowledgements.   The research leading to these results has received funding from the European Union's Seventh Framework Programme (FP7/2007–2013) under grant agreement no. 606796 (SOTERIA Project).

References

1. Przybyszewski, M., Stachowicz, A., Olejniczak, T., Choraś, M., Zych, J.: Application "POMOC" – emergency calls with geo-location. In: Proceedings of the 13th International ISCRAM Conference, Rio de Janeiro, Brazil (2016)
2. Special Eurobarometer 423 Cyber Security (Fieldwork: October 2014 Publication: February 2015). http://ec.europa.eu/public_opinion/archives/ebs/ebs_423_en.pdf
3. Special Eurobarometer 431 Data Protection (Fieldwork: March 2015 Publication: June 2015). http://ec.europa.eu/public_opinion/archives/ebs/ebs_431_en.pdf
4. Citizen Survey Summary Report: Project EmerGent. http://www.fp7-emergent.eu/wp-content/uploads/2014/05/CITIZEN-SURVEY-SUMMARY-REPORT.pdf
5. Negahban, M., Nourjou, R.: Internet of Things for next-generation public safety mobile communications. In: Proceedings of the 13th International ISCRAM Conference, Rio de Janeiro, Brazil (2016)

6. Romano, M., Onorati, T., Díaz, P., Aedo, I.: Improving emergency response: citizens performing actions. In: Proceedings of the 11th International ISCRAM Conference – University Park, Pennsylvania, USA (2014)
7. Selfies, smartphones bring comfort to migrants on balkan route. http://www.vocativ.com/225532/smartphones-selfies-migrants-syria-europe-balkans/
8. Survey of emergency service staff attitudes towards social media: Project EmerGent. http://www.fp7-emergent.eu/publications/

Modelling and Simulation

SPRITE – Participatory Simulation for Raising Awareness About Coastal Flood Risk on the Oleron Island

Carole Adam[1]([✉]), Franck Taillandier[2], Etienne Delay[3],
Odile Plattard[4], and Mira Toumi[5]

[1] Laboratoire d'Informatique de Grenoble, UMR 5217, Univ. Grenoble-Alpes,
Grenoble, France
carole.adam@imag.fr
[2] Univ. Bordeaux, I2M, UMR 5295, 33400 Talence, France
franck.taillandier@u-bordeaux.fr
[3] GEOLAB, UMR 6042, Université de Limoges, Limoges, France
etienne.delay@unilim.fr
[4] Univ. Paris 1, UMR 8504 Géographie-Cités, Paris, France
odileplattard@gmail.com
[5] Groupe de Recherche en Droit Economie et Gestion, Université Côte d'Azur,
Nice, France
mira.toumi@unice.fr

Abstract. Coastal flood is a major risk for the French Atlantic coast and its island territories, and its management is a key issue for local authorities. Good management of this risk requires understanding the need for a trade-off between occupant safety, attractiveness of the island, environmental development, costs minimisation and population satisfaction. But such a trade-off can be difficult to find and to understand, for both decision makers and the population. SPRITE is a serious game aiming to answer this problem by placing the player in the role of a decision maker and letting them explore various (more or less balanced) policies. The knowledge gained from playing SPRITE can benefit both decision makers, enabling them to make more informed decisions, and residents, helping them to understand the issues involved in territory management.

Keywords: Agent-based model · Participative simulation · Coastal flood · Territory management · Isle of Oléron

1 Introduction

In 2010, the Xynthia storm hit the Atlantic littoral, causing important human (53 deaths in France), material (4800 flooded houses, 120 km of coastline damaged, 40 km of departmental roads flooded), and economical (457 M€of public expenses) damage [1]. Xynthia had a particularly strong impact on the islands of the Atlantic littoral, specifically the island of Oléron. Indeed, the combination

© Springer International Publishing AG 2016
P. Diaz et al. (Eds.): ISCRAM-med 2016, LNBIP 265, pp. 33–46, 2016.
DOI: 10.1007/978-3-319-47093-1_4

of a barometric depression (977 hpa), strong South-West wind (over 110 km/h with gusts around 140 km/h to 160 km/h), and high tidal coefficient (102) produced a particularly high tide, 50 cm to 70 cm over predictions [2], leading to the flooding of a part of the island and important damages. Before Xynthia, only few extended submersion events had happened recently, the last remembered one being the Martin storm in 1999 (and unlike Xynthia its resulting damages were mainly due to the wind rather than coastal flood). The submersion risk was therefore largely underestimated by both the local authorities and the population, and as a result mostly ignored in territory planning and management policies [3], leading to an increase of both the risks and the island vulnerability (construction in flood-prone areas, failure to maintain dykes, etc.) [2].

Xynthia highlighted the risk of submersion which became a priority for local councillors of the island of Oléron, and even more so with global warming that leads to an increase in the number of extreme meteorological events and the probability of occurrence of coastal flood [4]. Local councillors must meet various competing objectives: ensure the residents' safety, respect a limited budget, preserve fauna and flora, promote the island and make it attractive to tourists and new residents, etc. They can use various actions (e.g. building dykes, modifying the local landuse plan to forbid construction in flood-prone areas, etc.), each of them having both positive and negative effects with respect to the different objectives (e.g. building a dyke protects the littoral from submersion but induces maintenance costs, degrades landscape and has a negative impact on fauna and flora; changing the landuse plan reduces vulnerability in unconstructible areas also reduces attractivity of the island and increase pressure on constructible areas). There is therefore no optimal solution answering all (competing) objectives simultaneously; good management requires a combination of actions to reach a balanced compromise between them, but it might be difficult to find for the councillors, and to understand for the population. Indeed, councillors are not experts of everything, and they tend to favour some solutions at the expense of others depending on their history, convictions, knowledge and culture. Understanding the need to reach a balance is therefore an important stake, both for the local councillors to build better land management policies, and for the island residents to better understand (and therefore accept) the policies they are subjected to, even when they have direct short-term negative consequences for them.

SPRITE (Participatory Simulation of Territorial Risks) seeks to answer that challenge: it is a serious game placing the player (population or elected representative) in the role of a local councillor to raise their awareness about the risk of coastal flood and the notion of balanced management of that risk.

This paper is structured as follows: Sect. 2 briefly discusses some literature about the use of participatory simulation for raising awareness; Sect. 3 introduces our conceptual model of the island and its population; Sect. 4 describes the serious game based on this model and its game design and evaluation; finally Sect. 5 concludes about this serious game and future prospects.

2 Participatory Simulation for Raising Awareness

Computer simulation is a great tool for crisis management and offers many benefits. Compared to full-scale simulation exercises, it is much less costly, less dangerous, and easier to organise, yet it still allows to discover knowledge by exploring several "what-if" scenarios before an actual crisis happens, with complete control on all parameters. Participatory simulation is a kind of simulation where human users interact with the simulated world by controlling some of the agents in the system. Participatory simulation is therefore a type of serious games, *i.e.* games that are used not for entertainment but for learning, training, or understanding mechanisms [5].

Serious games have several benefits over more classical approaches to teaching or raising awareness. They follow a constructivist logic in which the players build their own knowledge by confronting a problem in a simulated world. A meta-analysis gathering 193 articles about serious games [6] has shown the following benefits: favouring the development of social and human relationships and communication skills; increasing learning motivation, self-esteem and self-confidence, engagement and persistence; developing problem-solving skills; helping learners to structure, build and represent knowledge; and helping learners to integrate information by developing the capability to build links and transfer knowledge from other contexts.

Simulation-based serious games are particularly interesting for raising awareness of various types of risks [7]. By being placed in a risky situation and allowed to try several ways of managing it, the players can better comprehend the risks and their possibility of occurrence, but also the consequences of their actions of these risks. For major risks such as coastal flood, exploring different strategies and their impact in a serious game provides players with some experience, simulated but close to the real world mechanics. Such experience would be hard to acquire from real crisis in such a short time, due to the long duration between events, and the stakes involved that prevent from trying. An important aspect of serious games and participatory simulations is to rely on a pedagogical scenario integrated in the game design to answer a specific pedagogical objective [8]. Moreover, a number of rules must guide the player's experience by specifying objectives, conditions of victory or failure, possible interactions with the game and the other players (if any), and mechanisms for the evolution of the game world. These rules can be integrated in the computer model, provided externally (*e.g.* note card to be referred to when needed), or both.

3 Conceptual Agent-Based Model

The SPRITE model contains four types of agents: Parcel, Territory, Player, and Resident, as well as a global World agent, all described below. The human player plays the role of the mayor of the territory by controlling the Player agent; all other agents are autonomous.

3.1 Geographical Model

Island. The game board is a grid made up of square cells (the `Parcel` agents) that is built automatically from real Geographical Information System (GIS) data (planimetric and altimetric information, density of buildings, etc.) as illustrated on Fig. 1. To reduce the game initialisation time, the grid is built once by an external module, and does not need to be re-built before each game.

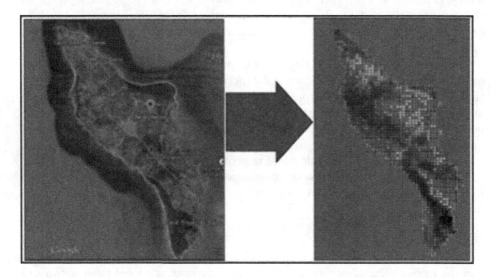

Fig. 1. From the map to the game board

`Parcel` agents have the following (physical) attributes: altitude, water height, dykes (height, status), constructibility, number of residents (current and max), distance to the sea, etc. Some of them are illustrated on Fig. 2. Parcels also have 3 values corresponding to the different competing objectives of the mayor: safety, ecological value, and attractivity.

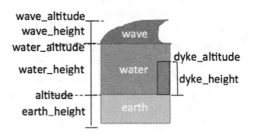

Fig. 2. Parcels attributes

`Territory` agents are composed of a set of parcels. The sea is one territory, and the island itself can be split in several land territories (one per town). At the moment there is only one island territory, so the player manages the entire island and does not interact with other players (a multi-player version of this game is considered for future work). `Territory` agents have the following attributes: number and list of parcels, number of residents, tax rate, budget, as well as global safety, ecology and attractivity values averaging those of their parcels.

Submersion Model. Each year, there is a chance of a submersion occurring (random probability or forced by the pedagogical scenario). Our submersion model is based on [4]; it receives as inputs the wind strength and direction, barometric pressure, and tidal coefficient, and computes water height and wave height from these. The submersion is then simulated based on an overflow algorithm following 4 stages: initialise weather conditions (barometric pressure, tidal coefficient, wind...); propagate water (in all directions to the 8 neighbours cells, see Fig. 3); propagate waves (only in wind_wave direction, see Fig. 4); end submersion. The different cases depending on relative water, wave and dyke altitudes are illustrated below. The algorithm also considers the status and resistance of dykes: water pressure and waves have different effects but both can damage dykes and lead them to break with a certain probability. Broken dykes offer no more protection against future submersion, and increase the insecurity feeling in residents; dykes can be maintained or repaired by the player to keep them in an operational state.

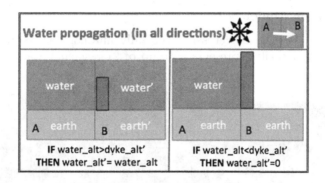

Fig. 3. Submersion algorithm: 2 cases of water propagation (no wave)

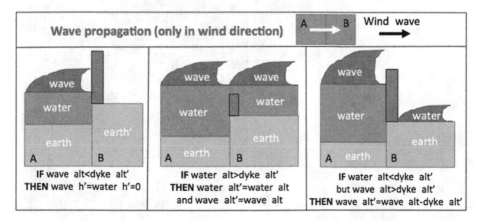

Fig. 4. Submersion algorithm: 3 cases of wave propagation

At the end of the submersion, SPRITE shows the map of impacted areas, and computes total submersion damage as the sum of damages induced on each parcel, which is function of water height, building density and number of residents.

Validation of Our Submersion Model. In order to validate our submersion model, we compared its prediction with real submersion data recorded for Xynthia. We used OSM data about the actual position of dykes on the island, and fed the model with the meteorological data as measured during Xynthia on the Oléron island: atmospheric pressure 969 HPa, wind speed 140 km/h, and tidal coefficient 102. Figure 5 shows the real submersion map as recorded on the island after Xynthia (left) and the submersion predicted by our model from the input data (right). We can see that the submersed areas are almost identical on both maps. Of course a proper validation would require to perform further experiments on other events, but these first results are encouraging.

3.2   Population Model

Residents. The Resident agents are the only autonomous cognitive agents. Each such agent actually represents a group of 21 residents. Each resident has

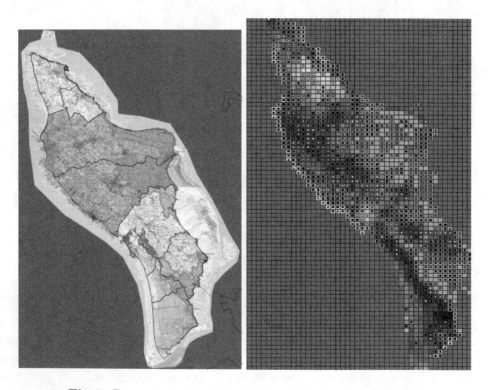

Fig. 5. Comparing real and simulated submersion during Xynthia

personal preferences for the 4 indicators (ecology, safety, economy, attractiveness), and can dynamically assess satisfaction with the current situation based on the events and actions of the mayor. For instance the satisfaction of expropriated residents will decrease significantly; residents protected by dykes will feel much safer, unless these dykes are damaged; residents are attracted to sea-side parcels even though they might be unsafe. Concretely, residents' satisfaction is computed as a function of their parcel value and current water height, and their number of relocations (each relocation further decreases satisfaction). Parcel value is a personal value, computed by each resident based on several indicators weighted by the resident's personal preference for each indicator:

- **ecology**, environmental value of the parcel (ecological development actions, low density of buildings...);
- **safety** of the parcel (protection by dykes, altitude, distance from sea...);
- **economical** value (tax rate);
- **attractivity** of the parcel (sea side, low density of buildings, promotion campaigns, low number of submersions in the past...);
- rate of residents arriving or leaving.

For instance, some residents might be very sensitive to ecological questions and not so much to safety, while others will be mainly interested in a low tax rate.

Residents can make various decisions based on their assessment of the situation: do nothing; move to a different parcel (or territory in future versions), for instance if feeling unsafe; or leave the island altogether. There is some degree of randomness in their behaviour: a satisfied resident can also leave the island for various reasons (*e.g.* finding a job on the continent); new residents can also randomly arrive on the island.

Player. The player represents the mayor of the territory, and has competing objectives, different actions to fulfill them, and a limited budget that constrains how many actions he can perform. The budget is expressed in a virtual money called kopecs. The `Player` agent is controlled by the human player through user commands (see Sect. 4). The available actions, along with their cost and effects, are described below:

- Local actions on a specific parcel:
  - **Build a dyke:** (3 different types) to improve residents' safety:
    - concrete dykes are higher and more durable but have a negative impact on touristic attractivity and on the environment; they cost 10 kopecs;
    - rip-raps have a medium height and durability but are cheaper (6 kopecs); they also have a negative touristic and environmental impact;
    - sand dunes are the most expensive (15 kopecs) and can only be built on the shore; they have a medium height and durability; unlike other types of dykes, they have no negative touristic or environmental impact;

- **Demolish a dyke:** (1 kopec for a rip-rap, 2 kopecs for a concrete dyke, 3 kopecs for a dune); removes the feeling of insecurity coming from damaged dykes, and allows to build a new dyke on that parcel;
- **Repair a dyke:** that was damaged by submersion (cost of 3 kopecs for a rip-rap, 6 for a concrete, 9 for a dune), restoring both protection from submersion and feeling of safety;
- **Environmental development:** increases environmental value (only once per parcel);
- **Allow construction:** makes it possible for the player or for private real estate companies to construct buildings, increasing attractivity (possibly at the expense of safety)
- **Forbid construction:** on an (unsafe) parcel: no further buildings can be added, pre-existing buildings are destroyed (cost of 1 to 5 kopecs depending on density), and their residents expropriated; this increases territory safety but significantly decreases satisfaction of expropriated residents;
- **Construct buildings,** which increases the number of residents that can live on that parcel
- Global actions on the whole territory:
  - **Promote:** the territory (costs 20 kopecs): increases territory attractivity, more new residents will arrive and less residents will leave;
  - **Change the tax rate:** increasing tax rate will increase the available budget but reduce resident satisfaction and territory attractivity; decreasing tax rate will increase these but less budget will be available for actions;
- **Finish turn:** when the player has no more actions to perform.

As one can see, each action has a mix of positive and negative effects, and progressing one goal often leads to impeding another one.

4   Serious Game

In this section we explain the game design of the SPRITE serious game based on this multi-agent simulation. The player has the role of the mayor and manages the island for a number of turns (each turn is one year). Our goal is to make the game engaging to better immerse the player in the experience, and improve knowledge acquisition and understanding of the key concept in that situation: the need to find an appropriate balance between the different objectives involved (economy, ecology, attractivity, safety). At the end of the game, the player can also access note cards explaining the balance mechanisms between actions and objectives. This knowledge delivered in a more classical way completes the experience, turning the game into a motivation factor to acquire knowledge [9].

4.1   Implementation

The simulation and serious game were implemented with GAMA [10], an opensource multi-agent geographical simulation platform. GAMA offers an integrated programming language and development framework, allowing even noncomputer scientists to simply design and maintain elaborated models, with up to

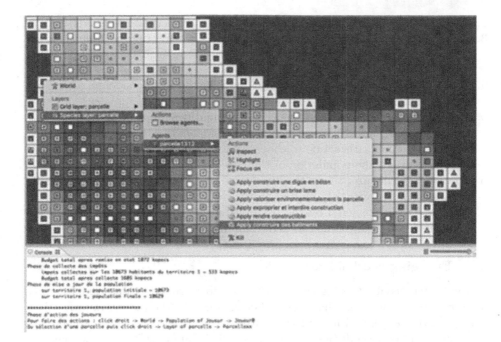

Fig. 6. Interface du jeu (Color figure online)

several millions of agents. GAMA also provides native management of GIS (Geographical Information Systems) data allowing to integrate geographical data files into simulations. Finally, GAMA offers interactive functions (user commands) enabling the use of the participatory dynamics required in SPRITE.

Figure 6 shows the game interface: game board and console. The console (at the bottom) provides the player with useful information during the whole game, and an overlay on the map shows the current values of all indicators and number of residents. The game board (at the top) is presented as a grid of parcels whose colour indicates their altitude (the darker the higher). Triangles of different colours represent dykes of different types. Squares represent the buildings (darker squares for higher construction density). Circles represent the population (darker circles for more densely populated parcels). Actions can be performed on the map by right clicking on the target. Parcel actions (building a dyke, etc.) become available by right clicking that parcel. Territory actions (change tax rate, etc.) become available by right clicking the player icon. Right clicking on a parcel also allows to see the values of all its attributes.

4.2 Game Dynamics and Interactivity

Each turn of the game (one year on the island) follows the same process:

1. **New turn:** the current year is incremented, and the console displays a message with the new year, and an alert if it is the last turn.

2. **Elections:** in election years (set in scenario), an election is triggered.
3. **Submersion:** if a submersion must happen this year (random chance or set in the scenario) it is triggered (see Sect. 3.1), submersion map and computed damage are shown to the player, and the world is then restored.
4. **Tax collection:** taxes are automatically collected from residents, at the tax rate set by the player, and added to the available budget.
5. **Residents:** each parcel might receive new buildings (depending on its attractivity) and welcome or lose residents; the residents then perform their behaviour (assess their satisfaction to choose to leave the island, move to a different parcel, or stay); the population of the parcel is updated as a result.
6. **Player interaction:** this is the interactive phase when the player can realise a number of actions (only limited by the available budget).
7. **End of turn:** triggered by the player when he is done; victory and defeat conditions are then checked to determine if the game should continue.

4.3 Engaging Mechanisms

Beyond interactivity, turning the simulation into a proper serious game requires adding some engaging mechanisms to better immerse the player, improve their learning experience, and maximise acquisition of knowledge, which is the main goal of SPRITE. Brandtzaeg et al. [11] studied "funology", *i.e.* enjoyment in human-computer interaction, by using Karasek's model of engagement and well-being at work. They found that the same three factors influenced engagement in both types of activities: **demands** on the worker or player (challenge and surprise but not overwhelming); level of **control** they have (controlled interaction, timely feedback); and **support** they receive (social interaction, no isolation). These criteria are also in agreement with Garris *et al.* 's model of motivation in educational games [12]. In order to match these criteria we have introduced several engaging elements:

– **Demands:** actions are constrained by a limited budget, yet sufficient to succeed; elections add some level of randomness and challenge; obtaining a good score requires finding a balance between various indicators;
– **Control:** the interactive map lets the player control the parcels; the console provides immediate and useful feedback on cost and remaining budget; different pedagogical scenarios of different difficulties can be selected;
– **Support:** an online high-score table allows comparison with other players; future versions will provide multi-player experience by splitting the island into several territories that can compete to attract residents.

These engaging elements are detailed below: pedagogical scenarios (Sect. 4.4); constrained budget (Sect. 4.5); elections (Sect. 4.6); and scores (Sect. 4.7).

4.4 Pedagogical Scenarios

The player can control the difficulty of the game by choosing an appropriate scenario. Four scenarios have been defined and integrated in the game, ordered by increasing difficulty. Each scenario has specific values of: **duration** (number of years/turns); **election years**; probability of occurrence, or list of years of occurrence, of **submersion** events; **defeat conditions** that might stop the game before the scripted number of turns; **game parameters** (*e.g.* residents' level of intransigence, or level of environmental damage after a submersion). We have also defined a special "cheat mode" where the player has 10 years with an unlimited budget and no submersion, where he can explore various strategies.

4.5   Budget

The player can perform as many actions as he wants at each turn, only constrained by his available budget. The game uses a virtual currency called 'kopec'. The budget exclusively comes from the taxes collected from the residents. It can be spent to pay for different actions: building or repairing dykes, promoting the island, etc. Having a limited budget means that choices need to be made every year as to which actions (*i.e.* which objectives) have more priority. Proper management of the budget is therefore a key aspect of the serious game.

The player can control the tax rate on his territory. Increasing the tax rate will increase the available budget but decrease residents' satisfaction, who might then leave as a result, therefore decreasing the amount of taxes collected the next year. Decreasing tax rate will increase immediate satisfaction but decrease the mayor's available budget to take required actions. The challenge is therefore to find an appropriate balance between having enough budget to act to satisfy the population, without overwhelming them with a too high tax rate.

4.6   Elections

Another engaging mechanism in SPRITE is the organisation of elections. The residents can vote for their new mayor every fifth year (generally at the end of the game), and the player might lose points if he is not reelected. The election process is quite basic for now but adds some fun to the game.

Apart from the player, there are 4 predefined **candidates** each focusing on one indicator: Mr Green (ecology), Mrs Gold (economy), Miss Grey (safety), and Mr Blue (attractivity). The player's score on each indicator (value between 0 and 5) is computed from his actions; the other candidates' scores are set to 3 on their focus indicator and to 1.8 on all others. The elections proceed in 2 turns. In the **first turn**, residents that are satisfied vote for the player, while neutral and unsatisfied residents choose the candidate that has the best score on their main interest. For instance an unsatisfied resident whose highest preference is on the ecology indicator will vote for Mr Green. The two candidates with the most votes move on to the second turn of the election. In the **second turn**, satisfied residents again vote for the player (if qualified after the first turn); unsatisfied residents vote for the opponent; neutral residents (or all residents if the player is not qualified) compare weighed scores (sum of scores on each indicator weighed by the resident's preference for that indicator) of both candidates to choose their favourite. The candidate with the most votes in this second turn **wins** the election. If the player is not reelected, his final score is decreased.

4.7   Victory and Defeat Conditions, Scoring and Feedback

At the end of each turn (each year), SPRITE checks the defeat conditions defined in the pedagogical scenario, and game might end immediately if some of these defeat conditions are met. In particular, some minimal threshold values of the different satisfaction indicators (ecology, attractiveness, safety, economy) are set in each pedagogical scenario. If the game stops prematurely because of one of these conditions, the player receives explanations about why he failed. On the contrary, if the player manages to reach the last turn (as defined in the scenario), the game stops with a victory message and the final score of the player is computed and displayed, along with detailed scores on each objective for each year. This detailed feedback helps the player understanding his strengths, weaknesses, and which actions contributed to increasing or decreasing his score. Finally, we also intend to provide the player with note cards explaining the balancing mechanisms at play, in order to complement the serious game.

Concretely, final score is a balanced function of the average ecology and safety values of all territory parcels, the mayor's popularity (satisfaction of his residents), and the number of residents of his territory. This score is placed on a qualitative scale (*e.g.* "average" or "good", mapping depends on the scenario) allowing the player to better understand its meaning, and motivating him to replay and try to improve his management. Motivation is even reinforced by an online "High scores" table that allows players to compare to each other, and contributes to the social support component of Karasek's model of engagement.

Evaluation and competition are key factors to improve player's engagement [11] as well as motivation and learning capability [13]. Detailed feedback improves knowledge acquisition about the risk of submersion and how to deal with it. The realism of the underlying model means that the knowledge acquired in the game should be valid and transferable to real life [14].

4.8   Preliminary Evaluation

SPRITE serious game was tested by a small number of heterogeneous participants in order to calibrate the rules, scoring and overall balance of the game, and to improve game design and engagement (*e.g.* adding elections). Further evaluation of engagement with more players is still ongoing. In the future, we will also evaluate knowledge acquisition and understanding by presenting players with a questionnaire about submersion risk and its management. We will compare learning by subjects using only the note cards, only the game, or a combination of both. The questionnaire is currently under development.

5   Conclusion

In order to raise awareness of both population and elected representatives on the island of Oléron, we designed SPRITE, a participatory simulation tool. It allows the user to play the role of the mayor and manage the island for a number of years, with the mission of finding an appropriate balance between popularity, economy, attractivity, safety and ecology. SPRITE has a double pedagogical mission: informing the player about a major but often under-estimated risk (coastal flood); and forcing him to reflect on policies for managing this risk. It provides elected representatives with elements of reflection to design an efficient and balanced management strategy, and allows residents to better understand (and therefore accept) the policy carried out by their representatives.

The model is fully implemented in GAMA and the game is already playable. The evaluation of engagement and learning is still preliminary but encouraging. Short term future work will mainly be dedicated to this evaluation and subsequently improving the model, while longer term prospects include the refinement of the mechanisms involved in the residents' decision-making.

Acknowledgements. SPRITE was initially developed by a multidisciplinary team at the CNRS MAPS 8 thematic school (https://maps.hypotheses.org/evenements-maps-passes/maps-8) organised by the MAPS network dedicated to multiagent modelling applied to spatial phenomena. SPRITE then served as a basis for the LittoSim project (directed by Nicolas Bécu and Marion Amalric) funded by CNRS Défi Littoral call 2015, that developed a new, refined, and multiplayer model. Further refinement of SPRITE (in particular with hydrological and political factors) is ongoing in the MAGIL project (directed by Eric Barthelemy) funded by CNRS Défi Littoral call 2016.

References

1. Bersani, C., Coll.: Tempête Xynthia: retour d'expérience, évaluation et propositions d'action. Technical report, Ministére écologie, dév. durable et mer (2010)
2. Vinet, F., et al.: Le processus de production du risque "submersion marine" en zone littorale: l'exemple des territoires Xynthia. NOROIS **222**, 11–26 (2012)
3. Duvat-Magnan, V.: Les impacts de la tempête Xynthia sur les plages de l'île d'oléron: les réalités du terrain. Institut du Littoral et de l'Environnement, Technical report (2010)
4. Le Cozannet, G., et al.: Evaluating uncertainties of future marine flooding occurrence as sea-level rises. Environ. Model. Softw. **73**, 44–56 (2015)
5. Michael, D., Chen, S.: Serious Games: Games that Educate, Train, and Inform. Thomson Course Technology, Boston (2006)
6. Sauve, L., Renaud, L., Gauvin, M.: Une analyse des écrits sur les impacts du jeu sur l'apprentissage. Revue des Sciences de l'Éducation **33**(1), 89–107 (2007)
7. Crovato, S., Pinto, A., Giardullo, P., Mascarello, G., Neresini, F., Ravarotto, L.: Food safety and young consumers: testing a serious game as a risk communication tool. Food Control **62**, 134–141 (2016)
8. Chadli, A.: Micro jeux et simulation multi-agents participative : apprentissage des procédures de lutte contre les rongeurs arvicoles. Ph.D. thesis, Université des Sciences et de la Technologie d'Oran (2015)
9. Wouters, P., Spek, E., Oostendorp, H.: Current practices in serious game research: a review from a learning outcomes perspective. In: Games-based learning advancements for multi-sensory human computer interfaces: techniques and effective practices, pp. 232–250. IGI Global (2009)

10. Grignard, A., Taillandier, P., Gaudou, B., Vo, D.A., Huynh, N.Q., Drogoul, A.: GAMA 1.6: advancing the art of complex agent-based modeling and simulation. In: Boella, G., Elkind, E., Savarimuthu, B.T.R., Dignum, F., Purvis, M.K. (eds.) PRIMA 2013. LNCS (LNAI), vol. 8291, pp. 117–131. Springer, Heidelberg (2013). doi:10.1007/978-3-642-44927-7_9
11. Brandtzaeg, P.B., Folstad, A., Heim, J.: Enjoyment: lessons from karasek. In: Blythe, M.A., Overbeeke, K., Monk, A.F., Wright, P.C. (eds.) Funology: From Usability to Enjoyment. HCI, vol. 3, pp. 55–65. Springer, Rotterdam (2006)
12. Garris, R., Ahlers, R., Driskell, J.E.: Games, motivation, and learning: a research and practice model. Simul. Gaming **33**(4), 441–467 (2002)
13. Koster, R.: A Theory Of Fun For Game Design. Paraglyph Press, Scottsdale (2005)
14. van Ruijven, T.: Serious games as experiments for emergency management research: a review. In: ISCRAM, May 2011

BDI Modelling and Simulation of Human Behaviours in Bushfires

Carole Adam[1]([✉]), Geoffrey Danet[1], John Thangarajah[3], and Julie Dugdale[1,2]

[1] Grenoble Alpes University, LIG, 38000 Grenoble, France
{carole.adam,julie.dugdale}@imag.fr,
geoffrey.danet@gmail.com
[2] University of Agder, Kristiansand, Norway
[3] RMIT University, Melbourne, Australia
john.thangarajah@rmit.edu.au

Abstract. Each summer in Australia, bushfires burn many hectares of forest, causing deaths, injuries, and destruction of property. Emergency management strategies rely on expected citizens' behaviour which differs from reality. In order to raise their awareness about the real population behaviour, we want to provide them with a realistic agent-based simulation. The philosophically-grounded BDI architecture provides a very suitable approach but is little used due to the lack of adapted tools. This paper uses this case study to illustrate two new tools to fill this gap: the Tactics Development Framework (TDF) and GAMA BDI architecture.

Keywords: ABMS · BDI architecture · Bushfires · Human behaviour

1 Introduction

Societies can manage crisis and emergency situations in several ways: adopt urban and territory planning policies to reduce the risks (*e.g.* forbid construction in exposed areas); raise awareness and prepare the population in advance; or create efficient emergency management policies to deal with crisis when they happen. **Modelling and simulation** offer tools to test the effects and complex interactions of these different strategies without waiting for an actual crisis to happen, without putting human lives at risk, with limited cost, and with a great degree of control on all conditions and the possibility to reproduce exactly the same situation as many times as needed.

When modelling human behaviour, mathematical, equation-based models are too limited [1]; on the contrary, **agent-based models** offer many benefits [2]. They allow to capture emergent phenomena that characterise such complex systems; they provide an intuitive and realistic description of their behaviour; they are flexible, offering different levels of abstraction by varying the complexity of agents. However, the agents used are often too simplistic, reacting to environmental stimuli without any long-term reasoning. On the contrary, crisis situations involve complex individual decision making, influenced by emotions (sometimes causing irrational actions), and by the social context (effect of group, family).

© Springer International Publishing AG 2016
P. Diaz et al. (Eds.): ISCRAM-med 2016, LNBIP 265, pp. 47–61, 2016.
DOI: 10.1007/978-3-319-47093-1_5

The BDI (belief, desire, intention [3]) architecture is more sophisticated and realistic. It describes agent behaviour in terms of mental attitudes, and has also been used to formalise emotions [4]. BDI provides the perfect level of abstraction to describe human behaviour in terms of folk psychology, which is the preferred level of description for humans [5]. It therefore addresses the problem of the scarcity of (quantitative) behaviour data by using qualitative data such as witness statements or expert reports. Despite these advantages making it very suitable for social simulation, BDI has had limited use in this field due to the **lack of adapted tools** to harness its complexity [6]. We propose to fill this gap by introducing to the emergency management community two new tools that are still under development in the field of agent-based modelling and simulation (ABMS): the TDF methodology that allows the designer to capture informal descriptions of human behaviour into a conceptual agent-based model; and the GAMA simulation platform that allows even non-computer scientists to implement a BDI model in an intuitive modelling language and conduct simulations.

We illustrate these tools on a particular case study: modelling the population behaviour during the bushfires that burn every summer across many states in Australia. Concretely, we focus on the so-called Black Saturday, 7th February 2009, when particularly strong bushfires killed 173 people and destroyed hectares of bush and many properties in the state of Victoria. Reports [7] showed that emergency management policies were designed based on an (ideal) expected behaviour that differed from the residents' actual behaviour on the day. It is therefore important to provide deciders with a simulation to raise their awareness about residents' decision making, and let them try different strategies. For such a simulation to lay valid results, it is important that the underlying human behaviour model be as realistic as possible [8]. Currently, the available data is mostly in the form of witness statements [9]. Given all of this, BDI based agent-models are an ideal choice.

In previous work [10], we have shown how the TDF methodology could be adapted to capture civilians' behaviour in the fires. We used this methodology to model the 6 archetypes of behaviours identified in the population [7] as 6 possible roles for the agents of the system, each with their own goals and plans. However, that report did not provide any statistics about the representation of the profiles in the population, or their possible links with demographics attributes, so it did not make it possible to initialise a representative simulation with the real distribution of profiles. As a result, in the current paper we adopt a different approach: we develop a single general behaviour for all of the civilians that captures the different ways in which a civilian could behave in the case of a fire. We then randomly initialise civilian agents with different beliefs that will guide them along different paths of the possible behaviours at runtime. We observe and log the behaviour of the agents, and use these logs to infer the different profiles that emerge from them. The profiles are therefore not prescribed but observed. Our hypothesis is that if our general behaviour model of the population is valid, then we should observe the emergence of the same profiles of behaviour as the ones identified from the population interviews after the Black Saturday bushfires.

2   BDI Modelling Methodology: TDF

In this case study, we aim to model the behaviour of the civilian population in the Black Saturday bushfires, as gathered from witness statements from the affected population following the bushfires [9]. When designing a conceptual model for computational simulation, UML is the most widely used tool, mostly because of its generality and ease of use, allowing one to describe entities in terms of attributes and actions; but it is not well suited for modeling human behaviour which is what is often required in disaster management and evacuation simulations such as our case study. On the other hand, as mentioned earlier, agent-based software development methodologies that develop systems using mental attitudes of goals, events, plans, beliefs, capabilities etc. are well suited for these systems. This is particularly relevant when transcribing behaviours described by human witnesses as is the case here, since humans naturally tend to explain their behaviour in terms of mental attitudes. For instance, take this extract: *"I looked out the window and saw some hazy smoke to the north-west. Gary said that he thought it was just dust but we went outside and straight away we noticed that we could smell smoke. It was about 12.45pm when we smelt the smoke and as soon as that happened, Gary agreed to go and get the fire pump"*. We can make the mental attitudes involved more explicit: Gary (wrongly) **believed** for a while that the smoke was just dust, but **planned** to get more information; after going outside they **perceived** smoke and realised that it was coming from a fire (**belief update**). As a result, he adopted the **goal** to get ready for the fire, and started on their **plan** whose first **action** is to get the fire pump.

Whilst there are several agent-oriented software engineering methodologies such as Prometheus, Tropos, O-MaSE, GAIA and others [11] here we introduce a more recent methodology purpose built for eliciting and encoding tactical/strategic behaviour in dynamic domains – TDF (Tactics Development Framework) [12,13]. TDF is based on the Prometheus methodology [14], a mature and popular agent-oriented software engineering methodology. A pilot study has shown that TDF significantly improves comprehension of behavior models, compared to UML [12]. Although TDF was initially designed to capture and model military behaviour, we have shown in previous work [10] that this framework can be adapted to model civilians' descriptions of their behaviour in crisis situations. The TDF methodology proceeds in following 3 phases as relevant to our case study: *System specification*: Identification of system-level artefacts, namely goals, scenarios, percepts, actions, data, actors and roles; *Architectural design*: Specification of the internals of the system, namely the agents that play the different roles, the interactions between the agents (via protocols) if any, and messages between agents; and *Detailed design*: Definition of the internals of the agents, namely capabilities, plan diagrams and internal messages/sub-goals. We now illustrate how we modelled our case study in TDF below.

2.1   System Specification: Analysis Overview

The purpose of this diagram is to identify the actors (entities external to the system), the inputs (percepts) to and outputs (actions) from the system, and identify scenarios (use-cases) that describe possible runs of the system. In our case, the scenarios are examples of behaviours that we want to observe. A given scenario will comprise a sequence of steps, where a step could include goals, actions, percepts and sub-scenarios. Figure 1 illustrates part of the analysis overview diagram related to a scenario where the civilian defends his property and Fig. 2 illustrates the detailed steps of the "Defend Property" scenario.

2.2   System Specification: Goal Overview

In the next step, we develop the goals for the agents (civilians) in the system. The goal overview diagram illustrates how the high-level goals are decomposed into more concrete goals. Figure 3 illustrate the goals that civilians adopted, as extracted from the interviews. The different behaviours described in these interviews result from two high-level goals: **Defend Property** (stay and defend it), and **Stay Alive** (protect life of self and family). The relative priorities of these goals depend on individual differences in various factors: awareness of fire risk, fire training, physical condition, family situation (children to protect), motivations to defend property (family house, livelihood), etc. These two high-level goals are then decomposed as shown. The sub-goals of a goal can be either **OR**, **AND** or **CON** decompositions. **OR** goals are a disjunction: a civilian can try to stay alive by either taking cover at home, or by going to a shelter. **AND** goals are a (possibly ordered) conjunction: to get to a shelter, one must first prepare their house and themselves, then know a shelter location, then know a safe route to get there, then finally follow that route. **CON** goals are concurrent goals where several sub-goals must be pursued in parallel: to fight the fire, one must concurrently monitor their health, the state of their house, and fight the fire (spraying water).

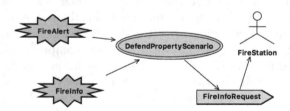

Fig. 1. Partial analysis overview diagram

Type		Name	Description
☐	Percept	FireAlert	The civilian becomes aware of a fire
☐	Goal	DefendProperty	Commits to defending the property
☐	Goal	PrepareProperty	Begin preparation to fight the fire
☐	Action	FireInfoRequest	Request more information from the firestation
☐	Percept	FireInfo	Information regarding the fire
☐	Goal	FightFire	Begin steps to fight the fire if the fire is close

Fig. 2. Example scenario: civilian defending property (detailed steps)

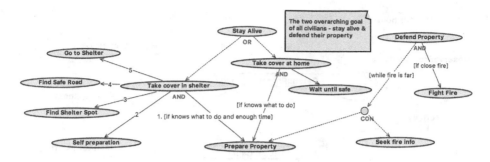

Fig. 3. Goal overview for civilians: decomposition of 2 main high-level goals, "Stay Alive" and "Defend Property"

2.3   System Specification: Role Overview

Having identified the goals, we next determine the roles to which these goals are relevant: the 6 profiles of behaviour identified by [7] from the witness statements. Usually, these roles will then be assigned to agents, however, in our case we only model a single agent that can play any of these roles at run-time.

2.4   Architectural Design: System Overview

Figure 4 outlines the system overview, which shows the inputs and outputs to the Civilian agent type. In general, when there are multiple agent types, this diagram also captures the interactions between the agents via protocols. However, in our case we have only one (type of) agent.

2.5   Detailed Design: Agent Overview

The next step consists in designing the agent overview for each agent type which details the capabilities and plans of the agents used to achieve their goals. The plans can be distributed in several capabilities, and each agent can be endowed with one or more capabilities. Figure 5 shows the different capabilities that civilians are endowed with and the inputs and outputs relevant to each capability.

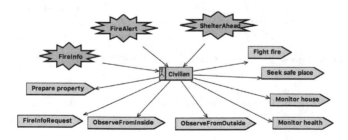

Fig. 4. System overview

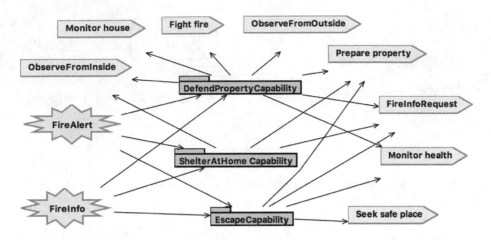

Fig. 5. Agent overview, illustrating the capabilities of a Civilian agent

2.6 Detailed Design: Capability Overview

Figure 6 details the plans and sub-goals involved in the "defend property" capability. This diagram shows the flow of activities and also specifies the data elements required, for example the "FireData" that is read by the "DefendProperty" and written to by the "ContactFireStation" and "ObserveSurroundings" plans. Note that this capability contains a sub-capability called "FightFire" that handles the "fight fire" goal.

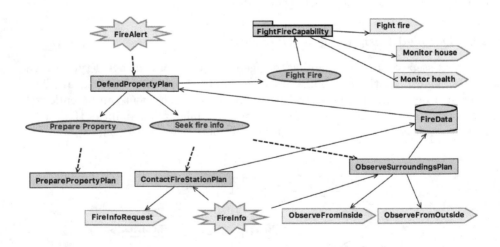

Fig. 6. Details of the "DefendProperty" capability

2.7 Detailed Design: Plan Diagrams

Finally, each plan is detailed in a plan diagram, that is essentially a process diagram, that can be directly translated into implementation code. A plan can be triggered by external percepts or by internal goals, and is composed of several (sequential or concurrent) steps. Steps can be atomic actions (external), activities (internal processes, *e.g.* write data), or sub-goals. TDF allows to design one plan diagram per plan; these diagrams are quite similar to UML activity diagrams.

Figure 7 shows the plan diagram for the "Defend Property" plan. It illustrates that the plan is triggered by the "FireAlert" percept, and then concurrently adopts goals to "PrepareProperty" and "Seek Fire Info". Having adopted the goals, it monitors the "FireData" information for when the fire is close enough to adopt the goal to "Fight Fire".

Figure 8 shows the plan diagram for the "ObserveSurroundings" plan. It illustrates a decision node where the agent considers if it safe outside before choosing a mode of observation, followed by a merge node where the plan proceeds to the next step, which is an activity that updates the agent's fire data.

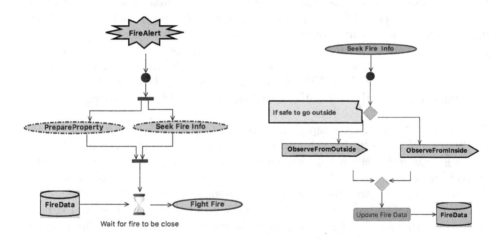

Fig. 7. DefendPropertyPlan   **Fig. 8.** ObserveSurroundingsPlan

3 Simulation Platform: GAMA

3.1 GIS and Agent-Based Modelling Architecture (GAMA)

GAMA [15, 16] is an open source platform for agent-based modelling and simulation of complex spatialised systems. It provides built-in functions for using Geographical Information Systems (GIS) data, such as OpenStreetMap (OSM) for fast and precise mapping of the environment. Simulations built with GAMA are scalable, since the platform can deal with several thousands of agents, depending on the level of complexity of their architecture. Further, GAMA provides a very simple and high level programming language called GAML, that allows even non-programmers to simply build and maintain their own models. As a result, it is widely used by designers from many different fields. Finally, it is supported by an active development team that is progressively improving the software.

In particular, GAMA was recently extended with a BDI plugin [17,18] to allow designers to easily create BDI agent models in the GAML language. They can specify logical predicates, initialise their agents with beliefs and desires, describe the effect of new percepts on the agent beliefs, and provide them with a plan library. The BDI engine then lets the agents perceive their environment, update their beliefs and desires, select an intention based on relative priorities of their goals, and choose and execute an adapted plan to reach that goal.

3.2   Implementation of the Model

Environment. The BDI implementation for this particular case study is based on our previous simulation [19] which used a finite-state machine (FSM) for the agent architecture. Only the environment is the same: a square grid of 50 by 50 cells with two safe shelters and a number of houses each inhabited by one resident, where a fire starts in a few initial cells and then propagates to neighbouring cells at a speed that can be set as a parameter. The focus of this paper is not on the realism of the environment or the fire behaviour, but on illustrating the use of the GAMA BDI plugin to simply design complex human behaviour models such as that developed using the TDF methodology.

Population. Residents are represented by a GAMA species `Civilian`. Their attributes include: a health value which decreases due to injuries caused by the fire or its radiant heat; a velocity when moving; a random awareness of risks (perception radius); a random ability to fight fires (defense radius); a level of determination to protect their property; a random risk aversion; and a reference to its property. Civilians also maintain their own list of known fires and known shelters. At the start of the simulation, all agents are unaware of any fires (since there is none yet) and are waiting at home until they perceive one.

The next paragraphs illustrate how the model designed with TDF precisely map with concepts provided by the BDI agent architecture of GAMA.

3.3   Mapping TDF Design with GAML Code

Predicates. In GAML, the designer first needs to describe the different logical predicates that will be manipulated by the agent. This is basically the ontology of the domain. The code snippet in Fig. 9 illustrates some predicates for our bushfire domain. Predicates can be associated with a priority: here staying alive has a priority based on the agent's danger aversion, while protecting the property has a priority based on the agent's determination.

```
predicate fire_position ← new_predicate(''Know the fire
position'');
...
predicate stay_alive ← new_predicate(''Stay alive'')
        with_priority rnd(danger_aversion);
predicate protect_property ← new_predicate(''Protect property'')
        with_priority rnd(determination);
```

Fig. 9. Code snippet: predicates for domain ontology

Percepts. Agents can then be given perceptions, that explain how they interpret stimuli coming in. These perceptions can add new beliefs or goals. They match the percepts in TDF that represent the stimuli coming in from the environment and triggering the agent's plans. The code snippet in Fig. 10 shows how the civilian agents perceive new fires (that are not yet in their list of known fires): they add them to their list, and create a belief that there is a fire, and a desire to get more information.

```
perceive target:(list(fire) - known_fires) in: perception_radius
{
    add self to: myself.known_fires;
    ask myself
    {
        do add_belief(fire_position);
        do add_desire(get_information);
    }
}
```

Fig. 10. Code snippet: perception of an unknown fire

Actions. Agents are endowed with a number of actions, as specified in TDF. There is no concept of capability to group actions together in GAML. The snippet in Fig. 11 illustrates 2 actions of civilians: prepare their building (the effect value is computed based on some parameters not detailed here, and added to their building resistance); and prepare themselves (similarly, a value is computed and added to their total health, to simulate *e.g.* wearing protective clothes).

Plan Library. Similarly to TDF, actions are combined in plans. The agents are endowed with a library of plans to achieve their goals. Each GAML plan is defined with several features: the goal that it achieves (keyword intention); a context condition (keyword when) that describes when this plan is applicable; and a success condition (keyword finished_when). The code snippet in Fig. 12

```
action prepare_building {
    int prepEffect ← ...;
    ask myBuilding {
        resistance ← min([max_resistance,resistance+prepEffect]);
    }
}
action prepare_self {
    int preparationEffect ← ...;
    health ← min([health+preparationEffect,max_health]);
}
```

Fig. 11. Code snippet: actions to prepare building and self

illustrate the plan to prepare to defend one's property against fire: it realises the goal to prepare one's property, by executing the 2 actions defined above (preparing the building and preparing oneself); it is applicable when the individual knows how to fight fire, his house is still standing, and the fire is not in the immediate vicinity; it succeeds when resistance and health reach the maximum possible value. It could also be interrupted when the fire gets too close and the civilian changes intention to "fight fire".

```
plan prepare_property
    intention: prepare_property
    when: (knows_how and empty(known_fires at_distance
defense_radius) and !self.myBuilding.destroyed)
    finished_when: myBuilding.resistance=max_resistance and
health=max_health
{
    do prepare_building;
    do prepare_self;
}
```

Fig. 12. Code snippet: plan to prepare property

Reflexes. This is not specific to BDI agents but common to all agent architectures in GAMA. Reflexes allow an agent to directly and quickly react to some events. They are useful to implement fast reactions that do not need deliberation. For instance in our model we implemented a reflex (shown in Fig. 13) that set the agent to "dead" when their health decreases to 0 or less; its beliefs, desires and intentions are cleared as a result.

```
reflex death when: health <= 0 and !is_dead {
    do clear_bdi();
    ...
    self.is_dead ← true;
}
```

Fig. 13. Code snippet: reflex to die when health decreases to 0

3.4   Results and Validation of the Model

In order to validate the model, we have run a number of simulations (to smooth the randomness in fire behaviour) and logged the behaviour of the civilian agents, tracking in particular the plans they used, and for the ones who died, what was their last plan. We have then categorised the agents in the profiles identified by [7] based on their logged behaviour: unaware reactors are conscious of the fires but do nothing; threat avoiders immediately adopt the plan to go to a shelter without trying anything else; threat monitors stay home and seek information without trying to defend, but they can evacuate to a shelter eventually; can-do defenders know how to fight the fire, they stay home to prepare and fight, but might take shelter if needed; livelihood defenders stay home to fight the fire and defend their property seen as their livelihood, they will never evacuate but might shelter at home; considered defenders fight the fire but are less knowledgeable, they might evacuate late when they cannot deal anymore. We have run 2 scenarios with different parameters for the fire, and were able to observe the emergence of these profiles, with a different distribution depending on the intensity of fires. However, the difference between livelihood defenders and can-do defenders is mainly in the type of motivation to defend their property (determination vs livelihood) so we were not able to differentiate them at runtime.

Figure 14 we show the distribution of the 5 remaining profiles for a small fire (left) and a more intense fire (right). We can see in particular that there are much less unaware reactors in a more intense fire (when it is harder to fail to notice it). There are a bit less can-do defenders in a more intense fire, probably because this profile corresponds to more experienced residents who can recognise when a fire is too intense to be dealt with, and subsequently escape. Indeed, there is more threat avoiders and threat monitors in the more intense fire. The number of considered defenders is stable, probably due to their lack of experience which does not let them adapt their behaviour to the intensity of the fire. This confirms that the choice of a profile by civilians is indeed dynamic, linked to the situation (fire) and not to demographic features (which did not change between the 2 scenarios). In both scenarios, we also observed that most victims died while doing nothing (53 % in a smaller fire, and over 65 % in a bigger fire, when they have more risks of being surprised), which is consistent with the statistics after the Black Saturday bushfires [20,21].

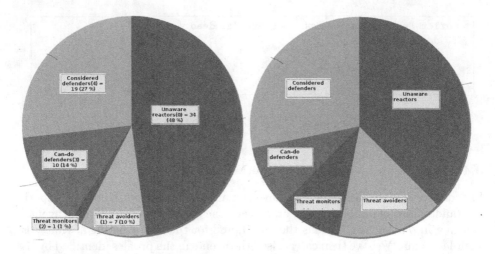

Fig. 14. Dynamic distribution of profiles in the population facing low vs intense fire

4   Discussion and Conclusion

Results. Our results are consistent with the statistics from the actual Black Saturday bushfires, therefore demonstrating the validity of our model. Our detailed case study thus shows that TDF and GAMA BDI can successfully help designers to conceive and implement a BDI agent-based model of civilian behaviour in crisis situations. TDF provides a visual tool offering a variety of diagrams to support design (illustrated in Figs. 1, 2, 3, 4, 5, 6, 7 and 8), and tailored for BDI agents. GAMA BDI offers an intuitive language to implement the same concepts modelled with TDF, allowing an easy translation from diagrams to code (as illustrated in code snippets of Figs. 9, 10, 11, 12 and 13). The innovative combination of these two tools as described here therefore works very well, and our study is very promising.

Related Work. Kuligowski *et al.* [22,23] showed the importance of modelling human behaviour in crisis situations. To design realistic behaviour models, it is important to use a sophisticated model such as BDI [6], and various works have recently looked into how to integrate BDI agents into simulations, but most authors develop *ad hoc* platforms. Tsai *et al.* [24] develop their own framework called ESCAPES to integrate BDI agents into a 3D simulator of airport evacuation to be used by security officers. Okaya *et al.* [25] use Robocup Rescue simulation platform to implement BDI agents into building evacuation scenarios and study human relationships and altruism. Singh *et al.* [26] use their middleware [27] that connects Jack (an agent-oriented development framework) with the Phoenix fire simulator to plan population evacuation in bushfires.

These tools are often complex to use and limited to computer scientists. On the contrary, TDF provides a visual tool for simply conceptualising models, and GAMA provides a simple and intuitive language to implement these models.

Moreover, in most papers in ABMS, little detail is given on the actual tools that were used. On the contrary in this paper we intended to describe in sufficient details two tools that we believe could be useful, and we illustrated them on a real case study which should enable others to develop similar models for their own applications.

Limitations. The case study also allowed us to identify some limitations of the tools, that are currently being addressed. The TDF tool used here was a proto-type and was sometimes unstable, however a new web-based version is currently being redeveloped and will be released by the end of the year. The BDI archi-tecture for GAMA used was a beta-version, and it is also still being improved.

Future work. In future works we will further develop these tools, and most importantly conduct a user-based evaluation to validate their combined use with respect to usability and maintainability. In the longer-term, in relation with the case study exposed here, we intend to turn this simulation into a serious game to raise deciders' awareness and let them try various strategies and explore their effects. TDF allows to model external users as actors of the system, while the GAMA simulation platform offers interactive capabilities to let users play an active role in the system. The innovative combination of these two tools proposed here is therefore very promising for our project and others in crisis management.

Acknowledgements. This work was supported by the ANR ACTEUR project and AGIR SWIFT project. The authors also thank Patrick Taillandier and Benoit Gaudou for their help with GAMA.

References

1. Dyke Parunak, H., Savit, R., Riolo, R.L.: Agent-based modeling vs. equation-based modeling: a case study and users' guide. In: Sichman, J.S., Conte, R., Gilbert, N. (eds.) MABS 1998. LNCS (LNAI), vol. 1534, pp. 10–25. Springer, Heidelberg (1998). doi:10.1007/10692956_2
2. Bonabeau, E.: Agent-based modeling: methods and techniques for simulating human systems. Proc. Natl. Acad. Sci. **99**(3), 7280–7287 (2002)
3. Rao, A., Georgeff, M.: Modeling rational agents within a BDI-architecture. In: 2nd International Conference on Principles of Knowledge Representation and Reason-ing, pp. 473–484 (1991)
4. Adam, C., Herzig, A., Longin, D.: A logical formalization of the OCC theory of emotions. Synthese **168**(2), 201–248 (2009)
5. Norling, E.: Folk psychology for human modeling: extending the BDI paradigm. In: AAMAS, New York (2004)
6. Adam, C., Gaudou, B.: BDI agents in social simulations: a survey. Knowl. Eng. Rev. **31**(3), 207–238 (2016)
7. Rhodes, A.: Why dont they do what we think they should? In: AFAC, Emergency Management Victoria (2014)

8. van Ruijven, T.: Serious games as experiments for emergency management research: a review. In: 8th International ISCRAM Conference, Lisbon, Portugal need for realism of underlying model to get valid results, transferable to real life situations, May 2011
9. Exell, S.: Witness statements. http://vol4.royalcommission.vic.gov.au/index03a1.html?pid=111
10. Adam, C., Beck, E., Dugdale, J.: Modelling the tactical behaviour of the Australian population in a bushfire. In: Bellamine Ben Saoud, N., Adam, C., Hanachi, C. (eds.) ISCRAM-med 2015. LNBIP, vol. 233, pp. 53–64. Springer, Heidelberg (2015). doi:10.1007/978-3-319-24399-3_5
11. DeLoach, S.A., Padgham, L., Perini, A., Susi, A., Thangarajah, J.: Using three AOSE toolkits to develop a sample design. Int. J. Agent-Oriented Softw. Eng. **3**(4), 416–476 (2009)
12. Evertsz, R., Thangarajah, J., Yadav, N., Ly, T.: A framework for modelling tactical decision-making in autonomous systems. J. Syst. Softw. **110**, 222–238 (2015)
13. TDF: Tactics development framework. http://agentprojects.com/tdf/
14. Padgham, L., Winikoff, M.: Prometheus: a methodology for developing intelligent agents. In: Giunchiglia, F., Odell, J., Weiß, G. (eds.) AOSE 2002. LNCS, vol. 2585, pp. 174–185. Springer, Heidelberg (2003). doi:10.1007/3-540-36540-0_14
15. Grignard., A., Taillandier, P., Gaudou, B., Huynh, N., Vo, D.A., Drogoul, A.: Gama v. 1.6: advancing the art of complex agent-based modeling and simulation. In: PRIMA (2013)
16. GAMA: Gis and agent-based modelling architecture. http://gama-platform.org
17. Caillou, P., Gaudou, B., Grignard, A., Truong, C.Q., Taillandier, P.: A Simple-to-use BDI architecture for agent-based modeling and simulation. In: The Eleventh Conference of the European Social Simulation Association (ESSA 2015), Groningen, Netherlands, September 2015
18. A BDI Agent architecture for the GAMA modeling, simulation platform. In: International Workshop on Multi-Agent-Based Simulation, Singapore, Malaysia, MABS, May 2016
19. Adam, C., Gaudou, B.: Modelling human behaviours in disasters from interviews: application to Melbourne bushfires. In: Social Simulation Conference (SSC), Rome, Italy, September 2016
20. Victorian Bushfires Research Commission: Final report, volume i: The fires and the fire-related deaths. Technical report, VBRC (2009). http://goo.gl/TW1N9b
21. Teague, B., McLeod, R., Pascoe, S.: Final report, Volume I, Part 2: The people who died. Chapter 21: lessons learnt. Technical report, 2009 Victorian Bushfires Royal Commission (2009)
22. Kuligowski, E., Gwynne, S.: The need for behavioral theory in evacuation modeling. In: Klingsch , W.W.F., Rogsch , C., Schadschneider, A., Schreckenberg, M. (eds.) Pedestrian and Evacuation Dynamics, pp. 721–732. Springer, Heidelberg (2008)
23. Kinateder, M.T., Kuligowski, E.D., Reneke, P.A., Peacock, R.D.: A review of risk perception in building fire evacuation. Technical report, National Institute of Standards and Technology NIST Technical Note 1840, September 2014
24. Tsai, et al.: Escapes: evacuation simulation with children, authorities, parents, emotions, and social comparison. AAMAS **2**, 457–464 (2011)
25. Okaya, M., Takahashi, T.: Human relationship modeling in agent-based crowd evacuation simulation. In: Kinny, D., Hsu, J.Y., Governatori, G., Ghose, A.K. (eds.) PRIMA 2011. LNCS (LNAI), vol. 7047, pp. 496–507. Springer, Heidelberg (2011). doi:10.1007/978-3-642-25044-6_40

26. Singh, D., Padgham, L.: Community evacuation planning for bushfires using agent-based simulation: demonstration. In: AAMAS, pp. 1903–1904 (2015)
27. Padgham, L., Nagel, K., Singh, D., Chen, Q.: Integrating BDI agents into a MAT-Sim simulation. Front. Artif. Intell. Appl. (ECAI) **263**, 681–686 (2014)

Obtaining Optimal Bio-PEPA Model Using Association Rules: Approach Applied to Tuberculosis Case Study

Dalila Hamami$^{(\boxtimes)}$ and Baghdad Atmani

University of Oran 1 Ahmed Ben Bella, Oran, Algeria
dhamami8@gmail.com, atmani.baghdad@gmail.com

Abstract. The computational modelling has been applied in several works, which exert considerable positive impact, particularly in epidemiological field. However, modelling epidemics is very sensitive where selecting appropriate feature and model structure is challenging task for experts and epidemiologists. To overcome this limitation, we presented in previous work a methodology combining computational modelling and decision tree techniques. The approach has been validated on tuberculosis case study. Therefore, as comparative study, we propose here to apply association rules algorithms. The results indicate the epidemiological relevance of the extracted rules. Thus, the enhanced Bio-PEPA model demonstrates the robustness of the proposed approach.

Keywords: Modelling and simulation · Bio-PEPA · Data mining · Association rules · Tuberculosis

1 Introduction

Epidemiological field has received a great attention from computational modelling, where large studies have been achieved to predict complex diseases and analyse their dynamics [1–4]. However and instead of successful results, the massive increase in epidemics datasets and their complexity, lead to a tedious task to perform accurate models. In fact, associating between different features of specific diseases or detecting the perfect correlation between treatment and diseases make designing a rigorous model structure and using an appropriate set of parameters cumbersome for both developer and epidemiologist where the uncertainty remains the main trial. To overcome this issue, more support should be provided to the expert for better understanding and analysis the epidemics dataset. In this context, data mining seems to be the perfect candidate [5].

Association rules are well-known data mining technique to find predictive rules, frequent sets from large datasets and causal relationship among individuals [6–8]. Association rules algorithms have been widely used in epidemiological field. Nahar et al. [9] applied Apriori, Predictive Apriori and Tertius to analyze the main factors identifying the hearth disease depending on gender. Authors reported significant rules indicating that males have more chance of being a subject of heart disease then females. Duby [10] reported a strong correlation between HIV and tuberculosis medications.

© Springer International Publishing AG 2016
P. Diaz et al. (Eds.): ISCRAM-med 2016, LNBIP 265, pp. 62–75, 2016.
DOI: 10.1007/978-3-319-47093-1_6

Author found out that overlapping medication toxicities and immune reconstitution inflammatory syndrome complicate the treatment of both diseases. Ordonez et al. [11, 12], applied Apriori algorithm to heart disease data. The goal of their experiment was to improve the current medical diagnosis by finding a relation between patient characteristics and vessel disease. They report that the resulting medical knowledge was important, since they enrich the current knowledge. Asha et al. [13] argued, by using association rules on tuberculosis data, that several symptoms such as chronic caught, weight loss or prolonged fever are mostly associated to pulmonary tuberculosis.

This paper presents an extensive experimental evaluation by using association rules on tuberculosis data. The main findings are a set of pertinent attributes which are explored in optimizing our computational tuberculosis model using Bio-PEPA formalism (see Appendix for more details about Bio-PEPA formalism).

As expand of our previous work [5], where computational tuberculosis model has been evolved by using decision tree induction, this work provides comparison between decision tree and association rules. The selected attributes found by association rules are more abundant than attributes induced by decision tree. We investigate the usefulness of our findings by optimizing our Bio-PEPA computational model using the different attributes. Based on our Bio-PEPA simulation results, we demonstrate that the model is deeply refined than with decision tree induced attribute.

This paper is structured as follows: Sect. 2, divided into two parts. First, a brief recall of our previous work and its limitation. Second, a description of the different steps performed to refine our initial Bio-PEPA model using association rules. Section 3 describes the experimental results followed by conclusions.

2 Method

In support of this work, we based our study on the model and data provided in our previous work [5]. This section presents first a brief recall of modelling limitation provided in our previous work [5] and then a description of the approach based on association rules.

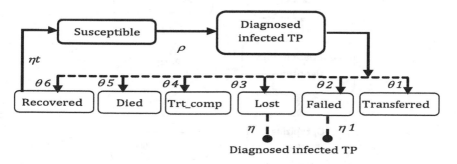

Fig. 1. Simplified tuberculosis compartmental model (Taken from [5])

2.1   Bio-PEPA Model Combined with Decision Tree: Problem Definition

Tuberculosis model described in our previous work [5] and illustrated in Fig. 1, indicates that by using only expert knowledge, the model results do not fit the observed data. In addition, it was argued that some knowledge and features can be hidden to the expert/epidemiologist, which leads to inaccurate prediction. To overcome this limitation, the proposed approach, in our previous work explores deeper data derived from cohort study using decision tree induction. The conclusion derived is that the model uncertainty can be controlled by mining tuberculosis data, where only the most pertinent information is extracted.

As argued in our previous study, using decision tree is in great help. Indeed, decision tree algorithms are flexible, understandable and provide useful prediction [8]. Decision trees deal better with categorical attributes [14] and their structure as tree makes the interpretation clearer. The above characteristics are the most well known offered advantages compared to other decision-making tools. However, we find out that decision tree are limited to one output per attribute, which highlight their inability to represent rules that refer to two or more different objects. In addition, to find the best predictor, a laborious comparison has been undertaken between different classifiers. Choosing the highest accuracy is not automatically evident. This was argued in our previous work, where the rule induced from the best classifier (J48) [6] relying to the highest accuracy does not bring additional information to our model. To overcome these limitations, we propose here to apply association rules algorithms.

2.2   Bio-PEPA Model Combined with Association Rules: Solution

In the aim to achieve the objective of this paper, the approach proposed in our previous work has been modified by integrating association rules step in the optimization process. Figure 2 shows the modified structure of the methodology. We recall that the typical steps of our approach include:

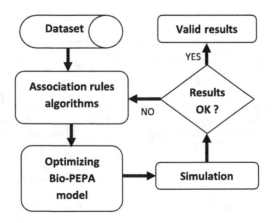

Fig. 2. Modelling and simulation process

1. Interaction expert/developer: To help developer to construct the model, an extensive exchange is performed between epidemiologist and developer.
2. Bio-PEPA modelling: the knowledge provided by the expert in the previous step (inputs, outputs and rules) leads to build the formal Bio-PEPA model.
3. Simulation and analysis: the constructed model is analysed by comparing the resulting outputs with observed data.
4. Optimisation: in the aim to provide an accurate representation of the real system, the model achieved in the previous steps is refined. This step is performed using information gained by applying association rules to tuberculosis data.

We recall that the aim of this paper is to optimise existing computational model using association rules. Therefore the initial Bio-PEPA model built in our previous work is reused for optimisation step. Thus the steps 1, 2 and 3 are already performed and we focus only on the step 4 described above.

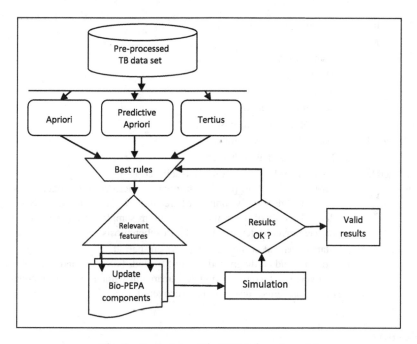

Fig. 3. Optimizing Bio-PEPA formal model

Optimisation Using Association Rules. As argued in Sect. 2.1, association rules algorithms are used in this study. For this purpose, a range of algorithms are proposed, the most commonly reported in literature [9, 15–20] are: Apriori, Predictive Apriori and Tertius.

Once the rules resulting from the algorithms listed above are generated, their significance and performance is evaluated. To this end and according to the algorithms used, three primordial measures assuring rules certainty are used [9, 21]: confidence, accuracy and confirmation.

By using the above measures, a comparison is carried out between rules within each algorithm. The best selected rules are analysed where the pertinent attributes are extracted. In general, the epidemiologist could intervene to make a selection as being the primary expert of the domain. At this step, the extracted information is integrated into the initial Bio-PEPA model.

It is worth noting that integrating the relevant attributes to the Bio-PEPA model includes restructuring the model (new compartment and new functional rates) and recalculating parameters.

Figure 3 summarizes optimizing Bio-PEPA formal model.

Table 1. Model attributes and description (Taken from [5]).

Attributes	Description
Attributes used in the study	
Age	Age of individual
Sexe	Male/Female
Com	City
Daira	Municipality
Address	Flat nimber, Zip code, etc.
Mois	Month of detection
Trim	Season of detection
Annee	Year of detecting disease
Date_Debut_TRT	Date of starting treatment
Typmal	New/Relapse/Failure/Other
Bacil1, Bacil2, Bacil3	Baciloscopy1, Baciloscopy 2, Baciloscopy 3. MM: negative, MP: positive, known as microscopy for Bacilli, test performed during six months of treatment by using a microscope to detect bacteria of tuberculosis in sputum samples. This test is used to manage mycobacterial infections of tuberculosis
AretTRT	State of patient at the end of treatment period: Lost: individual diagnosed but not treated, failed: treated but not recovered, Trt_comp: completed treatment without proving recovery, died, transferred: resistant TB, recovered

3   Results

To demonstrate the validity of our approach, tuberculosis data set obtained from the SEMEP[1], the Service of Epidemiology and Preventive Medicine of Mostaganem (Algeria) is used. This data records the details of 998 individuals infected by tuberculosis (TB) in different location, from 2008 to 2012, where each individual is described by 23 attributes.

---

[1] SEMEP: Service d'Epidémiologie et MEdecine Préventive.

Before applying association rules algorithms, data should be pre-processed. This can be achieved by applying data cleaning and data transformation. By using either manual process or WEKA algorithms, some of irrelevant variables were removed and some others were transformed. After removing nine of them and transforming one, in total, it remains fourteen attributes, illustrated in Table 1. These were input to the association rules algorithms. Attributes are classified into three types according to the information they contain. Attributes correspond to personal individual details, attributes correspond to TB test and attributes correspond to the state of the individual at the end of treatment. The goal is to detect mined patterns expressing correlation between attributes and leading to one of the final state of individual (Lost, recovered, died, … etc.).

3.1 Rules Extraction and Attributes Selection

While in our previous work, we considered classification as solution to improve the Bio-PEPA model, in this paper, we observe the most relevant association between attributes. For this purpose, we run experiments on algorithms illustrated in Fig. 3.

These were achieved under two considerations. First, the extracted rules indicate attributes in highest association. Second, as Bio-PEPA simulation performed in our previous work detected that the lost state is the most inaccurate part of the model, specifically for both years 2010 and 2012, then experiments are performed to discover rules based on the final state of individual described on Table 1 (Lost, Recovered, Died, … etc.).

As specified above (taken from our previous work), the Bio-PEPA simulations related to the years 2010 and 2012 show discrepancies with observed data; therefore, two series of experiments are carried out in WEKA. The first series concern mining the range of data set from 2008 to 2010 and the second series from 2008 to 2012.

Table 2 (resp. Table 3) shows the best rules extracted for the first series of experiments for dataset up to 2010 (resp. the second series of experiments for dataset up to 2012). As there can be many rules, only rules observing the lost state (as stated above) were selected.

For the Apriori experiments (series 1), rules 1–6 show that Bacil 1–3 and Daira are those relevant attributes inducing the lost state. However, it is well known from epidemiologist knowledge that if the entire tests, Bacil 1–3, are unavailable then individual is defined as Lost. Therefore, the attribute Daira is the only new pertinent feature. In the same line of this analysis the remaining rules show that the attributes Sex and Com are also pertinent but with lower confidence.

Although Predictive Apriori experiments (series 1) performed higher accuracy than other algorithms, the resulted rules show similar group of pertinent attributes with an exception of the attribute AGE.

Tertius experiments (series 1) show relatively different results, where the attribute age is not depicted as relevant. Even if the confirmation degrees related to Tirtius experiments seem low compared to other algorithms measures, according to [22] those degrees are relatively highly confirmed where some are well satisfied such as the rule 2 (number of counter instances = 0.01). Overall, the three algorithms generated similar rules with similar set of selected attributes.

Table 2. Experiments series 1 - Extracted rules from Apriori, Predictive Apriori and Tertius

Algorithms	Rules	Measure
Apriori	1. If (DAIRA = KHEIREDDINE, BACIL1 = NF, BACIL2 = NF, BACIL3 = NF) ==> ARETTRT = Lost	conf:(0.84)
	2. If (DAIRA = KHEIREDDINE, BACIL1 = NF, BACIL2 = NF) ==> ARETTRT = Lost	conf:(0.81)
	3. If (DAIRA = KHEIREDDINE, BACIL1 = NF, BACIL3 = NF) ==> ARETTRT = Lost	conf:(0.75)
	4. If (DAIRA = KHEIREDDINE, BACIL2 = NF, BACIL3 = NF) ==> ARETTRT = Lost	conf:(0.74)
	5. If (DAIRA = KHEIREDDINE, BACIL1 = NF) ==> ARETTRT = Lost	conf:(0.72)
	6. If (DAIRA = KHEIREDDINE, BACIL2 = NF) ==> ARETTRT = Lost	conf:(0.71)
	7. If (SEXE = M, BACIL1 = NF, BACIL2 = NF, BACIL3 = NF) ==> ARETTRT = Lost	conf:(0.65)
	8. If (COM = SAYADA, BACIL2 = NF, BACIL3 = NF) ==> ARETTRT = Lost	conf:(0.52)
Predictive Apriori	1. If (AGE = A3, SEXE = F) ==> ARETTRT = Lost	acc:(0.96)
	2. If (AGE = A3, COM = SAYADA, DAIRA = KHEIREDDINE) ==> ARETTRT = Lost	acc:(0.96)
	3. If (AGE = A3, COM = SAYADA, BACIL1 = NF, BACIL2 = NF) ==> ARETTRT = Lost	acc:(0.93)
	4. If (SEXE = F, COM = SAYADA, DAIRA = KHEIREDDINE, BACIL2 = NF, BACIL3 = NF) ==> ARETTRT = Lost	acc:(0.93)
	5. If (AGE = A3, DAIRA = KHEIREDDINE, BACIL1 = NF) ==> ARETTRT = Lost	acc:(0.93)
	6. If (AGE = A3, SEXE = F, COM = SAYADA, DAIRA = KHEIREDDINE, BACIL1 = NF, BACIL2 = NF, BACIL3 = NF) ==> ARETTRT = Lost	acc:(0.93)
Tertius	1. If DAIRA = KHEIREDDINE ==> COM = SAYADA or BACIL1 = NF or ARETTRT = Lost	Confi:(0,53)
	2. If (DAIRA = KHEIREDDINE and BACIL1 = NF) ==> COM = SAYADA or ARETTRT = Lost	Confi:(0,50)
	3. If DAIRA = KHEIREDDINE ==> COM = SAYADA or ARETTRT = Lost	Confi:(0,50)
	4. If (DAIRA = KHEIREDDINE and SEXE = M) ==> COM = SAYADA or ARETTRT = Lost	Conf:(0,42)
	5. If (DAIRA = KHEIREDDINE and BACIL1 = NF and BACIL2 = NF) ==> ARETTRT = Lost	Confi:(0,41)

Table 3. Experiments series 2 - Extracted rules from Apriori, Predictive Apriori and Tertius

Algorithms	Rules	Measure
Apriori	1. If (DAIRA = KHEIREDDINE, TYPMAL = N, BACIL1 = NF) ==> ARETTRT = Lost	conf:(1)
	3. If (DAIRA = KHEIREDDINE, TYPMAL = N, BACIL1 = NF, BACIL2 = NF) ==> ARETTRT = Lost	conf:(1)
	4. If (DAIRA = KHEIREDDINE, TYPMAL = N, BACIL1 = NF, BACIL3 = NF) ==> ARETTRT = Lost	conf:(1)
	7. If (DAIRA = KHEIREDDINE, TYPMAL = N, BACIL1 = NF, BACIL2 = NF, BACIL3 = NF) ==> ARETTRT = Lost	conf:(1)
Predictive Apriori	1. If (DAIRA = KHEIREDDINE, TYPMAL = N, BACIL1 = NF) ==> ARETTRT = Lost	acc:(0.99)
	2. If (AGE = A5, SEXE = M) ==> ARETTRT = Lost	acc:(0.98)
	3. If (AGE = A1, BACIL1 = NF) ==> ARETTRT = Lost	acc:(0.97)
	4. If (DAIRA = KHEIREDDINE, TYPMAL = N) ==> ARETTRT = Lost	acc:(0.92)
	5. If (DAIRA = KHEIREDDINE, BACIL1 = NF) ==> ARETTRT = Lost	acc:(0.92)
	6. If AGE = A0 ==> ARETTRT = Lost	acc:(0.91)
Tertius	1. TYPMAL = N and BACIL1 = NF and BACIL3 = NF ==> ARETTRT = Lost	Confi: 0,31
	2. TYPMAL = N and BACIL1 = NF and BACIL2 = NF ==> ARETTRT = Lost	Confi: 0,31
	3. TYPMAL = N and BACIL1 = NF ==> ARETTRT = Lost	Confi: 0,29
	4. DAIRA = KHEIR EDDINE and TYPMAL = N and BACIL1 = NF ==> ARETTRT = Lost	Confi: 0,25
	5. DAIRA = KHEIR EDDINE and BACIL1 = NF and BACIL2 = NF ==> ARETTRT = Lost	Confi: 0,24
	6. DAIRA = KHEIR EDDINE and TYPMAL = N and BACIL2 = NF ==> ARETTRT = Lost	Confi: 0,21
	7. TYPMAL = N and BACIL2 = NF ==> ARETTRT = Lost	Confi: 0,21
	8. SEXE = M and TYPMAL = N and BACIL1 = NF ==> ARETTRT = Lost	Confi: 0,21

Apriori experiments (series 2) show highest confidence comparing all other algorithms. However, the attributes influencing the lost state are relatively different than experiment of series 1. The extracted rules depict that the attribute TYPMAL has high association with Daira attribute, where SEX and COM have no impact on the lost state.

Predictive Apriori (series 2) indicate that the attributes Daira, TYPMAL and AGE have an influence on the Lost state, where the attribute SEX and COM are not considered. However, Tertius experiments (series 2) show the attributes Daira, TYPMAL and SEX as pertinent features.

Table 4. Relevant features.

Experiments	Algorithm	Selected attributes
Series 1	Apriori	Daira, Sex, Com
	Predictive Apriori	Daira, Sex, Com, Age
	Titrius	Daira, Sex, Com
Series 2	Apriori	Daira, TYPMAL
	Predictive Apriori	Daira, Age, TYPMAL
	Titrius	Daira, TYPMAL, Sex

It is worth noting that as the aim of this analysis is to enrich the expert knowledge and refine the computational model, the most interesting rules were reported. Most remaining, however, were ignored as they confirm expert knowledge.

Selected attributes are summarized in Table 4. These features will be the input of the computational model refinement.

3.2   Bio-PEPA Model Optimization

As described in Sect. 2.2, taking in consideration the selected attributes the Bio-PEPA model is updated by optimizing its components (parameters, species and functional rates). Recall that our goal is to validate the usefulness of using association rules. Therefore, we focus on simulation results. The full Bio-PEPA models (initial and updated version) are available online [23].

Following each selected attribute the optimization is achieved. Regarding to Bio-PEPA components, species can be grouped in compartments. Thus, for each attribute, the population will be restructured according to the attribute modality. However, restructuring the model according to each modality is tedious. For example, the attribute COM is described by seven modalities. Consequently, seven compartments (species) should be defined and for each compartment all the functional rates duplicated and parameters recalculated. To overcome this issue, we suggest expressing in Bio-PEPA only modalities appearing in the extracted rule. For example, in experiments series 1, the attribute COM is related to the modality "Sayada", which leads to define in Bio-PEPA two compartments, Sayada and Others. The former concerns only population located in Sayada and the latter regroups the rest of population in one compartment.

Table 5. Selected modalities

Experiments	Selected attributes	Selected modalities
Series 1	Daira	Kheireddine (KH), Ain Tedles (AT)
	Sex	Male (M), Female (F)
	Com	Sayada, Other
Series 2	Daira	Kheireddine (KH), Ain Tedles (AT)
	TYPMAL	New, Other

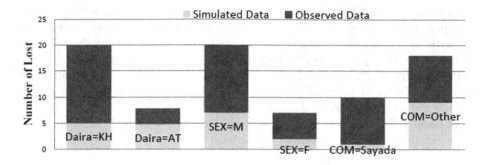

Fig. 4. Histograms for tuberculosis model for 2010

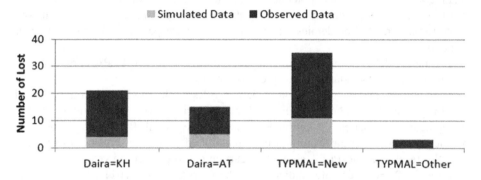

Fig. 5. Histograms for tuberculosis model for 2012

Moreover, as first part of this paper, we suggest to take in consideration the common attributes between the three algorithms, the rest will be the purpose of the future works. This leads to optimize Bio-PEPA model using the attributes Daira, SEX, COM for the series 1 and the attributes Daira and TYPMAL for the series 2. Table 5, illustrates the modalities reported for each attribute.

The analysis can now be conducted on the revised models using Bio-PEPA simulations (100 stochastic simulations) and compared to 2010 data (resp. 2012 data).

Histograms in Fig. 4 (resp. 5), illustrate comparison between simulated and observed data for selected attributes related to series 1 (resp. series 2). As can be seen from Fig. 4, the gap between simulated and observed data is more important for Lost individuals:

– located in Kheireddine, than those located in Ain Tedles,
– located in Sayada than in other cities.

However, the attribute SEX does not show significant gap. Normalizing the number of observed data for male and female indicates that male is characterized by gap of 60 % of infected when female is characterized by 56 % of infected. In contrast, for example the attribute COM shows that Sayada is characterized by gap of 90 % where other is characterized by 0 %. This confirms that no significance differences between discrepancies of predicting male and female in contrast of predicting Sayada and other. Therefore, optimizing the Bio-PEPA model using gender does not enrich the epidemiologist knowledge neither developer understanding, where using the attributes Daira and COM lead to specify where exactly the expert has to investigate more research and which parameters should be updated.

In parallel, Fig. 5 shows that both attributes Daira and TYPMAL indicate significance gap, thus the same conclusions are derived.

4 Discussion

This work highlights the usefulness for using association rules to understand the dynamic of the tuberculosis epidemics. Tuberculosis data reported by the SEMEP is used to extract relevant patterns. It is urgent to identify pertinent sources which contribute to the spread of epidemics for making decision, deeper investigation and better predictions.

Combining data mining, in particular decision tree with Bio-PEPA computational modelling has been validated in our previous work.

This current study combines association rules with Bio-PEPA computational modelling applied to tuberculosis case study in Algeria between 2008 and 2012. The results detected a series of attributes enriching the initial Bio-PEPA model and specifically uncovering the main part of population affecting the dynamic of tuberculosis. We recall that Bio-PEPA simulation carried out to predict the years 2009, 2010, 2011 and 2012 show accurate prediction for the years 2009 and 2011 where 2010 and 2012 depicted discrepancies with observed data, those are the subject of this study.

To optimise the model, we undertook experiments using three association rules algorithms: Apriori, predictive apriori and Tertius. The analysis of resulted rules based on the measures: confidence, accuracy and confirmation, reveal that the attributes Daira, Com, SEX and TYPMAL are mostly affecting the study.

The first aim of this work is to optimise the initial Bio-PEPA model where discrepancies between simulated and observed data have been detected for the Lost state. Integrating the selected attributes to the model reveals that the discrepancies above are frequently due to population located in Daira Kheireddine and COM Sayada where the majority of Lost individual are defined as new infected. However, the Bio-PEPA simulation shows that no significant evidence can be provided related to the attribute SEX.

The second aim of this work is to compare the current results with the work achieved in our previous study [5].

By using decision tree [5], the branches leading to the Lost state revealed for both years of prediction 2010 and 2012 only Daira attribute, whereas association rules showed the attributes Daira, COM, TYPMAL and SEX. However, applying TYPMAL to our Bio-PEPA model do not inform which part of population (Male or Female) is in more concern. Indeed, when dividing the Bio-PEPA model in two compartment (Male and Female), we observed that the proportion of male are similar to female, therefore we were not able to derive any conclusion about anomalies observed in the initial simulation. In addition, the attributes listed above and related to association rules experiments are those chosen for our convenience. Experiments depicted in Tables 3 and 4, show various associations with different attributes such as rule 3 (Predictive Apriori in series 1) where AGE, COM and Daira are all associated to the Lost state. It is worth noting that optimising Bio-PEPA model leads to redefine all its components: species, functional rates and parameters. To achieve this process using such large set of selected attributes is tedious and time consuming. As argued by Sullivan [7]: "the number of association rules that can be elicited from even a small dataset can quickly become huge". We need further investigation to meaningfully identify the rule in greater pertinence. Even if decision tree experiment revealed only one attribute, this was in great help to explain anomalies and define relevant patterns.

Using data mining techniques confirms the pertinence of our approach. Indeed, combining such algorithms to computational modelling enrich and simplify the inter-action between expert and developer to achieve accurate predictive model. Specifically, when the expert is unable to provide useful knowledge.

Appendix: Bio-PEPA Formalism

A Bio-PEPA model is described by a set of species, which execute a set of activities. The latter define the dynamic behaviour of the species. Conventionally, Bio-PEPA formalism is described by the following syntax:

S :: = (α, κ) op S | S + S | C
op = << | >> | (+) | (−) | (.)
P :: = P >< P | S(x)

For more clarity, we explain the above syntax through an example of a generic SEIR (Susceptible Exposed Infected Recovered) compartmental disease model taken from [24] and illustrated in the program code as below:

```
crw = 6.015;
ir = 0.133;
rr = 0.154;
kineticLawOf contact : (crw * S * I) /(S +E +I +R);
kineticLawOf incubation : (ir * E);
kineticLawOf recover : (rr * I);
S = contact  << S;
E = contact  >> E + incubation << E;
I = contact(.)I +incubation >> I +recover << I ;
R = recover >> R;
     I [5] < * > S[508000] < * > E[0] < * > R[0]
```

As defined in [24], a Bio-PEPA model is structured by defining a set of numeric rates (e.g. *crw*), functional rates (introduced by kineticLawOf) and species definitions (S, E, I and R). The activities executed by the species are contact, incubation and recover. The contact activity, decreases (resp. increases) the level of species S (resp. E), by using the operator ≪(resp.)≫. The incubation activity decreases (resp. increases) the level of species E (resp. I) and finally, the recover activity decreases (resp. increases) the level of species I (resp. R). The operator (.), used in I, indicates that I participates in contact, but this does not affect its level. The operator '+', allows a choice between activities (contact, incubation and recover) based on rate (faster activities are more likely to occur). The last line of the model is the model component, defining interaction between species (* means activities are shared where possible) and their initial levels.

References

1. Anderson, R.M., May, R.M.: Infectious Diseases of Humans: Dynamics and Control. Oxford University Press, Oxford (1991)
2. Weber, A., Weber, M., Milligan, P.: Modeling epidemics caused by respiratory syncytial virus (RSV). Math. Biosci. **172**(2), 95–113 (2001). http://www.ncbi.nlm.nih.gov/pubmed/11520501
3. Keeling, M.J., Rohani, P.: Modeling infectious diseases in humans and animals. Princeton University Press, Princeton (2008)
4. Hamami, D., Atmani, B.: Tuberculosis modelling using Bio-PEPA approach. WASET, Int. J. Med. Health Biomed. Bioeng. Pharm. Eng. **7**(4), 183–190 (2013)
5. Hamami, D., Atmani, B., Shankland, C.: Decision support based on Bio-PEPA modeling and decision tree induction: a new approach, applied to a tuberculosis case study. Manuscript accepted April 2016, IJSSS **9**(2) (2017, in-press)
6. Witten, I.H.: Data Mining: Practical Machine Learning Tools and Techniques, 3rd edn. Morgan Kaufmann, San Francisco (2011)
7. Sullivan, R.: Introduction to Data Mining for the Life Sciences. Springer, Heidelberg (2012)
8. Gorunescu, F.: Data Mining: Concepts, Models and Technique, vol. 12. Springer, Heidelberg (2011)
9. Nahar, J., Imam, T., Tickle, K.S., Chen, Y.P.: Association rule mining to detect factors which contribute to heart disease in males and females. Expert Syst. Appl. **40**(4), 1086–1093 (2013)
10. Dubey, A.: Association rules for diagnosis of Hiv-Aids. Comput. Mol. Biol. **4**(4), 26–33 (2014)
11. Ordonez, C., Omiecinski, E., De Braal, L., Santana, C.A., Ezquerra, N., Taboada, J.A., Cooke, D., Krawczynska, E., Garcia, E.V.: Mining constrained association rules to predict heart disease. In: ICDM, vol. 1, no. 1, pp. 433–440 (2001)
12. Ordonez, C.: Comparing association rules and decision trees for disease prediction. In: ACM Proceedings of the International Workshop on Healthcare Information and Knowledge Management, pp. 17–24 (2006)
13. Asha, T., Natarajan, S., Murthy, K.N.: Optimization of association rules for tuberculosis using genetic algorithm. Int. J. Comput. **12**(2), 151–159 (2014)
14. Phyu, T.N.: Survey of classification techniques in data mining. In: Proceedings of the International Multi-conference of Engineers and Computer Scientists IMECS, Hong Kong, vol. 1 (2009)

15. Mutter, S., Hall, M., Frank, E.: Using classification to evaluate the output of confidence-based association rule mining. In: Webb, G.I., Yu, X. (eds.) AI 2004. LNCS (LNAI), vol. 3339, pp. 538–549. Springer, Heidelberg (2004)
16. Taihua, W., Fan, G.: Associating IDS alerts by an improved apriori algorithm. In: Third International Symposium Intelligent Information Technology and Security Informatics (IITSI), pp. 478–482. IEEE (2010)
17. Scheffer, T.: Finding association rules that trade support optimally against confidence. Intell. Data Anal. **9**(4), 381–395 (2005)
18. Flach, P., Maraldi, V., Riguzzi, F.: Algorithms for efficiently and effectively using background knowledge in Tertius (2006)
19. Han, J., Kamber, M.: Data Mining: Concepts and Techniques, 2nd edn. Morgan Kaufmann Publishers, San Francisco (2006)
20. Aher, S.B., Lobo, L.M.R.J.: A comparative study of association rule algorithms for course recommender system in e-learning. Int. J. Comput. Appl. **39**(1), 48–52 (2006)
21. Hastie, T., Friedman, J., Tibshirani, R.: Model assessment and selection. In: Hastie, T., Friedman, J., Tibshirani, R. (eds.) The Elements of Statistical Learning, pp. 193–224. Springer, New York (2001)
22. Flach, P.A., Lachiche, N.: Confirmation-guided discovery of first-order rules with Tertius. Mach. Learn. **42**(1–2), 61–95 (2001)
23. Hamami, D.: URL Bio-PEPA code (2015). http://www.cs.stir.ac.uk/~dha/
24. Marco, D., Scott, E., Cairns, D., Graham, A., Allen, J., Mahajan, S., Shankland, C.: Investigating co-infection dynamics through evolution of Bio-PEPA model parameters: a combined process algebra and evolutionary computing approach. In: Gilbert, D., Heiner, M. (eds.) CMSB 2012. LNCS, vol. 7605, pp. 227–246. Springer, Heidelberg (2012)

Optimization of Orchestration
of Geocrowdsourcing Activities

Kahina Bessai[✉] and François Charoy

University of Lorraine, LORIA-INRIA-UMR 7503, BP 239,
Vandoeuvre-les-Nancy, France
{kahina.bessai,francois.charoy}@loria.fr

Abstract. In this paper, we describe a process that can be used to assess a global situation on a map using a combination of services and user operations. We want to understand how best to distribute a limited amount of human actions between different kinds of tasks in order to get the most reliable result. Since it is difficult to conduct experimentation, we have decided to use simulation to reach a result that could be applied on the ground. This simulation relies on a geolocalised corpus of tweets. It provides some hints about how to deploy an exercise on the ground that are discussed as a conclusion.

Keywords: Crowdsourcing · GIS · Pattern · Simulation

1 Introduction

Calling to the crowd to conduct activities out of the reach of individuals or small groups is a very common practice. This kind of initiative is known under the generic name of crowdsourcing, or human computation [1]. It has been applied in catastrophic situations but can also be used in more controlled situations. The goal of this project is to develop and validate a method and a framework in order to get citizen to contribute to contextual city assessment activities at a large scale. More precisely, we want to be able to synthesize information regarding the state of a populated geographic area by coordinating in an optimized way volunteers actions. To achieve that kind of goal, we need to get information from the ground. People must execute actions at some places, mostly collect data. Other participant, connected to the system must then analyse the data to produce an aggregated result. People could use that framework for area status assessment during a crisis or as a preparedness activity, to measure phenomenon in a city at a defined point in time and to repeat that measure on a regular basis. They could combine it to other kind of sensors to conduct different kind of real time analysis. Real time means that the result could be used to take actions as the event unfold. This paper describes an ongoing work where we try to optimize the overall quality of a geographical area status assessment following a predefined process with a limited number of human resources. We have defined a crowdsourcing process and tested it with an existing dataset [2]. This was a

© Springer International Publishing AG 2016
P. Diaz et al. (Eds.): ISCRAM-med 2016, LNBIP 265, pp. 76–82, 2016.
DOI: 10.1007/978-3-319-47093-1_7

first experience to evaluate our framework. Here, we continue this work with a new dataset, with new parameters and with the objective to optimize the resource that we can leverage for such a process in order to get the best possible result. The rest of paper is organized as follows. The next section discusses some related works. Section 3 is devoted to the simulation model. In Sect. 4, we describe a subset of the results of our experiment and we discuss the best way to find compromise between the coverage of the assessment and its quality. Section 5 concludes the paper.

2 Related Works

People used crowdsourcing in a geographical context for a long time, even before the existence of computers. Bird watchers contribute to science by participating to counting activities periodically to create maps of birds populations and of their evolution. This activity has taken a new dimension with the advent of mobile phones, GPS and the Internet. The construction of maps like OpenStreetMap http://www.openstreetmap.org is a ten year old project that aims at building accurate maps calling to the crowd to contribute all kind of information. Each of these experiments are done in an ad-hoc way. Humanitarians organisations conduct more organized operations under the umbrella of the Digital Humanitarians [1]. They are able to call to volunteers to geolocalize information during crisis. Other sophisticated research use information produced on social media to make sense of what is going on a crisis area [3]. These are important steps toward a generalized approach regarding the use of crowdsourcing with a geographical context. The goal of other authors is to allow people to call to the crowd to answer more or less structured queries. In [4], the authors propose a prototype for location-based mobile crowdsourcing consisting of a Web and a mobile client. Through these clients, people from the crowd can search for tasks and submit solutions. Similarly, in [5], the authors design a framework for crowdsourcing location-based queries on the top of Twitter. The Framework relies on Foursquare to find the appropriate people to answer the query. In [6] Kazemi and Shahabi introduce a taxonomy of spatial crowdsourcing and propose three techniques for assigning the maximum number of tasks to the crowd. They also introduce a taxonomy for spatial data. This last work relies on the Gowalla dataset https://snap.stanford.edu/data/loc-gowalla.html for its simulation. Regarding, the selection of the *k-top* results several approaches have been proposed which can be classified in four categories: (i) heuristics-based approaches [7–10], (ii) machine-learning methods [11], (iii) extensions of heap-based methods [12–14] and (iv) combining rating and comparison based-algorithms [15,16].

3 The Simulation Model

The simulation of geolocalised actions is a difficult issue. We can do it by generating the actions on a map with a random distribution. This would not reflect the actual distribution of user geolocalised activities. The factors that influence

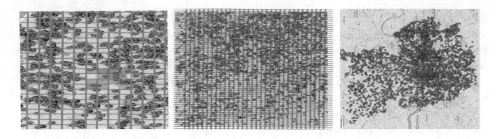

Fig. 1. 24 h of geolocalised tweets in Paris, the grid and the expected results

this distribution are not random. Another approximation would be to rely on actual location of user actions in geographical areas that are available through social network activities. Researchers have followed this path, relying on the well known Gollawa dataset and they refer to places and not precise location. We propose to use geolocalised tweets in urban areas. A geolocalised tweet correspond to a conscious action of someone at the corresponding location. Someone actually did post a message at that place. These actions are not evenly distributed. This gives us a sense of the kind of coverage we can expect. We are not considering the content, only the position. Figure 1 is an example of 24 h of geolocalised tweets in Paris.

The coverage is obtained by splitting the space in cells of equal size. We use the size of the cell to decide of the accuracy of the measure. We see on Fig. 1 the distribution of tweets on the map is not even. Some cells receive no action while others receive several. The same figure shows a detail that could be an intermediate results. Cells can be painted based on the assessment. Obviously, we won't get results for all cells since some of them have no data.

To simulate the process, we use tweets for geolocalised actions and we estimate a number of crowdsourcing actions that will be executed to complete the job. We estimate that if we have N tweets for a given period of time, we can count on $2N$ crowdsourcing actions that we can distribute between selection and assessment. We also execute some simulation with a varying number of workers (in our case from 20000 to 100000). The process evaluation consists in two steps: (i) the selection stage, where the user has to decide what, in his opinion is the more accurate data to reflect a situation and (ii) the assessment step, where the user grade the situation on a predefined scale based on the data that is provided to him. Of course, in a real situation, the description of the purpose of the selection and of the assessment would be of paramount importance but since we are simulating the actions, we consider that the users will have a good understanding of the context. However, the available workers do not provide the same quality.

The selection step consists to select the representative picture of a given situation. Formally this step can be described as follows. Without loss of generality, let a set of picture $p_1, p_2, ..., p_m$, belonging to the same geographical zone, where their quality are random variables with cumulative distributions functions denoted respectively F_{p_i} (and probability density functions f_{p_i}). Similarly, let a set of workers $w_1, w_2, ..., w_n$ where their quality are random variables with cumulative function $F(w_i)$. It is that if the workers votes of a given picture randomly in a uniform way, the number of votes follows a binomial distribution:

$$P(N_i = k) = C_n^k \left(\frac{1}{m}\right)^k \left(\frac{m-1}{m}\right)^{n-k}$$

where, $N_i, i \in \{1, ..., m\}$ are binomial random variables representing the number of votes of photos $p_1, p_2, ..., p_m$.

Regarding the assessment of a picture we use the following model. Photos are graded on a discrete scale $(0, 1, 2)$. The model assumes that the better the photo is, the more accurate the grading. We are just computing the chance that a user with a given worker quality W gives the right answer.

The correct result is assumed if $Pi * W > Random()$. Otherwise, we chose the resulting votes equi-probably between the two remaining choices.

3.1 Simulations

We have conducted several simulations using different kinds of parameters. The first parameter is the buckets size. We use squares of side length of 50 m, 100 m and 200 m. With smaller buckets, we can expect a more accurate map but a bad coverage. On our corpus (Paris) it represents respectively 50779, 12576, 3120 buckets. The number of votes k required to decide for a result $(1, 3, 5, 7, 9)$. Again, the more votes we require, the less result we will get since more actions will be required to take a decision in each area. On the other side, if we require more votes, we may expect more accurate results. Since we consider that we have a limited number of user actions, we can distribute them between selection and assessment, from 50/50 to 80/20. The more actions we allocate to selection, the more results we will have to assess. The worker quality is the last parameter that can vary. We assume that workers are doing their best but that may not have always a perfect judgement regarding the task to accomplish. Thus we assign a quality to workers that varies from 0.6 to 0.9 with a gaussian distribution.

4 The Experimental Results

The simulation has been executed using data collected on the area of Paris. We have collected tweets on this area on periods of 24 h. The number of geolocalised tweets collected did not vary much from one day to the other, around 60000 tweets per 24 h. It is very difficult to identify clear patterns in the distribution (cf. Fig. 1). The coverage in the city center is better than in the suburban areas. The same exercise done in other big cities like New York or London give the same kind of results. There is a high density of tweets in touristic areas or business districts. It means that we cannot expect a full coverage of a geographical areas with tweets. But since we want to compare the resulting coverage based on different distribution of actions, we are concerned with relative results more

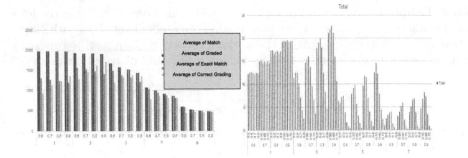

Fig. 2. Number of results depending on the workers quality and the number of votes

than with absolute results. We have conducted several experiments, varying the parameters. In Fig. 2, we vary the number of votes and the workers quality. Half of the actions are used for selection and half for the assessment. Match means that we have been able to select a picture. Exact match means that the best one has been selected by the voters. Graded means that the picture has been graded and Exact grading means that the grading is correct for the buckets. With one vote to make the selection, the number of actions is sufficient to select and grade pictures for every bucket. We see that in this case, and with the parameters that we have selected, the variation of the number of exact match does not vary much with the quality of the worker but the variation of the exact grading is much more important. With 3 votes, the number of results is lower but the number of exact match is higher in the end compared to 1 vote whatever the quality of the workers. With 5 votes, as it could be expected, the number of results decreased as well as the number of correct results. It is the percentage of good results compare to the overall results that increase. The more votes we use, the less results we get but of better quality. We vary also distribution of actions, quality and votes. This graphs shows the coverage of the correct results. It is the % of correct results. Varying the distribution of actions is interesting especially if we use several votes for each bucket. The more actions we use for selection, the more results we get for grading. We try to understand here how the percentage of correct grading vary based on the variation of these three parameters. Again the best result depends on the quality of the workers (W = 0, 9 and votes = 3). But we can observe than if we use one vote and good workers we get a lot of good results. We can also notice that with these parameters, the quality of the results decrease rapidly with the quality of the workers. In Fig. 4 we did the same simulation, varying the number of actions from 20000 to 100000. This figure presents the best results depending on the number of actions and on the workers quality.

Figure 3 represents the best results obtained for all the parameters (distribution, votes and number of actions) for a workers quality (the mean quality of a worker is fixed to 0.6). We can observe that the increase of the correct results by varying these parameters is very slow. The simulation suggests that when we

Number of actions	20000	40000	60000	80000	100000
Distribution	0.6	0,7	0.6	0.7	0.7
Vote	3	3	5	7	7
Best Result	13.37	15.95	17.06	18.04	19.4

Fig. 3. Best results by varying the number of actions and votes (workers quality fixed to 0.6)

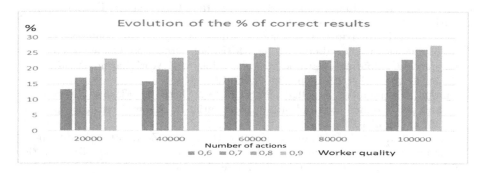

Fig. 4. Evolution of the number of correct results depending on the number of actions and on the workers quality

increase the number of actions done by workers, we must increase the number of votes to get better results. By varying workers quality, we notice that the percentage of best results increases. This percentage increases also according to the number of actions. However, as shown in Figs. 3 and 4, the gain slows above a certain number of actions. This trend is still consolidating for different values of workers quality Fig. 4 (0.7, 0.8 and 0.9).

As we can see in Fig. 4 it is interesting to note that the gain obtained when we increase the number of actions is less interesting than gain obtained when we have access to better workers. That would suggest that it is better to get access to a smaller number of skilled workers that to a large number of workers. In the results, we also note that when we have access to more actions, we obtain a better result when we increase the number of votes.

5   Conclusion

This paper presents a crowdsourcing simulation relying on a geolocalized corpus of tweets to obtain the best distribution of a limited amount of human actions between different tasks. The simulation we have done has been repeated several times on the same area with very similar results. This could be anticipated since a lot of data we use for the simulation are synthesized. Overall, based on our model and on the corpus we rely on, we can expect good results with 3 to 7 votes depending on the number of actions. Still, we see that the quality of workers is very important and that it's more efficient to select a reduced number of skilled workers. It means that it could be very valuable either to train the workers to increase their capacity to provide good results or to try to assess workers quality and distribute the work to the best ones first. To do that, we need to get more insight on the way workers behave with the kinds of tasks that we plan to ask them to execute.

References

1. Meier, P.: Digital Humanitarians: How Big Data Is Changing the Face of Humanitarian Response. Routledge, Boca Raton (2015)
2. Benouaret, K., Valliyur-Ramalingam, R., Charoy, F.: Answering complex location-based queries with crowdsourcing. In: 9th IEEE International Conference on Collaborative Computing: Networking, Applications and Worksharing, Austin, TX, USA, 20–23 October 2013, pp. 438–447 (2013)
3. Purohit, H., Hampton, A., Bhatt, S., Shalin, V., Sheth, A., Flach, J.: Identifying seekers and suppliers in social media communities to support crisis coordination. J. CSCW **23**, 513–545 (2014)
4. Alt, F., Shirazi, A.S., Schmidt, A., Kramer, U., Nawaz, Z.: Location-based crowdsourcing: extending crowdsourcing to the real world. In: Proceedings of the 6th Nordic Conference on Human-Computer Interaction: Extending Boundaries, NordiCHI 2010, pp. 13–22. ACM, New York (2010)
5. Bulut, M.F., Yilmaz, Y.S., Demirbas, M.: Crowdsourcing location-based queries. In: PerCom Workshops, pp. 513–518 (2011)
6. Kazemi, L., Shahabi, C.: GeoCrowd: enabling query answering with spatial crowdsourcing. In: SIGSPATIAL/GIS, pp. 189–198 (2012)
7. Guo, S., Parameswaran, A., Garcia-Molina, H.: So who won? Dynamic max discovery with the crowd. Technical report, Stanford University, November 2011
8. Pomerol, J.C., Barba-Romero, S.: Multicriterion Decision in Management: Principles and Practice. Springer, New York (2012)
9. Adelsman, R.M., Whinston, A.B.: Sophisticated voting with information for two voting functions. J. Econ. Theor. **15**(1), 145–159 (1977)
10. Eriksson, B.: Learning to top-k search using pairwise comparisons. In: Proceedings of the Sixteenth International Conference on Artificial Intelligence and Statistics, AISTATS 2013, Scottsdale, AZ, USA, 29 April–1 May 2013, pp. 265–273 (2013)
11. Pfeiffer, T., Gao, X.A., Rand, D.G.: Adaptive polling for information aggregation. In: AAAI (2012)
12. Ye, P., Doermann, D.: Combining preference and absolute judgements in a crowdsourced setting. In: ICML 2013 Workshop: Machine Learning Meets Crowdsourcing, June 2013
13. Davidson, S.B., Khanna, S., Milo, T., Roy, S.: Using the crowd for top-k and group-by queries. In: Proceedings of the Joint 2013 EDBT/ICDT Conferences, ICDT 2013, Genoa, Italy, 18–22 March 2013, pp. 225–236 (2013)
14. Feige, U., Raghavan, P., Peleg, D., Upfal, E.: Computing with noisy information. SIAM J. Comput. **23**(5), 1001–1018 (1994)
15. Khan, A.R., Garcia-Molina, H.: Hybrid strategies for finding the max with the crowd: technical report. Technical report, Stanford University, February 2014
16. Wauthier, F., Jordan, M., Jojic, N.: Efficient ranking from pairwise comparisons. In: Dasgupta, S., Mcallester, D. (eds.) Proceedings of the 30th International Conference on Machine Learning (ICML 2013), vol. 28, pp. 109–117. JMLR Workshop and Conference Proceedings, May 2013

Development of Information Systems

Visual Synthesis of Evolutionary Emergency Scenarios

Monica Sebillo[✉], Maurizio Tucci, and Giuliana Vitiello

Department of Computer Science,
University of Salerno, Fisciano, Italy
{msebillo,mtucci,gvitiello}@unisa.it

Abstract. During an emergency situation, decision makers are faced with the problem to quickly analyze large amounts of data related to the involved geographical area in order to grasp a comprehensive overview of the scenario of interest and manage the response activities. The success of those activities heavily depends on the availability of tools which allow them to extract and adequately represent relevant and timely information out of huge sets of (georeferenced) data. During the last 15 years researchers have long strived to define geovisual analytics methods and techniques, which support decision making in time-critical emergency response activities, such as evacuation planning and management. Such methods allow domain experts to visualize the status of the crisis, plan the evacuation and address people towards vacancies in emergency shelters. However, several issues remain to be addressed especially related to the need to make quick decisions in case of emergency scenarios which evolve differently from what one was expecting and from the devised emergency management plan. The research we are carrying out is meant to define an innovative paradigm for human-(geo)information discourse, which could expedite the analysis activities needed to make decisions on crisis management actions. The integrated visual system we describe in the paper allows domain experts, decision makers and any other emergency operator to analyze qualitative data about a geographical area, which may change vigorously with respect to both time and space and whose size represents a critical factor in the efficiency of management activities.

Keywords: Interactive geovisualization · Emergency response ·
Scenario-based interaction design

1   Introduction

During an emergency situation, decision makers are faced with the problem to quickly analyze large amounts of data related to the involved geographical area in order to grasp a comprehensive overview of the scenario of interest and manage the response activities. The success of those activities heavily depends on the availability of tools which allow them to extract and adequately represent relevant and timely information from huge sets of (georeferenced) data. During the last 15 years researchers have long strived to define geovisual analytics methods and techniques, which support decision making in time-critical emergency response activities, such as evacuation planning and management [1–3]. Such methods allow domain experts to visualize the status of the

P. Diaz et al. (Eds.): ISCRAM-med 2016, LNBIP 265, pp. 85–97, 2016.
DOI: 10.1007/978-3-319-47093-1_8

crisis, plan the interventions and distribute on-site responders, plan the possible evacuation and address people towards vacancies in emergency shelters. However, several issues remain to be addressed especially related to the need of making quick decisions in case of emergency scenarios which evolve differently from what one was expecting and from the devised emergency management plan.

The objective of the research we are carrying out in this context is to provide experts and operators with applications and tools addressed to support and improve their ordinary and extraordinary activities [5]. To achieve that goal we aim to define an innovative paradigm for human-(geo)information discourse, which integrates different modalities of visualization and navigation with visual metaphors representing geospatial data as well as their aggregations/syntheses.

An initial phase of our research has been devoted to investigate geovisualization methods and techniques addressed to users of mobile applications. In that case the major issue originated from the small size of screen which hinders the object visualization and requires some means to better support qualitative representation of geospatial information. In [7, 8] a visualization technique named *Framy* was proposed which underlies applications for mobile devices to simplify the detection of relevant elements. By applying *Framy*, sets of data can be summarized and qualitatively displayed on mobile devices by means of visual aggregates thus overcoming the limitations due to the screen size. The technique has been successfully embedded in different mobile applications where the need of summarizing large amounts of data is relevant to obtain information about a territory, thus corroborating the claim that applications based on a visual analytics approach are highly suitable to visually elaborate and communicate significant information to mobile users [9].

The interactive visualization technique we present in this paper leverages many of the benefits of *Framy* and its ability to support real time analysis of large data sets, but has been especially conceived to support central emergency management activities. *Beyond-the-Screen* is in fact the result of a contextual inquiry the authors conducted in the field of emergency preparedness and response involving a group of professionals, who handle both remote sensing images and thematic maps, and make decision on the basis of the detected phenomena and the objects distribution.

The involved professionals reported that when performing emergency management activities, they explore a geographic area by repeated panning and zooming of the corresponding raster image, towards more detailed portions. When, a possible area of interest is detected, the analysis is deepened possibly through additional tools. Such tasks often may cause user's disorientation due to the loss of context and, in the worst case, may lead to task failure. In order to efficiently speed up such tasks it would be useful to interact with both a rapid overview of qualitative distribution of data of interest and a detailed portion of the image. This implies a proper management of time and space parameters associated with the object distribution also through qualitative syntheses of geospatial data and phenomena.

The *Beyond-the-Screen* technique represents a solution to this specific requirement. It limits this drawback by visually summarizing information of interest, which can be used by the user as a guideline in performing the assigned activity. Maps are used to represent together the observed phenomena and their related geographic areas thus offering a unified map-related view of data resulting from information seeking or analysis tasks. Moreover, it offers the capability of switching among diverse views to analyze the evolution of an emergency scenario and make appropriate decisions.

The paper is organized as follows. Section 2 explains the problem domain analysis and the derived requirements. Section 3 describes the proposed interactive visualization technique. In Sect. 4 the use of the visualization tool is illustrated through a realistic interaction scenario. Conclusions are drawn in Sect. 5.

2 The Problem Domain Analysis

The participatory design process we have performed to derive the evolutionary visualization technique we present, has been mainly inspired by Rosson and Carrol's scenario-based design method [10]. Scenarios of usage were in fact chosen as our primary design objects, thanks to their simultaneous ability to guide design and to facilitate usability evaluation and assessment during the iterative development process. Starting from a field study conducted within potential real contexts of usage, we in fact built scenarios of emergency management practices. Our target users were those who operate in the Command and Control Centers (Centro Operativo Comunale, COC) and make strategic decisions. In the following subsection, we discuss the fieldwork results, and we describe the envisaged problem scenario and the derived users' requirements.

The field study

In 2012 we started a collaboration with the Civil Defence Agency of the town of Montemiletto, in the South of Italy, which led to development of a spreadsheet-mediated collaborative system for earthquake management activities which allows on-site responders to cooperate through mobile devices, share portions of data, apply for resources in a concurrent and reliable manner, and obtain real-time status updates from decision makers [5, 11].

The active participation of stakeholders and the knowledge capitalized from the former study led us to replicate it, this time focusing on the emergency management activities as they occur in the COC. We performed a contextual inquiry on the use of software applications for emergency management and on the processes performed for real time management. The main goal of the inquiry was to gain a comprehension of the extent to which information technologies support analysis and decision making during the emergency response process. A survey questionnaire was initially submitted to participants. The 6 subjects who took the questionnaire had different backgrounds and different roles inside the COC. Then we started the observation of:

- the physical settings where collaborative activities for emergency management are performed (e.g., the number of offices involved, whether co-located or distributed),
- the data which are continuously collected and analyzed, the information derived from the analysis, and
- how such an information is used for decision making purposes.

The kind of emergency response activities most of the interviewees described followed predefined protocols, that mainly relied on the use of a Web GIS platform, named SIRIO [12].

As a result of our study, we were able to understand that in common crisis management practices, SIRIO is used to understand the current situation and its evolution, based on heterogeneous data collected from different sources (e.g., local sensors, camera-enabled cell phones, etc.).

However, as some of the interviewees also reported, the effectiveness of the derived decisions often depends on the capability to quickly grasp the priority areas of intervention and establish the shelters locations and the rescue routes which may lead people there. If the emergency area is wide, COC operators may be forced to a high number of zooming and panning operations, shifting from the area overview to the detailed view and vice versa until full comprehension of the crisis situation is achieved and decisions are made. Moreover, as the emergency response actions take place, decision makers keep monitoring the area, ready to arrange for corrective actions if needed.

The problem scenario

In order to formalize the requirements elicited from the interviews, we capitalized the knowledge gained from the fieldwork and envisaged a scenario of emergency management practices, from which we could start our brainstorming activity for the design of a possible solution. Based on that knowledge, we built a persona, who could represent the 'decision maker', and, we envisaged his tasks inside a representative interactive emergency response scenario.

Persona Gino Rossi is a 55 years old Chief of the Civil Defence Agency for Montemiletto. He is an engineer and has a deep knowledge about the territory and has been covering the present role for the last 5 years. Supported by a team of experts, he coordinates the COC and makes decisions regarding evacuation, triage and any other action which can minimize the total extent of losses in case of a crisis. Data coming from different sources (telephones, cellular phones, fax as well as remote sensors) are made available through the SIRIO software platform, which provides him with both an analytical description and a synthetic view of the event evolution, also in the form of graphical representation. During critical situations Gino is forced to quickly elaborate the collected data and make timely decisions.

Scenario
A 4.5 magnitude earthquake has shaken Montemiletto, in South Italy, at 3:30 p.m. The event has happened during summer, on Sunday, in a touristic zone including the gathering area no.1, with many visitors in this period. The COC is immediately activated and the supporting team of professionals and volunteers are put on the alert according to the intervention model of the emergency plan.

Gino Rossi manages the conflicting recovery requests *coming from two on-site responders and makes appropriate decision on evacuees' destination.*
Gino is informed that today a music event occurred in that area, which attracted a higher number of visitors than expected. Therefore, the recovery actions scheduled in the original plan need to be dynamically adapted so as to face the crisis adequately. Approximately every 20 min he receives reports from the gathering areas.
At 4:15 p.m. he receives a data sheet from the gathering area no.2, where he reads a request for the recovery of 26 people at shelter no. 1. Gino asks the SIRIO GIS operator in his team to perform a number of zooming and panning steps to focus on the geographic area of interest, he approves the request and updates the number of

available beds at that shelter. At 4:35 he receives another request for 33 evacuees from the gathering area no.1 which is associated to the same shelter but he realizes that only 9 beds are left. The GIS operator zooms out to gain an overview of the surrounding areas and find an alternative sheltering site. He is then able to identify two possible shelters, one located to the North and the other to the East. After analyzing the derived information, through further zooming actions, Gino decides to redirect the 33 people to the northern shelter no. 3, which has still got 48 beds available and is closer to the gathering area no.1. He records the new data and notifies his decision to the on-site responders.

Finally, he asks the SIRIO operator to prepare a new report on the current status of the crisis management process, which is distributed to all the local responders. It includes the updates made to shelters no. 1 and no. 3.

At the end day 1 Gino has a plenary meeting at the COC *to collectively evaluate the evolution of the emergency situation since its beginning and the actions taken so far. The series of reports produced after each intervention are analyzed by the involved experts and an estimate is made of the actions which may be required next. As a result of the meeting, Gino and the other attendees agree that new teams of on site responders should be sent to the gathering area no 1.*

User requirements

The depicted scenario gave us the opportunity to reason on what claims about current practices emerged. In particular, they indicated that

- it takes too long to analyze details of a given area and relate that information to the surrounding territory
- in situations like the one described in the scenario, historical information on the evacuees allocation process performed at a given time can only be analyzed through the produced reports.

In fact, the first general requirement that all observed evacuation management activities seemed to raise is the necessity of innovative tools to visualize spatio-temporal information about emergency cases, that would yield an improvement in the efficiency of the related activities and, hence, of the overall emergency management process, while preserving the emergency management policies actuated so far. A second general requirement, strictly related to the former, which is also represented in the scenario, is that the visualized information should be easily interpreted by emergency managers, also with respect to the geographic and the temporal contexts, so as to provide effective support to rapid decision making. Those aspects would also imply limited learning efforts by emergency operators and satisfy the further requirement to minimize training costs and time needed for the actuation of the envisaged transformation, which also resulted from the interviews.

Summarizing the results of the field study, we were able to understand participants' main expectations for the improvement of current response processes:

- an interactive visualization tool should be built upon the current emergency management processes, supporting existing centralized decision making policies, with the goal to improve the real time comprehension of the current situation and the analysis of how it evolved.
- migration towards such an enhanced system should be as smooth as possible to COC operators.

In the following section we illustrate how the *Beyond-the-Screen* interaction technique has been exploited on top of SIRIO GIS platform to achieve an evolutionary geovisualization system satisfying the described requirements.

3 *Beyond the Screen* Visualization Technique

The described problem scenario highlights possible flaws in the emergency management process related to the number of exploration actions that professionals have to perform on an interface to gain an appropriate knowledge of the crisis situation. Typically, operators accomplish their activities through repeated panning and zooming towards more detailed portions of the image under investigation. When a possible area of interest is detected, the analysis is deepened also by additional tools. The contextual inquiry conducted with a team leader and his field workers revealed that such a (boring) combination of panning and zooming with either compression (the so-called *overview-detail* approach) or distortion operations (known as *focus-detail* approach) presents relevant limitations both in time necessary to reach a goal, and in the amount of backward operations one has to perform when changing the point of view and the identified directions. In order to speed up such tasks it would be useful to allow users to interact with both a rapid overview of qualitative distribution of data of interest and a detailed portion of the image, with an appropriate tradeoff between the zoom level needed to visualize the required features on a map and the amount of information which can be provided through the application.

The *Beyond the Screen* technique represents a solution to this specific requirement. It has been conceived to support analysis and visualization of huge volumes of geospatial data by combining interactive GeoVisualization methods [3, 4] with advanced computational techniques to support data exploration and decision-making processes. Moreover, it inherits the rationale underlying the *Framy* visualization technique [8] designed to face the limitation of the screen size of mobile devices exploiting an interaction metaphor for painting frames meant to provide hints about off-screen objects.

The *Beyond the Screen* technique adopts a similar approach by superimposing a frame to the currently displayed portion of the image, and adapts it by adding new features that guarantee a continuously available overview overlapped with a differently-scaled area under investigation, where the qualitative information is independent of the zoom level.

Given a buffer zone whose width can be either manually fixed or computed according to some parameters, the frame featuring *Beyond the Screen* is partitioned into several portions, corresponding to different sectors. Each sector is colored with a different intensity depending on both the quantity of POIs distributed within each map sector of the whole buffer zone, namely in-/off-screen objects, and the areal distribution of phenomena occurred within each map sector, expressed as the quantity of selected pixels in a raster image. It is also possible to customize the aggregate function by combining information from different layers thus improving the analysis results. As an example, a land use image can be overlapped with a vector theme and, on the basis of weights assigned to the different categories of land use and the presence of specific POIs (e.g. urbanized items), it is possible to identify and monitor zones with building constraints.

Figure 1 shows the adopted approach. It illustrates an area of interest partitioned into 8 sectors, *Pov* represents the center of the part of image displayed, S_i identifies the *i-th* sector and C_i is the corresponding frame portion. When the focus changes, *Pov* moves and the aggregate function is performed which first elaborates the value to assign to each S_i and then translates it into a color intensity associated to each corresponding C_i. The aggregate function associated to the frame calculates the target values independently of the part of image currently displayed thus guaranteeing an *ad hoc* overview cut out on the basis of objects and phenomena to display and properly balanced by the underlying aggregation function associated to the color intensity of the frame.

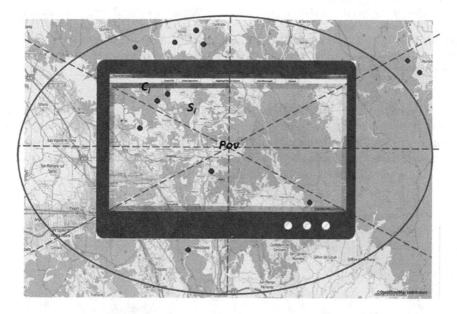

Fig. 1. The image partition according to the *Beyond the Screen* technique

As for the technological solution, *Beyond the Screen* is a server-side application interacting with SIRIO and has been developed as a Java project where classes mutually correlated have been packaged together. The most relevant modifications have been applied to the JMapViewer class of the OSM project [6].

4 Exploring Emergency Scenarios Through *Beyond the Screen*

To demonstrate the effectiveness of the proposed interactive visualization tool as a further support to centralized analysis activities and decision making, we performed a formative usability evaluation and tested *Beyond the Screen* prototype using an interaction scenario, which resulted from the transformation of the problem scenario described in Sect. 3. Again, at that stage we were able to rely on the active participation of the six subject who had responded to the initial questionnaire and gave us useful feedback on the appropriateness of the proposed technique.

Gino Rossi manages the conflicting recovery requests.

Gino has to modify the recovery actions scheduled in the original plan to face the crisis adequately, due to the fact that a higher number of people than expected was in one of the impacted zones.
At 4:15 p.m. he receives a data sheet from the gathering area no.2, where he reads a request for the recovery of 26 people at shelter no. 1. Gino asks the SIRIO GIS operator in his team to visualize real-time information about the geographic area of interest. Upon analyzing the situation, he approves the request and updates the number of available beds at that shelter.

The initial interface of *Beyond the Screen* is shown in Fig. 2. Displaying only the horizontal menu bar and the zoom slider one can visualize the widest map size. This approach satisfies the requirement of an initial overview to be offered to the user so that he/she can immediately recognize the area. The menu bar contains five buttons to invoke the application functionality as follows.

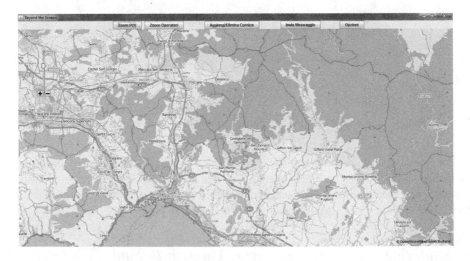

Fig. 2. The Beyond the Screen scenario

'Aggiungi/Elimina Cornice' (Add/Delete Frame) allows user to set up frames by selecting the associated layers. Figure 3 shows the selection of two frames, corresponding to the shelters and the gathering areas layers.

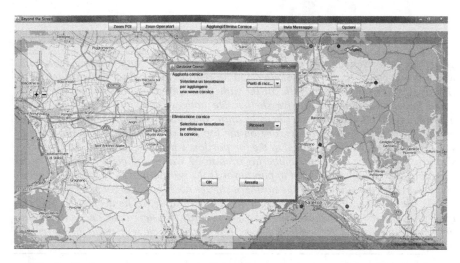

Fig. 3. Setting up frames corresponding to layers 'gathering areas' and 'shelters'.

Figure 4 shows the area of interest associated with a blue frame partitioned into 8 sectors. Data refer to the distribution of shelters and the different coloring of sectors immediately suggests the shelters which are closer. In particular, the up-right frame shows the most intense coloring thus indicating that a greater number of shelters have been set up along that direction.

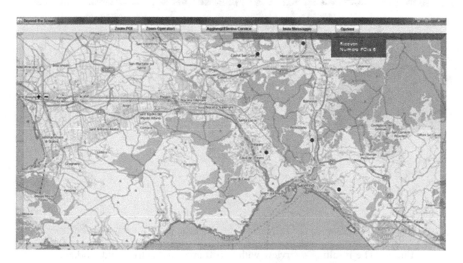

Fig. 4. An overview of a Beyond the Screen scenario

Going back to the scenario:

> *At 4:25 he receives another request for 33 evacuees from the gathering area no.2 which is associated to the same shelter and he realizes that only 9 beds are left. The GIS operator, who interacts with SIRIO with the support of Beyond the Screen, is asked to search for an alternative shelter. He notices that the frame summarizing information about the shelters (their location and their bed occupancy), has two portions with high color intensity, one on the top and one on the right of the screen. The highest intensity is associated to the top portion, which suggests that the northern shelter is the closest one to the gathering area no. 2 with a sufficient number of beds available. So, the operator is led to pan towards the northern area of the map. There, Gino can verify the situation of the northern shelter no.3, possibly zooming for further details. He discovers that it has still got 48 beds available, so he decides to redirect the 33 people to that shelter. The operator records the new data and notifies the decision to the on-site responders. A new report on the current status of the crisis management process, is distributed to all the local responders.*

Figure 5 shows the resulting interface where the zooming level has been automatically set up so as to contain all POIs involved within the area of interest. When clicking on a frame, the name and amount of POIs associated with it are displayed. Besides POIs recalled through these two (blue and red) layers, some additional (yellow) markers are displayed that correspond to the position of on-site teams of responders connected with COC.

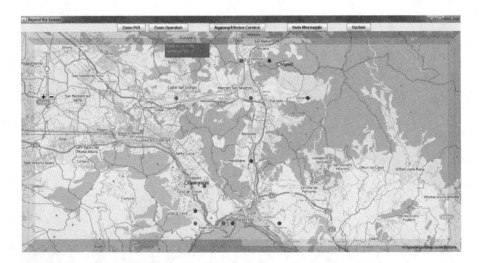

Fig. 5. The resulting overview with two frames and active field workers

In order to allow COC to send information to on-site responders, a message dialog box has been implemented. It is possible to select recipients (one, some, all) and edit the text message.

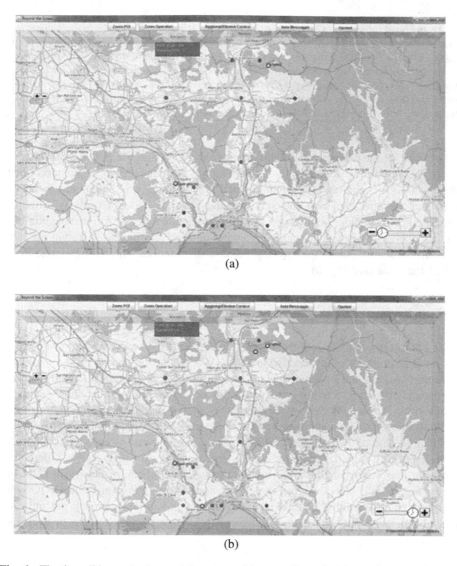

(a)

(b)

Fig. 6. The time slider on the lower right corner of the map allows decision maker to analyze the evolution over time of an emergency scenario.

The Zoom POI and Zoom Operatori (on-site responders) buttons set the map resolution at such a level that is contains all POIs and responders distributed within an area of interest. Finally, the Option function allows to set up some parameters, such as the size of the buffer zone corresponding to the area associated with the frame(s) and the layers features one wishes to visualize.

> *At the end of day 1 Gino has a plenary meeting at the COC* to collectively evaluate the evolution of the emergency situation since its beginning and the actions taken so far. By displaying the time slider experts are able to navigate through temporal sequences of the scenario of interest and monitor its evolution. The sequence revels that subsequent requests for evacuation routes originated from gathering area no.1. As a result, Gino and the other attendees agree that one more team of on site responders should be sent to that area as the next action.

This part of the scenario highlights the innovative feature of *Beyond the Screen*, namely the possibility to navigate through temporal sequences of a scenario thus allowing users to monitor its evolution. Such a functionality is paramount to better understand the effects of past interventions and make an ex-post analysis. Moving backwards the time slider on the interface, the user is able to recognize that the number of teams operating around the gathering area of interest has increased during the last few hours, probably due to the growing number of evacuees who have progressively reached that area (see Fig. 6)

5 Conclusion

Pan & Zoom represents one of the simplest and more used ways to perform analysis tasks on large amounts of information in a map. When decision makers need to monitor a territory to investigate a phenomenon, the width of the area of interest strongly affects the efficacy of his/her activities, independently of the technology available for data visualization. *Beyond the Screen* reduces the usage of repetitive operations by both providing users with hints about data and phenomena distribution around an area under investigation, and allowing a temporal and spatial comparison of evolving scenarios. This is especially important in case of emergency scenarios which evolve differently from what one was expecting and from the devised emergency management plan. In the next few months, the developed server-side application interacting with SIRIO will undergo a usability testing phase with the goal to validate the approach not only in terms of efficiency but also as an effective methodological enhancement of decision making processes.

References

1. Aedo, I., Díaz, P., Carroll, J.M., Convertino, G., Rosson, M.B.: End-user oriented strategies to facilitate multi-organizational adoption of emergency management information systems. J. Inf. Process. Manag. Int. **46**(1), 11–21 (2010)
2. Andrienko, N., Andrienko, G., Jankowski, P.: Map-centred exploratory approach to multiple criteria spatial decision-making. Int. J. Geogr. Inf. Sci. **15**(2), 101–127 (2001)
3. Andrienko, G., Andrienko, N., Bartling, U.: Visual analytics approach to user-controlled evacuation scheduling. Inf. Vis. **7**(1), 89–103 (2008)

4. Doshi, P., Rundensteiner, E., Ward, M., Yang, J., XmdvTool: visual interactive data exploration and trend discovery of high-dimensional data sets. In: Proceedings of ACM SIGMOD 2002 (2002)
5. Ginige, A., Paolino, L., Romano, M., Sebillo, M., Tortora, G., Vitiello, G.: Information sharing among disaster responders - an interactive spreadsheet-based collaboration approach. Comput. Support. Coop. Work (CSCW) **23**(4–6), 547–583 (2014). ISSN 0925-9724
6. OpenStreetMap. www.openstreetmap.org
7. Paolino, L., Sebillo, M., Tortora, G., Vitiello, G.: *Framy* – visualizing spatial query results on mobile interfaces. In: Ware, J., Taylor, G.E. (eds.) W2GIS 2007. LNCS, vol. 4857, pp. 175–186. Springer, Heidelberg (2007). doi:10.1007/978-3-540-76925-5_13
8. Paolino, L., Sebillo, M., Tortora, G., Vitiello, G.: Framy: visualizing geographic data on mobile interfaces. J. Location Based Serv. **2**(3), 236–252 (2008). doi:10.1080/17489720802487949. ISSN 1748–9725, Print/ISSN 1748–9733. Taylor & Francis
9. Paolino, L., Romano, M., Sebillo, M., Vitiello, G.: Supporting the on site emergency management through a visualization technique for mobile devices. J. Location Based Serv. **4**(03–04), 222–239 (2010). doi:10.1080/17489725.2010. Taylor and Francis Group Ltd.
10. Rosson, M.B., Carroll, J.M.: The Human-Computer Interaction Handbook: Fundamentals, Evolving Technologies and Emerging Applications. Lawrence Erlbaum Associates Inc., Mahwah (2002)
11. Sebillo, M., Vitiello, G., Paolino, L., Ginige, A.: Training emergency responders through augmented reality mobile interfaces. Multimedia Tools Appl. **75**, 9609–9622 (2016). doi:10.1007/s11042-015-2955-0. Springer Science + Business Media, New York
12. 3DGis: Sirio (2016). www.3dgis.it. Accessed May 2016

Modeling Emergency Care Process Taking into Account Its Flexibility

Asma Mejri[1(✉)], Sonia Ayachi Ghannouchi[1,2], and Ricardo Martinho[3,4]

[1] Laboratory RIADI-GDL, ENSI, 2010 Mannouba, Tunisia
mejri.assma@gmail.com
[2] High Institute on Management of Sousse, Sousse, Tunisia
sonia.Ayachi@isgs.rnu.tn
[3] School of Technology and Management, Polytechnic Institute of Leiria, Leiria, Portugal
ricardo.martinho@ipleiria.pt
[4] Center for Health Technology and Services Research (CINTESIS), Porto, Portugal

Abstract. It is widely recognized that the development of business processes (BPs), in the healthcare field, has a deep need of BP flexibility. This is due to changes that take place frequently. Hence, flexibility is one of the most overriding concepts in Healthcare. Since the Emergency departments are very complex, the processes structure has to be dynamically adapted and changed, specifically when dealing with crisis and disasters such as terrorist attack, earthquake, and hurricane, which often affect a high number of people. In such cases, the execution of the established plans is often perturbed. To allow flexible emergency care (EC) processes modeling, we have chosen the AristaFlow BPM suite as well as jBPM BPMSs.

Keywords: Healthcare · Emergency care process · Flexibility · BPMS

1 Introduction

In 2008, in a Dutch Mental Healthcare Institute, the death of a 47-year-old patient raised a storm of protestation [1]. Despite of having a certified quality management system, the investigation leaded to serious organizational and clinical quality problems. Such incidents and problems are an overriding reason that leads policy makers and health care leaders to redesign care [1]. Hence, BPM technologies have to be successfully used in the Healthcare sectors by taking into account methodological and practical considerations.

On the other hand, healthcare is more and more changing from isolated patient treatment episodes towards continuous treatment involving multiple healthcare professionals and institutions. Adopting BPM technology in the healthcare sector is starting to address some of the unique characteristics of healthcare processes, including their high degree of flexibility [2].

Healthcare processes are characterized by significant deviations, which constitute the normal case. Thus, physicians and nurses are acquainted to perform such deviations [3]. In this sense, it helps to adequately cope with both anticipated and unanticipated

© Springer International Publishing AG 2016
P. Diaz et al. (Eds.): ISCRAM-med 2016, LNBIP 265, pp. 98–104, 2016.
DOI: 10.1007/978-3-319-47093-1_9

exceptions and the possible deviations from the pre-specified treatment plan. A treatment plan comprises multiple diagnostic or therapeutic procedures [2]. Instances of a treatment plan need to be adapted to the specific needs of an individual patient [2]. It should also be possible to dynamically adapt it to the current situation of a particular patient at any time during process execution (i.e., to apply ad-hoc changes to the respective process instance) [4]. Consequently, BPs have to take into account that treatment plans need to be handled in an extremely flexible way [2].

It has become clearer that those systems have to be flexible and adaptable [5], because healthcare processes frequently change, and therefore the design of flexible healthcare BPs seems to be promising. We believe hence that flexibility has the potential to improve health care processes in order to deal with unexpected crisis. In this setting, we are going to model and execute flexible EC process models that can deal with the unexpected crisis and exceptional situations.

The remainder of this paper is organized as follows. Our emergency care process is described in Sect. 2. In Sects. 3 and 4, we reveal the emergency care process, modeled in a flexible way using consequently the ARISTAFLOW BPM suite and jBPM. We conclude in Sect. 5 with a summary and outlook on future work.

2   Emergency Care Process

In this section, we provide a description of the EC process and present its corresponding process model using the Activiti BPMS.

2.1   Description of the EC Process

In this work, we are going to consider the EC process which initiates with the patient registration and ends with her/his discharge of the emergency department. The EC process was analyzed and modelled at first in [6], using the BPMN language.

The main actors in this process are: physicians, nurses, paramedical providers and patients. Tasks of the EC process include: registration and payment, consultation, complementary Examinations, treatment and care, hospitalization, preparing of certificates: provide the patient with a certificate, depending on her/his situation, which includes the information about their emergency department use.

We have validated this process within the scope of this work, using observations and interviews with the main actors of the process. In addition, we arrived to a deeper understanding of the process and its different activities. The main activity that we have added was the sorting. This activity is done generally by physicians. It consists in sorting the patients, depending on their conditions, in order to send them to one of the following emergency department sectors: the delayed emergency, the waiting room, the crash room and the supervision room.

2.2   Crisis in the Emergency Care Process

Many examples were invoked in [7] regarding the emergency department of Farhat Hached. They cited these exceptional situations: the train accidents, fire victims, the collective food poisoning that occurred at the construction site of the airport and the AH1N1 pandemic. In such situations, the hospital has to treat all victims in time. In such situations, disruptions can take place, perturbing so the execution of the established plans [8]. In [7], author has studied four health crises faced by the emergency department of the Hospital Farhat Hached Sousse between 2007 and 2010. These crises provided significant changes to the EC process, including:

- Train accident: The accident occurred in the region of Sidi Bouali 19/11/2007, with several people injured. Carts and wheelchairs were prepared for moving victims within the service to consulting rooms or radiology unit. Victims could be also transferred directly to the crash room in case of life-threatening emergencies or need for resuscitation.
- Smoke poisoning: The fire that started in an academic home in 2008 resulting in many casualties/victims. The victims were put under high concentration masks in the halls of observation room. All the victims were kept under supervision for at least 12 h. One of the patients was hospitalized in the intensive care unit. The state of anxiety and panic among victims persisted despite their healing, which required the call of specialists in psychiatry. Psychiatric interviews were made for all the girls to calm and facilitate for them to return to the academic home where the disaster occurred.
- Collective food poisoning: The collective food poisoning occurred at the construction site of the airport in 2009. The victims, 156 people were taken. The reception room was reserved for victims of the poisoning. The sorting step depends on the severity of digestive and alteration in the level of consciousness of the patient's condition. To facilitate patient's management, special forms were issued to victims of poisoning containing certain personal data: their names, their ages, their nationalities and the suspect food. Moreover, another emergency form and medical form must be completed by doctors. They have to fill in the signs on physical examination, the requested balance sheets and its results, treatment, history and evolution of the victim.
- AH1N1 flu pandemic: The AH1N1 flu pandemic was between November 2009 and March 2010. It was considered essential to organize the triage of AH1N1 flu pandemic patients and create an isolation area to limit the transmission of the disease between the consultants of the service and the patients. To reduce the risk of transmission of the disease, a segmentation of the service was necessary. The waiting room has been converted into an isolation room for flu pandemic patients. This room accommodates a spaced dozen chairs. Patients had to be separated from their accompanying persons. A special form "AH1N1 sheet", containing information about epidemiological and clinical patients, has to be carefully and properly completed by the doctor.

3   Demonstrating Flexibility in the EC Model Using the AristaFlow BPM Suite

This process has been implemented using the AristaFlow BPM suite. The AristaFlow BPM suite is part of the ADEPT project which aim is to design a technology being able to flexibly cope with exceptions and dynamically adapt process instances at run-time. It was developed in 2008, with the purpose of having a powerful BPMS [9]. Accordingly, it provides advanced techniques for the modeling and the enactment of business processes. This BPMS adopted the ADEPT2 notation concepts. Therefore, the control flow of a process schema is represented as an attributed graph with different node and edge types. Based on these elements, model sequences, parallel and conditional branching could be modeled [10].

In [11], authors revealed that ADEPT2 is one of the leading technologies for realizing flexible and adaptive processes. Indeed, it allows the support of ad-hoc adaptations during the execution of particular instances. Therefore, this technology allows for modifications which would not be valid at design time. In this sense, various change operations were specified at a high level of abstraction. On the other hand, authors proved that it is possible to adapt the schema itself. This may lead to changes at the process instances based on the current process schema.

Figure 1 shows the EC process model in ADEPT2 notation. It comprises many activities which are connected through control edges. Generally, control edges specify precedence relations between activities. For example, activity order treatment and care is followed by activity complementary examinations, whereas activities registration and payment can be executed in parallel. Furthermore, the process model contains a loop structure, which allows for the repetitive execution of the depicted process fragment that contains the orientation, the consultation, the treatment and care, the complementary examination and the payment. If the status of the patient is not good, the patient should be reoriented to be examined. If his status is good, the patient can obtain a letter to an extern consultation or to be oriented to be hospitalized in a specialized department. Finally, data flow is modeled by linking activities with data elements. Respective data links either represent a read or a write access of an activity to a data element. In our

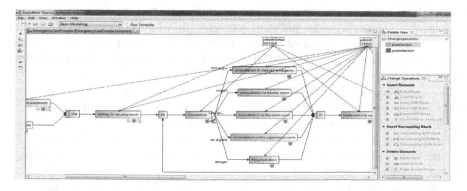

Fig. 1. A screen-shot of the EC process model in the AristaFlow BPM suite

model, for instance, activity "sorting" reads data element patientId, which is written by activity "registration".

To flexibly cope with exceptions, end-users may also dynamically change a process instance. ADEPT2 technology has been designed with the goal enabling the support of ad-hoc changes [4]. Physicians deviate from this process quite frequently, for example, in case a patient is victim of a smoke poisoning. Carts and wheelchairs were prepared for moving victims within the service to the radiology unit. In this former case, an additional activity concerning moving patients to the radiology units is added. Accordingly, patients were put under high concentration masks. The activity "wearing masks" was added during the execution of the process as shown in Fig. 2. The state of anxiety and panic among survivors persisted which required the use of specialists in psychiatry. Thus the activity "psychiatry interviews" and the actor "psychiatric physician" were added. The AristaFlow BPM suite allows thus for a great degree of flexibility during process execution. It provides a complete set of high-level change patterns for defining ad-hoc deviations. Users may dynamically add new activities or jump forward in the flow of control.

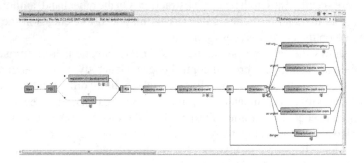

Fig. 2. A screen-shot of the EC process instance

4   Demonstrating Flexibility in the EC Model Using jBPM

In order to model our process, we used jBPM6. Since 2007, authors pointed out in [12, 13] that jBPM (java Business Process Management) is a pioneer example of open source products that are gaining more and more attention. jBPM could be downloaded from (http://www.jbpm.org/download/download.html). jBPM is a completely-defined, rich-functional workflow engine [14]. jBPM provides a large variety of nodes including events, activities, gateways, etc. [15].

We used frequently human task, rule task and ad-hoc sub-process in our implementation. Since most medical activities cannot be completely automated, but instead require a lot of user interaction, we frequently used human task for modeling clinical scenarios. Moreover, we use ad-hoc sub processes to realize our notion of workflow flexibility because it allows for EC participants (modelers and performers) to decide what should happen through the use of ad-hoc sub-process modeling elements. These elements enforce the flexibility by adding more steps and deviating from the proposed plan.

jBPM is closely integrated with Drools for specifying rule-based logic (in different formats, e.g. decision tables, rule files etc.). In our model, we have rule files (such as sorting-rule.drl). Drools rule files have a.drl (Drools Rules Language) extension.

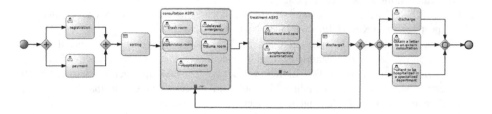

Fig. 3. The jBPM model

Figure 3 shows the modeled, in a flexible manner, EC process using jBPM. To ensure this, "consultation ASP1" and "treatment ASP2" are two composite activities that contain a number of atomic activities. The manner the contained activities will be executed and the order of their execution is unknown at design time. For instance, "consultation–ASP1" refers to the set of consultation activities that are likely to follow the sorting. Nevertheless, it is not possible to predict what types of consultation the doctor will do. Similarly, the complementary examinations and treatment and care activities cannot be predicted and depends on the status of the patient. Hence, the execution semantic for instantiating an ad-hoc sub-process is only known when this node is reached at the execution time. The procedure for patient treatment depends on her/his test results, further to diagnosis and medical history.

5   Conclusion and Future Work

In this paper, we specified first the importance of both BPM and flexibility in the healthcare domain. Then, we presented two prominent BPMSs that fortify flexibility. We presented next the EC process of the FarhatHached hospital in Tunisia. We demonstrated that the demand of flexibility is present in such processes, throughout several crisis situations that happened in the emergency department of the Hospital FarhatHached Sousse between 2007 and 2010. In this setting, business processes ought to be flexible enough to be adapted rapidly to such crisis situations. To cope with such situations, we have investigated therefore the modeling and execution of the studied EC processes, using prominent BPMSs: AristaFlow BPM suite and jBPM. We focused on the flexible features provided by these tools. Consequently, we demonstrated that the obtained models were dynamically handling real-world problems, disasters and unexpected situations.

In future work, it would be useful to consider other BPMSs such as YAWL (presented in [16]) and DECLARE (developed in [17]) BPMSs because they also care for flexibility. In addition, we are going to compare their degree of flexibility, while considering the modeled EC processes and the number of possible changes for each crisis.

References

1. Joosten, T., Bongers, I., Janssen, R.: Application of lean thinking to health care: issues and observations. Int. J. Qual. Health Care **21**(5), 341–347 (2009)
2. Lenz, R., Reichert, M.: It support for healthcare processes—premises, challenges, perspectives. Data Knowl. Eng. **61**(1), 39–58 (2007)
3. Reijers, H.A., Russell, N., van der Geer, S., Krekels, G.A.: Workflow for healthcare: a methodology for realizing flexible medical treatment processes. In: Rinderle-Ma, S., Sadiq, S., Leymann, F. (eds.) BPM 2009. LNBIP, vol. 43, pp. 593–604. Springer, Heidelberg (2010)
4. Reichert, M., Weber, B.: Enabling Flexibility in Process-Aware Information Systems: Challenges, Methods, Technologies. Springer, Heidelberg (2012)
5. Beyer, M., Kuhn, K.A., Meiler, C., Jablonski, S., Lenz, R.: Towards a flexible, process-oriented it architecture for an integrated healthcare network. In: Proceedings of the 2004 ACM symposium on Applied computing, pp. 264–271. ACM (2004)
6. Ghannouchi, S.A., Ghannouchi, S.E.: Une expérience de BPR dans un hôpital tunisien. Systèmes d'information & management **13**(1), 89–116 (2008)
7. Nouaouri, I., Nicolas, J., Jolly, D.: Reactive operating schedule in case of a disaster: arrival of unexpected victims. In: Proceedings of the World Congress on Engineering, vol. 3 (2010)
8. Ouni, A.B.: Plan blanc et gestion des crises sanitaires aux urgences. Ph.D. thesis, Faculté de médecine Sousse, Tunisia (2012)
9. Reichert, M., Weber, B.: AristaFlow BPM suite. In: Reichert, M., Weber, B. (eds.) Enabling Flexibility in Process-Aware Information Systems, pp. 441–464. Springer, Heidelberg (2012)
10. Reichert, M., Dadam, P.: Enabling adaptive process-aware information systems with ADEPT2. In: Handbook of Research on Business Process Modeling, pp. 173–203 (2009)
11. Dadam, P., Reichert, M., Rinderle, S., Jurisch, M., Acker, H., Göser, K., Kreher, U., Lauer, M.: Towards truly flexible and adaptive process-aware information systems. In: Kaschek, R., Kop, C., Steinberger, C., Fliedl, G. (eds.) UNISCON 2008. LNBIP, vol. 5, pp. 72–83. Springer, Heidelberg (2008)
12. Harmon, P.: Exploring BPMS with free or open source products. BPTrends **5**, 14 (2007)
13. Zhou, S., Gao, X., Li, G., Liao, M., Yang, L.: An application framework based on jBPM workflow engine. Appl. Mech. Mater. **2014**, 5968–5971 (2014)
14. De Maio, M.N., Salatino, M., Aliverti, E.: jBPM6 Developer Guide. Packt Publishing Ltd. (2014)
15. Adams, M., ter Hofstede, A.H., Rosa, M.L.: Open source software for workflow management: the case of YAWL. IEEE Softw. **28**(3), 16–19 (2011)
16. Pesic, M., Schonenberg, H., Van der Aalst, W.M.: Declare: full support for loosely-structured processes. In: 11th IEEE International Enterprise Distributed Object Computing Conference, EDOC 2007, pp. 287–287. IEEE (2007)

Information and Knowledge Management

Coordination Mining in Crisis: A Tool and a Case Study

Chihab Hanachi[1], Manel Tahari[2], and Meriem Riahi[2(✉)]

[1] IRIT, University Toulouse 1, Toulouse, France
Chihab.Hanachi@ut-capitole.fr
[2] ENSIT, Tunis, Tunisia
tahari.manel@gmail.com, meriem.riahi2013@gmail.com

Abstract. Crisis management systems are dynamic systems essentially build to support communication and coordination between heterogeneous, distributed and autonomous actors belonging to different organizations. In this paper, we are particularly interested in coordination. We show how the analysis of the interactions among the crisis actors can help discovering meaningful coordination patterns: organizational structures and interaction protocols. To do so, we use workflow mining techniques. Since workflow mining techniques are mainly focused on process (plan) discovery, we show how to extend them to be applied to the organizational and interactional dimensions. We use the Multi-agent paradigm to abstract these two dimensions in a uniform and coherent framework, and we provide a tool for their discovery. The contribution of this paper is three-folds: (i) a proposition of new log-file structure including Agent Communication Language performatives to capture interaction and relationships between actors; (ii) the design and implementation of a tool able to discover and analyze organizational structures and protocols; and (iii) the validation of this tool through a concrete example concerning the cooperative response of the Tunisian government to the terrorist attack of Bardo museum on March 18, 2015.

Keywords: Crisis management systems · Multi-agent systems · Workflow mining · Process models · Interaction protocols · Organizational structures

1 Introduction

Crisis management requires the coordination of several organizations evolving in a dynamic and open universe. New participants can dynamically join the crisis stakeholders, self-organizations can emerge while a relevant part of their activities can be possibly outsourcing. In this dynamic context with numerous formal and informal interactions, organizations have developed in the years different team collaboration tools based on information and communication technologies that facilitate the distribution of control and information exchanges and gathering. Given this highly dynamic context, despite the availability of these tools, it is difficult for the crisis management pilots to master the crisis management, and in particular to:

(1) Build an accurate view of the reality: deviations, vulnerabilities, organization evolution, interactions going on, etc.;

© Springer International Publishing AG 2016
P. Diaz et al. (Eds.): ISCRAM-med 2016, LNBIP 265, pp. 107–120, 2016.
DOI: 10.1007/978-3-319-47093-1_10

(2) Make rapid and appropriate decisions, coordinate and trigger the adequate response mechanisms;

(3) Understand, explain, justify and learn from past crises. Often there are possible deviances between the prescribed crisis plans and the performed ones. This leads responsible authorities to explain their behavior deviance and also learn from prior experiences to develop new coordination mechanisms.

Assuming the fact that we can record information about the actions and the formal and electronic interactions among the different actors involved in crisis, *the aim of this paper* is to show how the analysis of these actions and interactions can help to deal with the three previous issues, and in particular discover meaningful views about the coordination of crisis management.

Our approach combines workflow mining techniques [1] and multi-agent concepts [2]. Workflow mining techniques allow the analysis of execution traces of a collaborative system, in order to discover meaningful models regarding the organizational structures, the process models and the interactional protocols. The discovered models could be used for: (1) identifying and understanding coordination models that have emerged and that may constitute good practices, (2) analyzing the compliance between a prescribed coordination model and the performed one, (3) to improve existing coordination models.

Most of the work in this area focuses on the discovery of the process (procedural) perspective which corresponds to plan in our context. Very few of them are interested in the interactions between actors and on the organizational aspects which are of paramount importance in crisis management. To take into account these two last aspects, we turn to the multi-agent technology which is suitable for the design and development of cooperative systems. MASs [3] enable to model cooperation between (human and/or software) entities with a high level of abstractions, and so it's quite natural to refer to them in the workflow context. In this paper, we use the Fipa-ACL agent communication language [4] to record interactions between actors. We enrich workflow logs with FIPA-ACL performatives in order to integrate conversations between the actors within a process as [5]. However while [5] limits the discovery to organizational structures, we give means to evaluate qualitative properties of organizational structures (efficiency, robustness, flexibility) using Grossi's metrics [6], and also protocol compliance checking. Briefly, this paper proposes an implemented framework called COMIT (Coordination Mining Tool) enabling the discovering and analysis of procedural, interactional and organizational aspects of a workflow based on performative-based logs. We have validated this tool with the cooperative response of the Tunisian government to the terrorist attack of Bardo museum on March 18, 2015.

The remainder of this paper is structured as follows. In Sect. 2, we present the necessary background on workflow mining and its insufficiencies to capture interaction and organizational aspects. In Sect. 3, we propose a new enriched log file format illustrated with the terrorist attack of Bardo museum case study. In Sect. 4, we explain the architecture of the COMIT tool (i.e., Coordination Mining Tool), and we validate our work with the mentioned above case study. Finally, in Sect. 5 we conclude this paper.

2 Workflow Mining: Background and Insufficiency

2.1 Workflow Mining Principles

The workflow mining assumes that *a log file* recording past events related to a collaborative process is available. These kinds of files are available in most of the collaborative systems but we can also exploit a hand-made trace of a collaborative work. Most log file format, the XES standard included, are limited to four fields (cf. Table 1): (i) occurrence of a process (crisis in our context) also called case, (ii) task (performed activity), (iii) actor performing it, and (iv) timestamp of the event Also each line describes an event and events are temporary ordered. In the example of Table 1, we suppose that the three cases occur one after the other, which is not mandatory.

Table 1. A sample workflow log

Case identifier	Task	Perfomer	TimeStamp
Case 1	A: GiveSecurity	Police	T1
Case 1	B: RescuePeople	Military	T2
Case 1	F: TransportToHospital	Ambulance	T3
Case 2	A: GiveSecurity	Police	T4
Case 2	C: ClearTheGround	PrivateCompany	T5
Case 2	E: MedicalCare	FireFighter	T6
Case 2	F: TransportToHospital	FireFighter	T7
Case 3	A: GiveSecurity	Police	T8
Case 3	D: ExtinguishFire	FireFighter	T9
Case 3	E: MedicalCare	FireFighter	T10
Case 3	F: TransportToHospital	Ambulance	T11

In order to illustrate workflow mining principles, let us consider a toy example related to crisis management. A case refers to a particular crisis. In the example, we have recorded information about three crises. Let us illustrate the third crisis (case 3): as soon as the crisis started, the Police gives security (task A), then the Fire Fighters extinguish the fire (D) before providing medical care (E) to victims. Then, the Fire Fighters give duty to Ambulances to transport the surviving people to the Hospital (F). We can notice that we have three crises (C1 to C3) and each one follows its own emergency process but they also share some commons tasks. Existing workflow mining tools (like PROM [7] for example) can discover process diagrams [1] and also sociograms [8]. In our example, the process is represented by a conventional Petri Nets (see Fig. 1) able to play the three crisis cases. The sociogram (see Fig. 2) is a graph (P, R) where P is the set of actors and R a relation between actors, in our case it represents the work transfer from an agent A to an agent B.

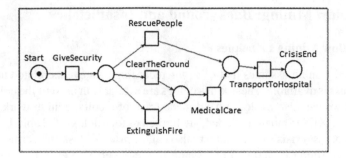

Fig. 1. Mined process represented with the Petri Net formalism

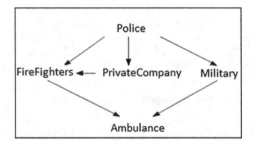

Fig. 2. Mined sociogram

A sociogram may be a weighted graph to underline the intensity of relationships. In this case, an additional function W is added to assign a value to each element of R. This relationship may also represent different kinds of collaboration [8]:

1. *The work transfer.* In a case (process instance) a work transfers from a person i to a person j *is* achieved if there are two successive activities where the first one is performed by i and the second one by j.
2. *Collaboration on common cases.* It quantifies how many times two persons i and j perform tasks in the same case. The more i and j work together, the more important the weight of the arc between i and j *will* be.
3. *Identical Profile.* The hypothesis here is the following one: actors doing similar things have a stronger relationship than if they do completely different things. A profile is assigned to each person according to his activities. The distance between two profiles can be measured using different metrics [8].

2.2 Workflow Mining Insufficiency

These deduced coordination models (process, sociogram) are interesting but adopt a strong and implicit hypothesis about actors' interactions. The log file doesn't keep any exchange traces (interactions and communications) between actors. In these conditions, considering the work transfer, nothing justifies that two successive activities of a same case really imply a transfer from one actor to another one, and several other interpretations may be considered [9]. In order to clarify this drawback, let us consider again the log file described in Table 1 and the *case3*: *Police* performs task A, then *FireFighters* task D and E and then Ambulance ends the case with task F. The classical interpretation considers that there are three work transfers: from *Police* to *Fire-Fighters*, self-transfer from *FireFighters*, and a third one from *FireFighters* to *Ambulance*. This interpretation assumes that two successive actors are in contact and they transmit to one another the control. In fact, many other interpretations may be provided according to the task assignment policy chosen:

1. *Arbitrary assignment of tasks* limited to competent actors (i.e. able to play the expected role: transport, security, etc.) and made by a supervisor.
2. *A Call for proposals* sent to all the competent actors, and the first volunteer does the task.
3. It may be based on *delegation*. For example, in case 3 the transportation of victims could have been allocated first to *FireFighters* who delegate it to *Ambulance*. Moreover, the delegation process could be multi-levels.
4. Actors perform a task and select the following actor according to *a protocol* that may be variable [10]: call-for-proposals, auctions, via a matchmaker, etc.

The assignment policy could also depend on the related organizational structure of the crisis management team in term of power, responsibility and authorities among the different actors.

In conclusion, the structure of current log files has an ambiguous semantics leading to numerous interpretations. More precisely, we don't find information related to the different task assignment policies or to the interactions between actors. Coordination mining are limited to process and sociograms, whereas we wish to be able to identify richer organizational structures and also interaction protocols. Thus, we argue that information exchanges that interleave tasks should be recorded and exploited. The remainder of our work is based on the idea that if a trace of these interactions is available, it will be probably possible to discover more fine-grained coordination models. Such mining requires an enrichment of log files integrating interactions of actors involved in the cooperation. This enrichment is detailed in Sect. 3.

3   Enrichment of Log Files for Improving Coordination Mining

Let us first present our example to better illustrate our proposition. The example corresponds to the Tunisian government response to the terrorist attack of 18 March 2015 in Bardo museum in city of Tunis. Three terrorists attacked the Museum, and took hostages. Twenty-one people were killed. This case study was based on information gathered from Tunisian media: in particular; interviews of the spokesman of the interior ministry.

According to this information, we draw manually a Petri Net to give a global and synthesized view on the actors involved and their interactions as illustrated in Fig. 3. This model is just a guide to check our method that does provide automatically (versus manually) different models from an enriched log file.

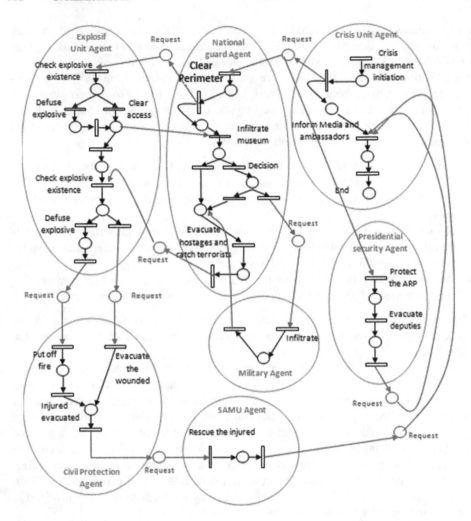

Fig. 3. Actors' behavior and their interactions during the reaction to the Bardo attack crisis

The six actors involved are: the Explosif Unit, the National Guard, the Crisis Unit, the Presidential Security, the Military, the Civil Protection and the SAMU (a medical emergency service). An ellipse surrounds the behavior of each actor. The Petri Net places, outside of the ellipses, correspond to communication places between actors. This model is executable and simulations can be done on top of it. Unfortunately, we have a unique model that couldn't help to distinguish and analyze clearly the different perspectives: process, interaction and also organizational perspectives. Besides, this manual modeling is not possible for a very large case in terms of actors and interactions. Also, we can't use mining techniques on top of conventional log files as they are ambiguous as discussed in Sect. 2. Giving all these observations, the question to address now is: What kind of log file structure could be defined to discover automatically process, interaction and also organizational perspectives?

The enrichment consists in enhancing workflow logs with further data, in order to discover more fine grained coordination models. In order to better understand the interest of this approach, Table 2 illustrates an enriched version about Bardo attack with a focus on the activity T4. The example shows six columns, "Case", "Activity" and "Time" which already exist in a conventional log structure. The enrichment consists in associating a performative to each task, and presenting the two actors (sender and receiver) involved in an interaction. We can distinguish two categories of tasks: *an interaction* which corresponds to a communication act between two agents, and *an action* which corresponds to a task executed by an agent. For communication acts (send, propose, delegate, reject, accept, broadcast, etc.) both the sender and the receiver are two human actors, while for an action (discernable with an *"execute"* value in the performative column) the sender correspond to the performer while the receiver is not a human actor but the system recording the action.

Table 2. Sample of the enriched workflow log

Case	Performative	Activity	Sender	Receiver	Time
C1	Cfp	T4: Clear perimeter	A1: Crisis Unit Agent	A2: Presidential Security Agent	12-10-2015 12:10:10.0015
C1	Cfp	T4: Clear perimeter	A1: Crisis Unit Agent	A3: National Guard Agent	12-10-2015 12:10:10.0016
C1	Propose	T4: Clear perimeter	A2: Presidential Security Agent	A1: Crisis Unit Agent	12-10-2015 12:10:10.0017
C1	Propose	T4: Clear perimeter	A3: National Guard Agent	A1: Crisis Unit Agent	12-10-2015 12:10:10.0018
C1 ,	Reject-proposal	T4: Clear perimeter	A1: Crisis Unit Agent	A2: Presidential Security Agent	12-10-2015 12:10:10.0019
C1	Accept-proposal	T4: Clear perimeter	A1: Crisis Unit Agent	A3: National Guard Agent	12-10-2015 12:10:10.0020
C1	Execute	T4: Clear perimeter	A3: National Guard Agent	System	12-10-2015 12:10:10.0021
C1	Inform	T4: Clear perimeter	A3: National Guard Agent	A1: Crisis Unit Agent	12-10-2015 12:10:10.0022

The example illustrated in Table 2 considers the interactions performed in the context of the task T4 (before and after its execution). It shows the first following sequence of interactions *Cfp.Cfp.Propose.Propose.Reject-proposal.Accept-proposal* before The *National Guard* Executes the action T4 and *Informs* the crisis unit of it. The first sequence of interactions could be interpreted as a call for proposal sent by A1 to A2 and A3 and leading to the execution of T4. The enrichment of log files allows one to interleave both interaction protocols (sequence of interactions such as auctions, contract nets, etc.) and processes (sequence of tasks) in the same file. Also, from the nature of communications acts, one could derive specific relationships between actors: power, coordination and control following Grossi framework [6].The power relation abstracts delegation patterns between actors. The coordination relation concerns the flow of information without commitments between actors (send, ask, etc.) The control structure can be derived when feedback performatives are used by an agent to account another one for his actions.

In order to elaborate a generic approach, we extended the standard XES log file format (http://www.xes-standard.org/) following the new meta-model of Fig. 4. In our meta-model, a log file is composed of multiple traces. Each trace (case) corresponds to a process instance that is composed of multiple events (lines). Each event consists on an activity (task), two actors, a timestamp and a performative that could be either an action or an interaction.

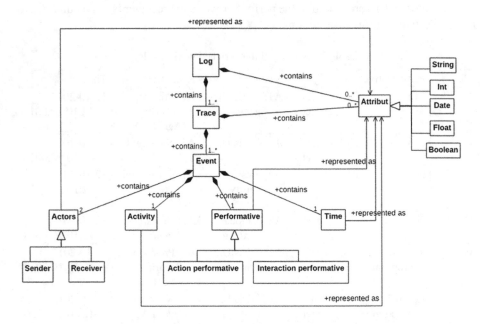

Fig. 4. Workflow log meta-model: an extension of XES

4   The Coordination Mining Tool: COMIT

In this section, we give an overview of the implemented tool COMIT. Figure 5 illustrates the architecture of our tool. Figure 5.a. gives a global architecture where the three modules appear, each one in charge of an aspect: organizational, interactional and procedural (or process). Two databases are used. The first one contains the structure of existing protocols in order to check their compliance with those discovered by COMIT. The second database records deduced organizational structures on top of which evaluations will be performed.

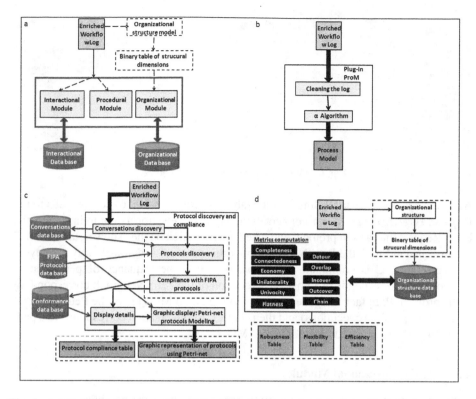

Fig. 5. (a) Global architecture, (b) architecture of the procedural module, (c) architecture of the organizational module, (d) architecture of the interactional module

4.1 The Procedural Module

This module (Fig. 5.b) corresponds to the process discovery model using our new log file format. To do so, we implemented a plug-in on top of ProM [7]. This plug-in is an extension of the alpha process mining algorithm [1]. Since we are using enriched log format, we operate a cleaning on the input log, keeping only the actions (versus inter-actions) and then we perform the alpha algorithm on it to get the process model.

4.2 The Interactional Module

This module (Fig. 5.c) generates from the log file a table composed of all interaction conversations discovered within the log file, and then elaborates their compliance with pre-recorded FIPA protocols as illustrated in Fig. 6. A conversation is a set of interaction performatives that work towards a common goal and operate under the causal depend-ency relation; if an interaction c1 belongs to a conversation C, then any interaction which causes c1 or is entailed by c1 also belongs to C. A protocol is a schema of conversations, and thus a conversation may be considered as an occurrence, or an execution of that Protocol. For example, the first conversation which occurs in the case C1 between A1 and

Protocol	Instance	Activity	Initiator	Participants	Start_time	End_time	Protocol Model
fipa request interaction protocol	C1	T2	A1	A2	2015-10-12 12:10:10.008	2015-10-12 12:10:10.011	Show Details
fipa request interaction protocol	C1	T3	A1	A2	2015-10-12 12:10:10.012	2015-10-12 12:10:10.014	Show Details
fipa contract net interaction protocol	C1	T4	A1	A2,A3	2015-10-12 12:10:10.015	2015-10-12 12:10:10.019	Show Details
fipa request interaction protocol	C1	T5	A3	A4	2015-10-12 12:10:10.023	2015-10-12 12:10:10.025	Show Details
fipa propose interaction protocol	C1	T8	A3	A4	2015-10-12 12:10:10.028	2015-10-12 12:10:10.029	Show Details
fipa request interaction protocol	C1	T11	A3	A4	2015-10-12 12:10:10.031	2015-10-12 12:10:10.034	Show Details
fipa request when interaction protocol	C1	T12	A4	A5	2015-10-12 12:10:10.036	2015-10-12 12:10:10.039	Show Details
fipa request interaction protocol	C1	T14	A6	A7	2015-10-12 12:10:10.041	2015-10-12 12:10:10.043	Show Details
fipa request interaction protocol	C1	T15	A7	A1	2015-10-12 12:10:10.044	2015-10-12 12:10:10.047	Show Details
fipa dutch auction interaction protocol	C2	T1	A1	A2,A3,A4,A5,A6,A7	2015-10-12 12:10:10.051	2015-10-12 12:10:10.074	Show Details
fipa request interaction protocol	C2	T2	A1	A2	2015-10-12 12:10:10.08	2015-10-12 12:10:10.082	Show Details
fipa request interaction protocol	C2	T3	A1	A2	2015-10-12 12:10:10.083	2015-10-12 12:10:10.086	Show Details
fipa contract net interaction protocol	C2	T4	A1	A2,A3	2015-10-12 12:10:10.087	2015-10-12 12:10:10.089	Show Details
fipa request interaction protocol	C2	T5	A3	A4	2015-10-12 12:10:10.094	2015-10-12 12:10:10.096	Show Details
fipa propose interaction protocol	C2	T8	A3	A3	2015-10-12 12:10:10.099	2015-10-12 12:10:10.1	Show Details
fipa propose interaction protocol	C2	T9	A5	A3	2015-10-12 12:10:10.102	2015-10-12 12:10:10.103	Show Details
fipa request interaction protocol	C2	T11	A3	A4	2015-10-12 12:10:10.107	2015-10-12 12:10:10.109	Show Details
fipa request when interaction protocol	C2	T14	A6	A7	2015-10-12 12:10:10.113	2015-10-12 12:10:10.116	Show Details
fipa request interaction protocol	C2	T15	A7	A1	2015-10-12 12:10:10.117	2015-10-12 12:10:10.119	Show Details

Fig. 6. Output of the interactional module

A2 in the context of task T2 (line 1 of the table illustrated in Fig. 6) corresponds to the *Request.Agree.Execute.Inform* conversation. This conversation is compliant with the FIPA Request Interaction protocol and when the user click on the "show details button" as illustrated in Fig. 7 the Petri Net describing this protocol is automatically displayed. A conversation C is compliant with a protocol P if the sequence of performative composing C corresponds to a possible execution of the Petri Net graph corresponding to the protocol P. In fact, we generate the marking graph MG [11] of the Petri Net (that gives all the possible executions) and then check if a conversation corresponds to a path going from the root node to a leaf node of MG.

4.3   The Organizational Module

In this module (Fig. 5.d), we do not try to retrieve or check the compliance with pre-existing organizational structures such as hierarchy, federation or coalition as already done in [12]. Here, we are interested in the quality of the organization set up in our log file whatever its structure. This module represent each actor as a node and its relations with others as an arrow. We consider three types of relation deduced from the types of communication acts existing between them: coordination, power and control. While *coordination* describes the flow of information between actors, the *power* refers to the delegation of tasks (i.e., agent a delegates a task to agent b, means that agent a have a power relation over agent b since he is entitled to assign tasks to him)and the *control* to an evaluation relation between two agents (i.e., agent a controls the work done by agent b, means that agent a can evaluate the behavior of agent b and so monitors the tasks performed by agent b). Figure 8 shows the different organizational structures deduced from our case study. Figure 8.1, 2 and 3 show respectively the coordination, control and power relations while Fig. 8.4 merges all of them in a unique diagram. The coordination relation looks like a "team" [13] with bi-directional relations between several actors. The control and power relations are "Hierarchy" [13] since they present one-way relations where A1 is the supervisor/delegator.

From this graph theory representation, a set of metrics (completeness, connectedness, economy, univocity, etc.) which formulas are given in [6] could be calculated to define the quality of the organization and in particular its robustness, flexibility and efficiency. *The robustness of an organization* requires a coordination structure highly connected and weakly economic and a power structure weakly univocal.

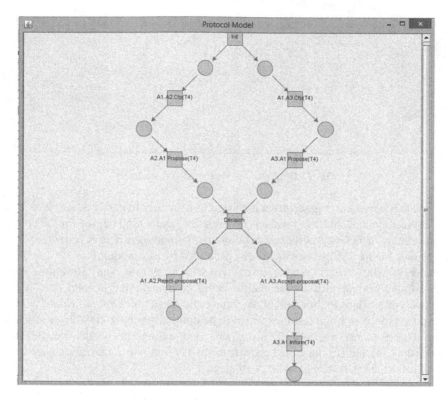

Fig. 7. Interaction protocol model conform to "FIPA Contract-Net" modeled with petri-net

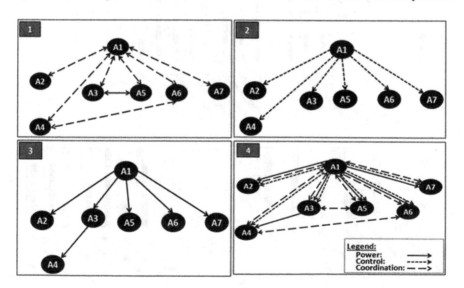

Fig. 8. The proposed organizational structure

Robustness			Flexibility			Efficiency		
Structural measures	Value obtained	Optimal value	Structural measures	Value obtained	Optimal value	Structural measures	Value obtained	Optimal value
Completeness_coord	0.42857143	1	Completeness_pow	0.14286715	0	Completeness_pow	0.14285715	1
Connectedness_coord	0.9285714	1	Connectedness_pow	0.9285714	0	Economy_pow	0.0	1
Univocity_pow	1.0	0	Chain_contr_pow	0.5	1	Economy_coord	0.33333334	1
Unilaterality_coord	0.0	0	Completeness_coord	0.42857143	1	Overlap_coord_pow	0.8333333	1
Univocity_contr	1.0	0	Connectedness_coord	0.9285714	1	Overlap_pow_coord	0.2777778	1
Flatness_contr	1.0	0	OutCover_pow_contr	1.0	1	Unilaterality_pow	1.0	1
Overlap_coord_pow	0.8333333	1				Univocity_pow	1.0	1
Chain_contr_pow	0.5	1				Economy_contr	0.0	1
Chain_contr_coord	0.85714287	1				Overlap_contr_pow	0.8333333	1
InCover_contr_coord	0.85714287	1				Overlap_pow_contr	0.8333333	1
OutCover_pow_contr	1.0	1						
OutCover_pow_coord	0.2857143	1						

Fig. 9. Output of the organizational module

The Flexibility of an organization is related to its ability to easily adapt. It requires alow degree of connectedness for the power relation, and a high degree for the coordination relation. *Efficiency* of an organization can be obtained if it is economic in all dimensions. Figure 9 illustrates the results generated by this module.

For each quality criteria, a table is displayed with 3 columns. The *"Structural measures"* column corresponds to the metric being computed, the second one *"Value obtained"* corresponds to the result of the computation, and the *"Optimal value"* column corresponds to the optimal result expected to be optimally robust, flexible or efficient. Figure 10 represents respectively histograms interpreting the results we obtained. Figure 10(a), (b) and (c) illustrated show respectively that our organizational structure is 58 % robust, 67 % flexible and 50 % efficient.

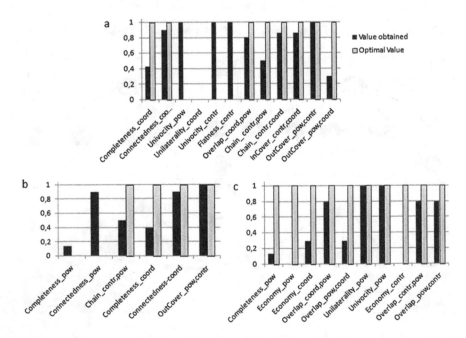

Fig. 10. (a) Histogram representing the robustness results (b) Histogram representing the flexibility results (c) Histogram representing the efficiency results

We meet a tradeoff. It's impossible to maximize all three criteria in the same organizational structure. For instance, the more the organization' nodes are well and directed connected from a coordination point of view, the more the organization is robust and flexible but the less efficient. This simulation is useful to test several scenarios with organization structures. According to the objective of the crisis cell (robustness, efficiency or flexibility), we could suggest to improve coordination, power or control relations in order to reach this objective.

5 Conclusion

In this paper, we have shown how the interactions among the crisis actors can be described with an Agent Communication Language, recorded in Log Files and exploited to discover and analyze meaningful coordination patterns: *evaluation* of organizational structures within Grossi framework [6] and *compliance checking* of interaction protocols with FIPA-ACL protocols. A tool COMIT has been implemented and has been used to analyze the terrorist attack of Bardo museum on March 18, 2015. To achieve our goal, we combined judiciously two paradigms: Workflow mining and Multi-agents system.

Also this work opens new perspectives and can be improved:

- *Managing the imperfections of log files*: the workflow log we used in our work is perfect (i.e., no event duplications, no missing messages, no noise). This kinds of logs are unusual. We usually find imperfect logs, so this is an issue that could be addressed.

- *Considering all FIPA protocols*: in our work we choose 5 FIPA protocols out of 11 to work with, so we could integrate the others for a more complete solution. Also, user-defined protocols could be considered.

References

1. van der Aalst, W.M.P., Weijters, A., Maruster, L.: Workflow mining: discovering process models from event logs. In: IEEE Transactions on Knowledge and Data Engineering, vol. 16, pp. 1128–1142. IEEE Xplore Digital Library (2004)
2. Divitini, M., Hanachi, C., Sibertin-Blanc, C.: Inter-organizational workflows for enterprise coordination. In: Omicini, A., Zambonelli, F., Klusch, M., Tolksdorf, R. (eds.) Coordination of Internet Agents: Models, Technologies, and Applications, pp. 369–398. Springer, London (2001)
3. Ferber, J.: Multi-Agent Systems - An Introduction to Distributed Artificial Intelligence, pp. 1–509. Addison-Wesley-Longman, Boston (1999)
4. FIPA. FIPA ACL message structure specification. FIPA agent communication language specifications (2002)
5. Andonoff, E., Bouaziz, W., Hanachi, C., Bouzguenda, L.: An agent-based model for autonomic coordination of inter-organizational business processes. Informatica Lith. Acad. Sci. 20(3), 323–342 (2009)
6. Grossi, D., Dignum, F.P., Dignum, V., Dastani, M., Royakkers, L.M.: Structural aspects of the evaluation of agent organizations. In: Noriega, P., Vázquez-Salceda, J., Boella, G., Boissier, O., Dignum, V., Fornara, N., Matson, E. (eds.) COIN 2006. LNCS (LNAI), vol. 4386, pp. 3–18. Springer, Heidelberg (2007)

7. van Dongen, B.F., de Medeiros, A.K.A., Verbeek, H., Weijters, A., van der Aalst, W.M.: The ProM framework: a new era in process mining tool support. In: Ciardo, G., Darondeau, P. (eds.) ICATPN 2005. LNCS, vol. 3536, pp. 444–454. Springer, Heidelberg (2005)
8. van der Aalst, W.M.P., Reijers, H.A., Song, M.: Discovering social networks from event logs. Comput. Support. Coop. Work (CSCW) **14**(6), 549–593 (2005). Springer
9. Hanachi, C., Khaloul, I.: Découvertes de protocoles et de structures organisationnelles dans le workflow. In: International conference NOuvelles TEchnologie de la REpartition, Lyon (2008)
10. Andonoff, E., Hanachi, C., Thanh, L.N.T., ibertin-Blanc, C.: Interaction protocols for human-driven crisis resolution processes. In: Camarinha-Matos, L.M., Bénaben, F., Picard, W. (eds.) PRO-VE, vol. 463, pp. 63–76. Springer, New York (2015)
11. Murata T.: Petri nets: properties, analysis and applications. In: Proceedings of the IEEE, vol. 77, no. 4, pp. 541–580, April, 1989
12. Hanachi, C., Gaaloul, W., Mondi, R.: Performative-based mining of workflow organizational structures. In: Huemer, C., Lops, P. (eds.) EC-Web 2012. LNBIP, vol. 123, pp. 63–75. Springer, Heidelberg (2012)
13. Horling, B., Lesser, V.: A survey of multi-agent organizational paradigms. In: The Knowledge Engineering, vol. 19, pp. 281–316. Cambridge University Press, Cambridge (2005)

A Rule-Based Computer-Aided System for Managing Home Accidents in Childhood

Baya Naouel Barigou[✉], Baghdad Atmani, and Fatiha Barigou

Laboratoire d'informatique d'Oran, Université d'Oran 1 Ahmed Ben Bella, Oran, Algeria
barigounaouel@gmail.com, atmani.baghdad@gmail.com,
fatbarigou@gmail.com

Abstract. Home accidents are one of the leading causes of death among children worldwide. First aids can in these situations help to initiate early treatment, which in turn may prevent death. Measures to improve emergency and medical treatment in the early phase may therefore help to save lives and reduce suffering. Home accidents require immediate attention but in Algeria, the problem is that majority of hospitals is usually concentrated around the urban areas and rural areas lack of emergency centers. In such situations, the parents must provide first aid until help arrives or carry the child to the nearest emergency center. Unfortunately, the first aid knowledge level among the parents is lower than expected. Therefore, the study aims to assist parents to the most common first aid emergency situations. We proposed a web-based expert system for the management of home accidents in collaboration with the pediatric intensive care unit of Oran's Hospital.

Keywords: Home accident · Children · First aid · Expert system · Web application

1 Introduction

World Health Organization defines accident as an unexpected and an unintended event causing physical and mental injuries.

Home accidents are defined as accidents that occur at home or its immediate surroundings. They commonly occur in children and concern mainly poisonings, falls, burns, and ingestion of foreign bodies. Statistics show that home accident is one of the leading causes of morbidity and mortality among children worldwide.

In Algeria, lack of safe storage for chemicals, complexity of the child's environment, smallness of the housing and the lack of a culture of health in many families all expose children to higher levels of risk. Also, the lack of accessible, affordable emergency health services increases the number of deaths and long-term deficiencies. Home accidents are the 2nd leading cause of hospitalization pediatric intensive care unit at the University Hospital of Oran [4]. Hence parental knowledge of first aids is required to initiate early intervention, which in turn may prevent death. Unfortunately, in Algeria the level of first aid knowledge among the parents, especially mothers, is lower than expected.

In this paper, the design of a rule-based clinical decision support system for Home Accident Management with a web-based version is proposed and described. Starting at

© Springer International Publishing AG 2016
P. Diaz et al. (Eds.): ISCRAM-med 2016, LNBIP 265, pp. 121–127, 2016.
DOI: 10.1007/978-3-319-47093-1_11

home, the place of the accident, the proposed system is intended for parents, who are the first people reacting during the accident, to help them to face the accident efficiently by giving them recommendation to help minimizing damage. Here are some of the facts that we've induced from our research and motivate our research:

- Home accidents are a major health problem in Algeria, resulting in more serious consequences in terms of mortality and handicap.
- The level of first aid knowledge among the parents is lower than expected.
- Rural areas lack emergency centers.
- No help systems are available for home accidents.

The paper is organized as follow; Sect. 2 is the related research and gives basic information about the concept of clinical decisions support systems and the related works. Section 3 presents our system and its architecture. Section 4 presents the conclusion.

2 Related Work

The growing amounts of data and knowledge with which physicians or medical staff need to work make the availability of proper information at the point of care greatest hurdles. This becomes more critical if the patient is in emergency situation. Studies suggest that as many as 18 % of medical errors may be due to inadequate availability of patient information [11]. Hence, clinical decision support systems (CDSS) can bridge this gap and can aid medical staff in gathering relevant data, making clinical decisions, and managing medical actions more effectively. CDSS has more than one definition provided by qualified professionals, institutes and non-profit standards-based organizations. Shortliffe gave the following definition: "*A medical decision-support system is any computer program designed to help health professionals make clinical decisions*" [13]. As stated by Conejar and Kim, CDSSs are expected to improve the quality of care by providing more accurate, effective, and reliable diagnoses and treatments, and by avoiding errors due to physicians' insufficient knowledge. In addition, CDSS can decrease healthcare costs by providing a more specific and faster diagnosis and by processing drug prescriptions more efficiently [5].

Systems from the 1970 s which inspire the modern systems provide a useful overview of the origin of work on CDSS. Three of those systems still are prevalent today. They are Dombal's system for diagnosis of abdominal pain [7], Shortliffe's MYCIN system [13] for diagnosis of the causes of infections, treatment and education, and the HELP system for delivery of inpatient medical alerts [10].

To our knowledge, there is no medical support system covering home accidents involving children but we found one work dedicated to injury [6] and other researches dedicated specifically to poisoning [1, 3, 12].

A French system called SETH [6] is developed at Rouen University in France to give end-users specific advice concerning treatment and monitoring of adult drug poisoning. SETH simulates the expert reasoning, taking into account for each toxicological class delay, signs and dose. MEDICOTOX-CONSILIUM [12] was developed for use in Bulgarian hospitals as a diagnostic system for first aid clinical toxicology. The system uses 1000 rules and scores provided by experts for diagnosis to identify poisons and supply the user with information about the appropriate treatment. A case-based CDSS for diagnosing poison cases caused by psychotropic [1] was built for use by the Russian Toxicology Information and Advisory Center in Moscow (Russia). Another system called ESP [3] was developed to overcome the lack of competent human resources and resource-intensive centers for the Toxicology domain in the Philippines. The system implemented as a rule-based expert system using CLIPS accepts signs and symptoms observed from a patient and present a list of possible poisoning types with the corresponding.

3 System Architecture

We propose a rule-based clinical decision support system for the home accident management. Our approach involves the use of a web client server model. By using an expert system, the server is dedicated to provide immediate information for parents and should help them make the right decisions to save the child or reduce the consequences of the accident. The client (parent) acts as a convenient user front-end.

This model simplify the client's task and put the core part of the system functions to the server to largely simplify the system development, maintenance, and use.

For a quick decision and ease of use, we have opted for a dynamic and interactive web application by integrating an adequate decisional system. The goal is to be able to respond to parents' requests effectively and efficiently. The key elements of the proposed system are:

- A web interface for the parent: Java Server Page on which the user can access the various features of the application.
- The Boolean expert system based on cellular automaton of CASI [2] which will be used to propose appropriate decisions in the case of a domestic accident.
- The Server and database.

The CDSS is implemented as a rule-based expert system with two major components - the knowledge base and the inference engine. But our architectural vision of the system is slightly different from the standard expert systems architecture. The main difference is the knowledge representation and the reasoning technique.

The implementation of the Boolean expert system consists of two modules. The first one is responsible for building the Boolean knowledge base following the principle of the cellular automaton CASI (Cellular Automaton for Symbolic Induction) [2]. The second one uses the Boolean inference engine of CASI to perform decision.

The CASI system [2]. In this study, we are only interested by its Boolean inference engine that is made of two finite arbitrary layers of finite state machines (cells) that are all identical. The operation of the system is synchronous, and the state of each cell at time $t + 1$ depends only on the state of its vicinity cells, and on its own state at time t. This automaton simulates the functioning of the basic cycle of an inference engine by using two finite layers of finite automata. The first layer, called CELFACT, is for representing the fact base, and the second layer, called CELRULE, is for representing the rule base. At every step, a cell can be active or passive, and can take part in the inference or not. The states of cells are composed of three parts: EF, IF and SF, and ER, IR and SR, which are the input, internal state and output parts of the CELFACT cells, and of the CELRULE cells, respectively. Any cell in the CELFACT layer with input EF = 1 is regarded as representing an established fact. Any cell of the CELRULE layer with input ER = 0 is regarded as a candidate rule. When ER = 1, the rule should not take part in the inference. Two incidence matrixes called RE and RS define the neighborhood of cells. They represent respectively the facts input relation and the facts output relation. They are used in forward chaining.

The input relation, noted RE[I, J] is formulated as follows: if (fact "I" ∈ Premise of rule "J"), then RE[I, J] = 1 otherwise 0. The output relation, noted RS[I, J] is formulated as follows: if (fact "I" ∈ Conclusion of rule "J"), then RS[I, J] = 1 otherwise 0. The cellular automaton as a cycle of an inference engine made up of two local transitions functions δfact and δrule, where δfact corresponds to the evaluation, selection, and filtering phases and δrule corresponds to the execution phase.

- The transition function δfact is defined as:

$$(EF, IF, SF, IR, SR) \rightarrow \left(EF, IF, EF, ER, + \left(RE^T \times EF\right), IR, SR\right) \tag{1}$$

- The transition function δrule is defined as:

$$(EF, IF, SF, IR, SR) \rightarrow \left(EF + (RS \times ER), IF, SF, ER, IR, \overline{ER}\right) \tag{2}$$

Our motivation to model rules with the Boolean principle adopted by the cellular automaton CASI is to reduce the storage complexity of these rules and also the response time while using them for inference. Effectively, the authors in [2] stated that CASI offers various benefits; the following are some of them: (i) the representation of data is simple, in the form of Boolean matrices requiring minimal treatment; (ii) the transition functions (δfact, δrule) are easy to use, of low complexity and effective. In order to be able to use the CASI system, we adopt the following steps: (1) Building of decision IF-THEN rules; (2) Boolean Modeling of constructed rules; (3) Boolean Inference for decision-making.

Building knowledge. For each type of accident (burn, fall, caustic ingestion and inhalation) we have identified the different signs and the first aids that the parent should know to save lives by giving basic treatment until professional medical help arrives. The knowledge base is expressed in the form of *IF-THEN* rules, where each type of accident is described by a separated set of rules. For example, in the case of falls, the parent must introduce the signs observed on the child; and then the system must decide accordingly the fall's nature and gravity to provide first aids. The fall may cause dislocation, fracture of a limb, vertebral fracture or a head injury.

Boolean Modeling of rules. To use the Boolean engine of CASI, we must first transform the IF-THEN rules in the format adopted by this machine.

- Every premise or conclusion of a rule is represented by a cell in the CELFACT layer.
- 0 initializes the EF state of each cell in CELFACT.
- Every rule in the original base constitutes a cell in the CELRULE layer.
- 0 initializes the ER state of each cell in CELRULE.
- For every fact "f" belonging to CELFACT and for every rule "r" in CELRULE, if "f" is a premise of "r" then RE[f, r] = 1 otherwise 0.
- For every fact "f" belonging to CELFACT and for every rule "r" in CELRULE, if "f" is a conclusion of "r" then RS[f, r] = 1 otherwise 0.

To illustrate this procedure, and for simplification, we consider that our knowledge base consists of only two rules:

- R1: IF *<Vomiting>* THEN *<Trauma Head>*
- R2: IF *<Deformed Joint>* and *<Swollen Joint>* THEN *<Dislocation>*

By applying the transformations mentioned above, the corresponding Boolean Knowledge base of R1 and R2 is given in Fig. 1. Four components form the Boolean knowledge base which can be used by the Boolean inference process.

CELFACT	EF	IF	SF
Vomiting	0	1	0
Deformed Joint	0	1	0
Swollen Joint	0	1	0
Trauma Head	0	1	0
Dislocation	0	1	0

CELRULE	ER	IR	SR
R1	0	0	1
R2	0	0	1

RE	R1	R2
Vomiting	1	0
Deformed Joint	0	1
Swollen Joint	0	1
Trauma Head	0	0
Dislocation	0	0

RS	R1	R2
Vomiting	0	0
Deformed Joint	0	0
Swollen Joint	0	0
Trauma Head	1	0
Dislocation	0	1

Fig. 1. The Boolean knowledge base

Boolean inference for decision making. We consider the Boolean knowledge base already built and shown in Fig. 1 and we suppose that the parent has selected the following signs: *"deformed joint"* and *"swollen joint"*. The process of inference, which operates by the method of forward chaining, consists of three phases. In the first phase, before launching the inference engine, the CELFACT layer is initialized. As illustrated in Fig. 2(a), for each sign selected by the parent, its corresponding cell is activated by setting the input state to true (EF = 1). In the second phase, called the filtering phase, the transition function δfact (see Eq. 1) is executed by selecting only activated facts (cells with EF = 1). Those facts will participate in the filtering step. The output state of the corresponding cells is in turn activated. In the Fig. 2(b) the SF of those cells is set to 1. Therefore, the input state in the CELRULE of rules having those facts in their premises is updated. According to the δfact equation, the new value of ER is calculated by the following formulae $ER = ER + (RE)^T \times EF$ where "+" and "×" are respectively the Boolean addition and Boolean product. This step corresponds to rule selection which corresponds to the action that matches the premises of the rules with all established facts. In our case, the rule R2 is a candidate and its input state is activated (ER is set to 1).

(a) CELFACT Initialization

"Deformed joint" and "Swollen Joint" cells
are activated ; EF = 1

CELFACT	*EF*	*IF*	*SF*
Vomiting	*0*	*1*	*0*
Deformed Joint	*1*	*1*	*0*
Swollen Joint	*1*	*1*	*0*
Trauma Head	*0*	*1*	*0*
Dislocation	*0*	*1*	*0*

(b) Filtering

CELFACT	*EF*	*IF*	*SF*
Vomiting	*0*	*1*	*0*
Deformed Joint	*1*	*1*	*1*
Swollen Joint	*1*	*1*	*1*
Trauma Head	*0*	*1*	*0*
Dislocation	*0*	*1*	*0*

CELRULE	*ER*	*IR*	*SR*
R1	*0*	*0*	*1*
R2	*1*	*0*	*1*

Rule "R2" is selected,; ER = 1

(c) Rule execution

CELRULE	*ER*	*IR*	*SR*
R1	*0*	*0*	*1*
R2	*1*	*0*	*0*

"*Dislocation*" is activated; EF = 1

CELFACT	*EF*	*IF*	*SF*
Vomiting	*0*	*1*	*0*
Deformed Joint	*1*	*1*	*0*
Swollen Joint	*1*	*1*	*0*
Trauma Head	*0*	*1*	*0*
Dislocation	*1*	*1*	*0*

Fig. 2. The Boolean inference process

During the execution phase, with respect to Eq. 2, the transition function δrule is started. At this stage, one or more rules that must be actually called are set. With respect to the example, the rule 2 is selected and, therefore, its output SR receives the value 0 (see Fig. 2(c)). The conclusion fact of that rule "*Dislocation*" is selected by setting the EF of this fact in the CELFACT base using the formulae $EF = EF + (RS \times ER)$ of Eq. 2. The CDSS generates recommendations based on the child's diagnosis. The recommendations specify actions to do in some order of priority and those to avoid in order not to aggravate the situation. Here, the CDSS will alert the parent to never attempt to back into place a dislocated joint. But it is necessary to proceed with the immobilization of the limb.

4 Conclusion

In conclusion, we can say that developing such system for home accidents can compensate the lack of emergency centers in the rural regions. And its implementation would extend the reach of the help even to the underserved regions. The findings of this work will be used in the improvement of the developed system for treating other domestic accidents like poisoning. This study was an important first step towards designing the system. We are convinced that CDDS can add value to the existing medical care by providing advice at the point of decision-making.

References

1. Althoff, K.D., Bergmann, R., Wess, S., Manago, M., Auriol, E., Larichev, O., et al.: Case-based reasoning for medical decision support tasks: the INRECA approach. Artif. Intell. Med. J. **12**(1), 25–41 (1998)
2. Atmani, B., Beldjilali, B.: Knowledge discovery in database: induction graph and cellular automaton. Comput. Inform. J. **26**, 171–197 (2007)
3. Batista-Navarro, R.T.B., Bandojo, D.A., Gatapia, M.J.K., Santos, R.N.C., Marcelo, A.B., Panganiban, L.C.R., Naval, P.C.: ESP: an expert system for poisoning diagnosis and management. Inform. Health Soc. Care **35**, 53–63 (2010)
4. Batouche, D., Khemliche, B., Sadaoui, L., Mentouri, E.: Accidents domestiques mortels chez l'enfant au CHU d'Oran. Archives de Pédiatrie **21**(5), Supplement 1 (2014)
5. Conejar, R., Kim, H.: A medical decision support system for ubiquitous healthcare diagnosis system. Int. J. Softw. Eng. Appl. **8**(10), 237–244 (2014)
6. Darmoni, S.J., Massari, P., Droy, J.M., Blanc, T., Leroy, J.: Functional evaluation of SETH: an expert system in clinical toxicology. In: Barahona, P., Stefanelli, M., Wyatt, J. (eds.) AIME 1995. LNCS, vol. 934, pp. 231–238. Springer, Heidelberg (1995)
7. De Dombal, F.T., Leaper, D.J., Staniland, J.R., McCann, A.P., Horrocks, J.C.: Computer-aided diagnosis of acute abdominal pain. Br. Med. J. **2**, 9–13 (1972)
8. Hayes-Roth, F.: The knowledge-based expert system. IEEE Comput. **17**, 11–28 (1984)
9. Haynes, R., Wilczynski, N.: Computerized clinical decision support system (CCDSS) systematic review team. Implement. Sci. **5**, 12 (2010)
10. Kuperman, G.J., Gardner, R.M., Pryor, T.A.: HELP: A Dynamic Hospital Information System. Springer, New York (1991). ISBN 0-387-97431-8
11. Musen, M.A., Middleton, B.A., Greenes, R.A.: Clinical Decision Support Systems. In: Shortliffe, E.H., Cimino, J.J. (eds.) Biomedical Informatics. Springer, New York (2014)
12. Monov, A., Iordonova, I., Zagorchev, P., Vassilev, V., Nissimov, M., Kojuharov, R., et al.: MEDIXOTOX CONSILIUM: an expert system in clinical toxicology. In: Lun, K.C., Degoulet, P., Piemme, T., Rienhoff, O. (eds.) MEDINFO 92, 7th World Congress on Medical Informatics, pp. 610–614. North Holland, Amsterdam (1992)
13. Shortliffe, E.: Computer programs to support clinical decision making. JAMA J. Am. Med. Assoc. **258**(1), 61–66 (1987)

Collaboration and Coordination

Building City Resilience Through Collaborative Networks: A Literature Review

Raquel Gimenez$^{(\boxtimes)}$, Leire Labaka, and Josune Hernantes

Industrial Management Department, TECNUN,
Paseo de Manuel Lardizabal, 13, 20018 San Sebastian, Spain
{rgimenez, llabaka, jhernantes}@tecnun.es

Abstract. Cities are interconnected and interdependent systems rather than isolated entities that face risks. Building resilient cities requires not only the government will, but also the involvement of different city stakeholders such as citizens, emergency services, academic, educational and scientific entities, and public and private organizations. Collaborative networks are relationships and partnerships between different stakeholders which provide opportunities to share information, knowledge, and to negotiate shared goals and issues. The involvement of the city stakeholders in collaborative networks during the emergency management phases (mitigation and preparation, response, and recovery) can contribute to improving city resilience. We carried out a literature review for obtaining an overview of the academic research that analyzes the contribution of collaborative networks and information systems to improving city resilience. Based on the literature review, this study suggests five resilience principles (*collaboration and networking, learning, training and preparedness, awareness* and *commitment*) that can improve through collaborative networks. Furthermore, specific examples of disasters and emergencies in which these principles have been implemented towards building resilience are illustrated.

Keywords: City resilience · Resilience principles · Collaborative networks · Information systems · Literature review

1 Introduction

Nowadays, the majority of the world's population live in cities and, according to forecasts, an increasing number of people will live in cities in the coming decades [1]. As cities across the globe continue to grow, they are facing an increasing variety of challenges ranging from acute shocks (that are sudden risk events) such as floods, droughts, and earthquakes, to chronic stresses (that are gradually unfolding risk events) such as climate change [1]. In this context, there is a growing interest in the implementation of measures to proactively reduce vulnerability and build the resilience of cities around the world [2, 3].

The term of resilience has been widely adopted by researchers and policy makers in an attempt to describe the way in which cities can reduce their vulnerabilities to shocks and stresses [4]. City resilience can be defined as the capacity of individuals, communities,

© Springer International Publishing AG 2016
P. Diaz et al. (Eds.): ISCRAM-med 2016, LNBIP 265, pp. 131–142, 2016.
DOI: 10.1007/978-3-319-47093-1_12

institutions, businesses, and systems within a city to survive, adapt, and grow no matter what kinds of chronic stresses and acute shocks they experience [1].

Current debate recognizes the limitations of uni-sectoral strategies and the need to engage multiple stakeholders from international, national and local governments, civil protection and emergency management organizations, public and private sector as well as professional associations in the process of making cities resilient to disasters [4, 5]. Approaches to building general resilience need to be bottom-up and top-down at the same time. Collaborative networks are relationships and partnerships between different stakeholders which provide opportunities to share information, knowledge, and to negotiate shared goals and issues [6, 7]. Furthermore, collaborative networks contribute to the development of social capital and sharing of assets and resources among involved stakeholders [8]. In this regard, the involvement of the different stakeholders of a city in collaborative networks during the emergency management phases (mitigation and preparation, response, and recovery) can contribute to the improvement of the city resilience [9, 10].

The development of information systems over the last few years has facilitated building collaborative networks among city stakeholders with numerous tools [11]. For instance, crowdsourcing tools and social media have become new sources to obtain information from citizens that can potentially enhance the response to disasters [12]. Nevertheless, future research is required to evaluate the impact of collaborative networks on improving resilience [13, 14].

In the following, this paper presents the findings from a literature review in which 126 journal articles related to the potential of collaborative networks in building resilience have been analyzed. Section 2 of the paper presents the research methodology, questions, and procedure carried out in the literature review. Section 3 presents the main findings of the literature review. Section 4 suggests five resilience principles to which collaborative networks contribute to. Furthermore, it illustrates specific examples of disasters and emergencies in which these principles have been implemented. Finally, Sect. 5 presents the main conclusions drawn from this research and identifies its limitations and further research lines.

2 Methodology

The scope of this research is obtaining an overview of the existing academic research on the possible contribution of collaborative networks to building city resilience.

Systematic Literature Reviews (SLRs) and mapping studies are two main techniques for carrying out a literature review. The first difference regarding these techniques are the objectives. While mapping studies aim at classifying and analyzing literature on a specific topic, SLRs aim at identifying best practices with respect to specific procedures, technologies, methods or tools by aggregating information from comparative studies [15]. Another difference between SLRs and mapping studies are the research questions. While the research questions in mapping studies are generic and related to research trends, research questions in SLRs are specifically related to outcomes of empirical studies. In addition to this, the scope in mapping studies and SLRs is also different. Mapping studies have a broader scope and focus on identifying papers related to a topic area and classifying the collected data. On the other hand, the scope in SLRs is to extract detailed information related to specific research questions [15, 16].

Taking into account the differences between mapping studies and SLRs, this research considers SLRs as an appropriate approach for gaining comprehensive insights on the contribution of collaborative networks to improve city resilience. The following paragraphs describe the stages conducted to carry out the SLR:

- Defining the research questions.
- Defining the filtering criteria for the search.
- Identifying articles based on filtering criteria.
- Reporting findings.

2.1 Defining the Research Questions

Following, the main questions that this research aims to answer by reviewing existing academic research are presented:

- RQ1: Towards which risks (e.g. natural, man-made, climate change) is resilience developed?
- RQ2: Which research methodologies are used for analyzing the contribution of collaborative networks to developing city resilience?
- RQ3: Which are the main findings obtained from analyzing the contribution of collaborative networks to developing city resilience?

2.2 Defining the Filtering Criteria for the Search

Emerald, Science Direct, and Scopus online databases were used with a combination of keywords to search for papers published in English. The combination of the following keywords was used: Resilience, Emergency management, City, Learning, Collaboration and Network in all the fields of journal articles. Regarding the used databases, Emerald, Science Direct, and Scopus databases were selected because the topic of our research is limited to social science and these databases provide a range of social science research. With regard to the time period, our research was limited to the last ten years (2005–2015).

Another filtering criterion in our research was the inclusion of only journal articles. Therefore, conference proceedings, book chapters, books, working papers, dissertations, projects, reports and thesis were not included in our research. The reason for limiting the literature to journal articles was that we primarily wanted to analyze high-quality research activities. In this regard, it was assumed that important results presented in thesis, projects, reports, conference proceedings, etc. would also be published in journal articles.

2.3 Identifying the Articles Based on Filtering Criteria

Having defined the boundaries of the SLR, the next steps consisted of identifying the articles fitting into our scope. Table 1 presents the steps carried out in the SLR in order to identify articles.

- The first step consisted of conducting a search with the defined combination of keywords in Emerald, Science Direct, and Scopus online databases in order to identify articles. Results from this search provided journal articles, book chapters, conference papers, editorials, call for special issues, and bibliographies of journals.
- In the second step, based on the filtering criteria previously defined, the results that were not journal articles were excluded.
- The third step consisted of reviewing the articles to exclude the irrelevant ones for °this study. For reviewing the articles, the title, the keywords, the abstract and the conclusions of the articles were read. Based on this information, there were some articles that could be rapidly excluded, since they provided clear evidence that such articles were not related to the topic. Doubtful articles were read thoroughly in order to determine whether the paper would be included in the definitive list.

As a result of these three steps, a total of 126 journal articles were selected to be analyzed in detail: 90 articles were selected from Science Direct database, 32 from Emerald and 4 from Scopus.

Table 1. Steps carried out in the SLR to select articles.

Journal databases	Keywords	1st step	2nd step	3rd step
Science direct	Resilience AND city AND emergency management AND learn AND collaboration AND network	121	113	90
Emerald		144	71	32
Scopus		46	8	4

3 Results

In the following sections, the main results from the analysis of the 126 journal articles that were analyzed in the SLR are presented. These results are presented according to the research questions defined in Sect. 2. The list of the 126 articles can be found in: https://www.dropbox.com/s/bb4ci9ciadp3tgt/List%20of%20papers.docx?dl=0. Table 2 shows the years in which the identified articles were published. It is clear that the topic has raised interest in the last four years. Approximately 88 % of the identified were published between 2012 and 2015. Furthermore, 35 % of the articles were published during 2015.

The 126 articles identified in this research are published in a total of 40 journals. *International Journal of Disaster Risk Reduction* is the journal with the greater amount of articles published. 21 % of the articles were published in this journal. In a second level, *International Journal of Disaster Resilience in the Built Environment* journal

Table 2. Number of articles published by year.

Year	Number of articles	% of articles
2015	44	35 %
2014	34	27 %
2013	20	16 %
2012	13	10 %
2011	3	2 %
2010	4	3 %
2009	3	2,4 %
2008	3	2,4 %
2007	0	0 %
2006	2	1,6 %

published approximately 10 % of the total number of the articles. Thirdly, *Urban Climate* journal published 9 % of the identified articles.

RQ1: To which risks (e.g. natural, man-made, climate change consequences) is resilience developed?

According to the findings of the SLR, natural disasters are the main concern for cities in terms of resilience-building efforts. As Table 3 shows, the majority of the articles addresses the resilience against natural hazards. Natural disasters apparently have affected communities, organizations, and cities, and forced them to continuously learn and improve their resilience, as shown in Table 3. Besides, there are 32 articles that use the concept of resilience applied to climate change adaptation (threats posed by climatological hazards such as extreme temperatures, drought and wildfires and the multi-faceted threats associated with sea level change). As Table 3 shows, there is a lack of studies about resilience against the man-made hazards.

The comparison of all publications from different continents shows that most publications from Asia, North America, Oceania and Africa are about natural disasters, i.e. 63.3 % (31 out of 49), 59 % (16 out of 27), 70 % (14 out of 20) and 60 % (3 out of 5) respectively.

The high numbers of publications analyzing resilience in Asia led us to investigate further what kind of topics and why the resilience discussions are so popular. Apparently, a couple of publications on resilience in Asia appeared for the first time in

Table 3. Classification of the articles based on the type of disaster and continent.

Type of disaster/continent	Asia	North America	Oceania	Africa	Europa	South America
Natural disaster	31	16	14	3	7	1
Climate change	12	6	6	2	5	1
All hazards	6	4	0	0	4	1
Man-made hazard	0	1	0	0	1	0
Total	49	27	20	5	17	3

2006 triggered by the major tsunami disaster in 2004. However, from 2006 to 2011, there are only six publications on the topic. After 2012, disaster resilience topic gains popularity and most of the publications (87 %) are published since then.

RQ2: Which research methodologies are used for analyzing the contribution of collaborative networks to developing city resilience?

The articles identified in the literature review were classified regarding the research methodology that was used in each of them (see Table 4). The majority of the articles (90 out of 126) use cases studies or action research to develop their study. Interviews, discussion, and focus group are the second most used type of methodology. It is important to point out that some articles use more than one methodology, thus, the total amount of articles that appears in Table 4 is higher than 126.

Table 4. Classification of the articles according to the research methodology.

Research methodology	Number of articles
Case study or action research	90
Interview, discussion or focus group	42
Concept description	18
Survey	11
Literature review	5
Grounded theory	4

RQ3: Which are the main findings obtained from analyzing the contribution of collaborative networks to developing city resilience?

The 126 articles analyzed in this research are classified in Table 5 according to the results they present. In order to do this classification, the results section of each of the articles was read in detail. It should be highlighted that some articles result in various findings, thus, the total amount of articles that appears in Table 5 is higher than 126. While 33 out of 126 articles present barriers identified to build resilience, 31 articles define policies or strategies to develop resilience. Furthermore, 29 articles present lessons learned from past events to improve resilience. Regarding frameworks for improving resilience, 24 articles develop new frameworks or models but only nine articles describe the application of existing frameworks to improve resilience. In addition, 13 articles develop different concepts of resilience and eight articles identify research gaps related to building resilience.

With regards to the use of information systems to build resilience, there are eight articles that present the development of tools to enhance collaboration, coordination, and networking among different stakeholders. According to the findings of these articles, information systems, social media and Web 2.0 tools are considered as suitable tools that allow stakeholders from different sectors learn from each other by sharing experiences and best practices [17]. In this context, [18] present an emergency management information system to support the coordination among different stakeholders in order to respond efficiently to emergencies. The system supports a fluent information

Table 5. Classification of the articles according to the research findings.

Research findings	Number of articles
Identification of barriers	33
Definition of policies or strategies	31
Identification of lessons learned	29
Development of a framework	24
Concept development	13
Application of a framework	9
Identification of research gap	8
Development of tools	8
Definition of resilience characteristics	4

flow among stakeholders to improve awareness so that involved agents understand what's going on in the emergency. Besides, [17] present a prototype of a decision support system for emergency operations. The system provides a trusted knowledge of risks and resources that allow emergency managers to develop an integrated perspective on shared risks and improve the inter-organizational resource allocation strategies. Furthermore, [19] proposes that social media can effectively support information sharing, communication, and collaboration in times of crises. Finally, there are four articles that propose characteristics of resilience that can be improved by collaborative networks.

4 Resilience Principles that can be Improved by Collaborative Networks

Following, we have selected the four articles identified in the literature review that present characteristics and aspects of resilience that can be improved through collaborative networks.

Authors [20] identify six characteristics of resilience in relation to climate change and flood risks. First, they recognize the need to learn from previous experiences, both positive and negative (ability to learn) and the ability to involve the public and foster their participation in policy decisions. Furthermore, they recognize the need to be aware and understand the existing conditions of the city (attention to current situation) and commit resources and initiate action to respond to issues such as climate change (ability to set goals and initiate actions). Finally, they emphasize the need to prepare for future disturbances on the basis of current information (attention to trends and future threats).

In terms of improving resilience towards flood risk management, [21] consider the following aspects. First, these authors recognize social learning as a key factor for awareness raising, and better preparedness and capacity building for increased flood resilience. Second, [21] recognize the role and importance of participatory governance and collaborative decision making for sustainable flood risk management. According to these authors, learning elevates overall environmental or risk awareness within communities and opens up possibilities for participatory decision making that may lead to commonly agreed alternatives, strategies, and measures.

In addition, [22] recognizes that strengthening community resilience is a dynamic process that is embedded within the day to day activities. In this vein, the author considers that resilience building process involves eight principles (preparedness, responsiveness, inclusion, connectivity, learning, self-organization, diversity and social cohesion) that enhance adaptive capabilities to respond and adjust to an increasing and unpredictable array of short terms shocks and long-term stresses.

Finally, [13] suggest that social resilience is composed of a variety of factors (see Table 6). The factors represent the ability of a community to cope with a disaster in minimizing social damage and returning back to the previous situation and even improve it.

Based on the previously analyzed articles, we can conclude that there are different principles which are important for improving city resilience and can be improved by collaborative networks. A variety of studies considers learning and collaboration and networking as central aspects of research and practice for the improvement of city resilience. Learning may increase the resilience of communities faced with risk from extreme events [23]. Furthermore, learning processes are stimulated by collaborative networks that enable interaction between individuals, organizations, agencies and institutions at multiple organizational levels to draw upon various knowledge systems [24].

In addition, the analyzed articles propose additional resilience principles that can be improved by collaborative networks. Training and preparedness, awareness, and commitment are also considered important aspects of resilience in most of the articles. On the one hand, fostering awareness among stakeholders increases understanding of the potential risks and vulnerabilities of the city and may contribute to the willingness and commitment of these stakeholders to assign resources and take actions to improve their capacity to deal with these risks. On the other hand, awareness of existing risks and vulnerabilities may also contribute to increasing training and preparedness for the stakeholders to be able to cope with unexpected events.

After analyzing the resilience aspects presented in the four articles, we propose five principles (*collaboration and networking, learning, training and preparedness, awareness* and *commitment*) that cover all the identified aspects of resilience in the analyzed papers (see Table 6).

- **Collaboration and networking.** Collaboration and networking entail ensuring effective integration of efforts among city stakeholders. Trust building, reaching consensus, establishing team spirit and improving mutual understanding via effective communication are essential actions for achieving involvement and effective collaboration between the different city stakeholders [13, 20].
- **Learning.** Learning is of crucial importance to building resilience as it entails internalizing lessons from past experiences and knowledge obtained from disasters, as well as developing new skills [20–22].
- **Training and preparedness.** Training and preparedness refer to the capacity of the city stakeholders to anticipate, deal with potential threats, and recover from disasters. To achieve this, working together and building expertise through previous planning and training programs are necessary [21, 22].

- **Awareness.** Awareness refers to how informed the city stakeholders are on the risks and vulnerabilities as well as on the resources and capacities of the city. In this context, education on disaster management is vital for the city stakeholders to develop a common understanding of the requirements to improve the city resilience [9, 13, 23].
- **Commitment.** Commitment refers to how committed city stakeholders are to initiate action and invest in building city resilience [20]. Committed stakeholders play a critical role in initiating action by advocating for change [25].

Table 6. Classification of the resilience aspects presented in the analyzed articles based on the identified five principles.

Author (Year)	Collaboration and networking	Learning	Training and preparedness	Awareness	Commitment
Lu and Stead (2013)	Involve public responses	Learn from previous experience	Attention to trends and future threats	Attention to current situation	Set goals and initiate actions
Evers et al. (2015)	Participatory and collaborative decision-making	Social learning	Preparedness and capacity development	Awareness raising	
Oxley (2013)	Connectivity, Inclusion, Diversity and Social cohesion	Learning	Preparedness		Responsiveness and self-organization
Khalili et al. (2015)	Exchange of information, Community participation, Trust, Sense of community and Social support	Learning		Shared information and education	

Implementation of the resilience principles

Based on the articles reviewed in this literature review, it has been possible to identify examples of disasters and crisis in which collaborative networks have improved the resilience principles. Following we provide examples of specific cases in which the resilience principles have been implemented. These examples have been obtained from the articles analyzed in the literature review.

On the one hand, collaboration and networking were of crucial importance in the aftermath of the 2011 Christchurch earthquake where community groups spontaneously organized to provide support to Christchurch residents. The Student Volunteer Army, Rangiora Express, and Farmy Army are examples of local groups that provided a substantial contribution to the disaster response. Services provided by these groups included recruiting and placing volunteers, digging liquefaction, providing transport as well as logistical support for the mainstream response, distributing food, hot meals, emergency supplies and essential items [26].

On the other hand, the need to learn from past experiences was totally evident in the early fall of 2013 in the Front Range of Colorado, where several communities experienced intense rainfall over a three-day period, exceeding annual average precipitation rates. During these days, extensive damage occurred to roads, infrastructure, parks, river corridors, homes and business throughout the region. In this context, successful response to extreme events relied on policy learning (i.e. changes in beliefs, attitudes, behaviors, and goals) in response to new information and experiences. Learning from these events led to the adaptation of local policies to increase the resilience of communities faced with risk from extreme events [23].

In terms of training and preparation, in Philippines, Indonesia and western Coast of America where they are used to experience the effects of tsunamis and earthquakes, they have established centers for preparedness and tsunami information systems. These countries recognize the need to take initiatives regarding preparedness from the government to reduce the impacts of shocks on communities [27].

Furthermore, the role of risk awareness in effective disaster reduction was demonstrated in the 2004 Indian Ocean tsunami. In this case, a small girl was able to warn her parents about the occurrence of the tsunami thanks to the education received in the school on this phenomenon. In this regard, the importance of involving stakeholders and providing disaster risk reduction programs at schools was evident [28].

Finally, in terms of commitment, cities such as Durban and Quito benefitted from the presence of committed stakeholders who agitated for action by effectively linking climate change risk to local agendas. These stakeholders achieved legitimacy by operating in close association with, the municipality and engaging the interest of a wider group of stakeholders. In other cities, technical or financial support has been obtained from donor or development agencies promoting resilience-building efforts (such as the Rockefeller Foundation) [25].

5   Conclusions

Cities across the world face a variety of challenges related to climate change, man-made and natural disaster occurrences. In order to improve city resilience towards these risks, efforts must be done to foster collaboration and collaborative processes among the different city stakeholders. The development of collaborative networks and the use of information systems among the city stakeholders can contribute to the improvement of the city resilience. This paper presents the findings from a literature review in which 126 journal articles about the potential of collaborative networks in building resilience have been analyzed. A great number of articles present case studies of specific disasters in which collaborative networks of stakeholder have contributed to successfully deal with disaster and emergencies. On the contrary, a limited number of articles propose characteristics and aspects of resilience that can be improved by collaborative networks. Based on the characteristics of resilience identified from these articles, this research suggests five resilience principles (collaboration and networking, learning, training and preparedness, awareness and commitment) that can be improved by collaborative networks. Furthermore, it has been possible to identify specific case studies of disasters and emergencies in which the resilience principles have been implemented. As a future research line, this research could be improved by analyzing to what extent information systems can enhance the implementation of the five resilience principles.

References

1. 100 Resilient Cities. http://www.100resilientcities.org/resilience#/-_/
2. UNISDR. http://www.unisdr.org/campaign/resilientcities/
3. Brown, A., Dayal, A., Del Rio, C.R.: From practice to theory: emerging lessons from Asia for building urban climate change resilience. Environ. Urban. **24**(2), 53–556 (2012)
4. Valdés, M.H., Amaratunga, D., Haigh, R.: Making cities resilient: from awareness to implementation. Int. J. Disaster Resilience Built Environ. **4**(1), 5–8 (2013)
5. Haigh, R., Amaratunga, D.: An integrative review of the built environment discipline's role in the development of society's resilience to disasters. Int. J. Disaster Resilience Built Environ. **1**(1), 11–24 (2010)
6. Kapucu, N.: Disaster and emergency management systems in urban areas. Cities **29**, 41–49 (2012)
7. Jung, K., Song, M.: Linking emergency management networks to disaster resilience: bonding and bridging strategy in hierarchical or horizontal collaboration networks. Qual. Quant. **49**(4), 1465–1483 (2014)
8. Cavallo, A., Ireland, V.: Preparing for complex interdependent risks: a system of systems approach to building disaster resilience. Int. J. Disaster Risk Reduct. **9**, 181–193 (2014)
9. Oktari, R.S., Shiwaku, K., Munadi, K., Shaw, R.: A conceptual model of a school–community collaborative network in enhancing coastal community resilience in Banda Aceh Indonesia. Int. J. Disaster Risk Reduct. **12**, 300–310 (2015)
10. Kapucu, N., Arslan, T., Demiroz, F.: Collaborative emergency management and national emergency management network. Disaster Prev. Manage. Int. J. **19**(4), 452–468 (2010)
11. Li, J., Li, Q., Liu, C., Khan, S.U., Ghani, N.: Community-based collaborative information system for emergency management. Comput. Oper. Res. **42**, 116–124 (2014)
12. Scifo, S., Salman, Y.: Citizens' involvement in emergency preparedness and response: a comparative analysis of media strategies and online presence in Turkey, Italy and Germany. Interact. Stud. Commun. Cult. **6**(2), 179–198 (2015)
13. Khalili, S., Harre, M., Morley, P.: A temporal framework of social resilience indicators of communities to flood, case studies: Wagga Wagga and Kempsey, NSW, Australia. Int. J. Disaster Risk Reduct. **13**, 248–254 (2015)
14. Sherrieb, K., Louis, C.A., Pfefferbaum, R.L., Pfefferbaum, J.D.B., Diab, E., Norris, F.H.: Assessing community resilience on the US coast using school principals as key informants. Int J Disaster Risk Reduct **2**, 6–15 (2012)
15. Kitchenham, B.A., Budgen, D., Brereton, O.P.: Using mapping studies as the basis for further research–a participant-observer case study. Inf. Softw. Technol. **53**(6), 638–651 (2011)
16. Webster, J., Watson, R.T.: Analyzing the past to prepare for the future: writing a literature review. Manage. Inf. Syst. Q. **26**(2), 3 (2002)
17. Chalfant, B.A., Comfort, L.K.: Dynamic decision support for managing regional resources: mapping risk in Allegheny county, Pennsylvania, Saf. Sci. (2015, in press)
18. Aedo, I., Díaz, P., Carroll, J.M., Convertino, G., Rosson, M.B.: End-user oriented strategies to facilitate multi-organizational adoption of emergency management information systems. Inf. Process. Manage. **46**(1), 11–21 (2010)

19. Dabner, N.: 'Breaking Ground' in the use of social media: a case study of a university earthquake response to inform educational design with Facebook. Internet High. Educ. **15** (1), 69–78 (2012)
20. Lu, P., Stead, D.: Understanding the notion of resilience in spatial planning: a case study of Rotterdam, The Netherlands. Cities **35**, 200–212 (2013)
21. Evers, M., Jonoski, A., Almoradie, A., Lange, L.: Collaborative decision making in sustainable flood risk management: a socio-technical approach and tools for participatory governance. Environ. Sci. Policy **55**, 334–344 (2015)
22. Oxley, M.: A "people-centred principles-based" post-hyogo framework to strengthen the resilience of nations and communities. Int. J. Disaster Risk Reduct. **4**, 1–9 (2013)
23. Albright, E.A., Crow, D.A.: Learning processes, public and stakeholder engagement: analyzing responses to Colorado's extreme flood events of 2013. Urban Clim. **14**, 79–93 (2015)
24. Rijke, J., Brown, R., Zevenbergen, C., Ashley, R., Farrelly, M., Morison, P., van Herk, S.: Fit-for-purpose governance: a framework to make adaptive governance operational. Environ. Sci. Policy **22**, 73–84 (2012)
25. Kernaghan, S., da Silva, J.: Initiating and sustaining action: experiences building resilience to climate change in Asian cities. Urban Clim. **7**, 47–63 (2014)
26. Kenney, C.M., Phibbs, S.: A Māori love story: community-led disaster management in response to the Ōtautahi (Christchurch) earthquakes as a framework for action. Int. J. Disaster Risk Reduct. **14**, 46–55 (2015)
27. Ainuddin, S., Routray, J.K.: Community resilience framework for an earthquake prone area in Baluchistan. Int. J. Disaster Risk Reduct. **2**, 25–36 (2012)
28. Lei, Y., Liu, C., Zhang, L., Wan, J., Li, D., Yue, Q., Guo, Y.: Adaptive governance to typhoon disasters for coastal sustainability: a case study in Guangdong. China Environ. Sci. Policy **54**, 281–286 (2015)

Towards Integral Security Concepts for Government Buildings Through Virtual Facility Reconstruction

Georgios Leventakis, George Kokkinis[✉], and Athanasios Sfetsos

KEMEA, Center for Security Studies, Athens, Greece
gleventakis@kemea.gr, {g.kokkinis,t.sfetsos}@kemea-research.gr

Abstract. This paper presents VASCO, a Virtual Studio for Security Concepts and Operations. It is based on an innovative multifunctional ICT platform that enhances security design and strengthens security measures for government buildings. VASCO enables security professionals to virtually reconstruct government buildings, their surrounding environment and overlay their existing security means. The security community can validate actual solutions and search for the best practices by simulating diverse types of threats in high-resolution, realistic though virtual environments. Responding to an emergency, which involves a multitude of affected stakeholders and actors necessitates the involvement of a number of state owned agents and organizations. The need for making decisions using a common operational view, sharing information, exchanging data and planning coordinated actions is prerequisite. VASCO is a solution aiming to provide an important leap from present-day security planning methodologies and tools, to more sophisticated and efficient security solutions.

Keywords: 3D representation · Security management plan assessment · Building security · Collaborative environment · Multi touch screen interaction · Threat response planning · Risk assessment

1 Introduction

Over recent years the demand for public and private building security continues to grow [1]. To fulfil this demand, there is a rapidly expanding supply of security technology products [2]. As a result, security related solutions are considered by a growing number of property owners and tenants, facility managers, construction professionals and government agencies. The growing demand for more secure facilities, in conjunction with recent advancements in Information and Communication Technology (ICT), necessitates the continuous evolution of existing security management plans (SMP) for civic facilities [3].

The security needs of a building must be determined as early as possible, as part of the facility planning and designing phases. Terrorism, crime, biohazards, workplace violence and many more threats expose, not only property but, human lives to risks [4]. As crime concerns increase each year, security professionals from both the public and private sectors are being called upon to address these concerns by incorporating security into the design and construction of all building types.

© Springer International Publishing AG 2016
P. Diaz et al. (Eds.): ISCRAM-med 2016, LNBIP 265, pp. 143–156, 2016.
DOI: 10.1007/978-3-319-47093-1_13

A comprehensive SMP focus on the protection of three main security pillars [5]. Focusing on the protection of each pillar separately will enhance the protection of the building, however greater efficiency is achieved when all pillars are planned and assessed together. Security professionals should be familiar with applicable codes and industry standards, understand the nature of threat assessments, risk and vulnerability analysis, methods of reducing liability exposure, and other preventative strategies. This is in line with 2007/124/EC, Article 4 "Specific Objectives" 3a and 3b.[1]

In this paper, we argue that virtual reality can overcome the obstacles which come with all these requirements, can enable collaborative planning and threat assessment, and thus expand the network of security experts. The proposed innovative ICT platform aims to enable security professionals and facility administrators to jointly formulate, test, and adjust security concepts and measures in a virtual environment [6]. Our solution provides a cost-effective and risk-free environment for a holistic view of a public building, broken down into three phases: (a) risk assessment and analysis phase, (b) emergency response planning phase and (c) test and effectiveness assessment of phases (a) and (b) for a variety of threats.

The rest of the paper is organized as follows. The next section focuses on highlighting related work in the building security theme. Section 3 lists the user requirements, the 3D visualisation enhancements and the solution requirements that drove the development of our solution. The solution, called VASCO (Virtual Studio for Security Concepts and Operations), has been designed as an ICT collaborative platform aimed to support the validation, testing and optimisation of existing SMPs. Section 4 describes the innovations and advantages that VASCO offers the security community. Finally, a discussion about the solution and recommendations for future work are touched upon in the last section.

2   Related Work

There are certain technology trends which will be introduced to explain the model of assessing security plans using interactive displays, GIS data and 3D representations of an urban environment. The necessity to ensure the integrity of building assets against loss, damage or other disruptions gives rise to the need for using advanced technology solutions for assessing security risks (including the risks associated with terrorism) and their impacts on service delivery [7].

The idea of using a GIS layer for studying and analysing a security plan has matured over time. Since 2002, GIS provide a range of geospatial tools and analysis methods. Work by Rauschert et al. [8] aimed for collaborative emergency management processes utilizing a GIS layer. However, the restricted range of users and lack of efficiency in task-solving was a decisive limiting factor.

Other advancements were introduced through the work carried out by Bader et al. [9], who introduced the concept of smart furniture in command and control centers. Again, technology limitations in 2008 were a limiting factor for the hand gesture

---

[1]   http://eur-lex.europa.eu/legal-content/BG/TXT/?uri=celex:32007D0124.

recognition system, while the interaction of users was limited. Nevertheless, the convergence of both GIS data and large interactive displays eventually took place. The latter came to be with uEmergency [10]. The user interface as a component in emergency planning was presented in 2012. A horizontal, large scale interactive display was implemented to assist end users from the security field to rapidly raise operational awareness using a simulation game and Google Maps as its GIS.

Following from the above, the concept of using a GIS background, large size interactive displays and simulations for emergency and security planning only came together very recently. TIPExtop constitutes a holistic integration of the aforementioned technological innovations [11]. The concepts of "Role-based collaboration", "Around-the-table interaction", "Geo-spatial representation", "Annotated design" and "Design history" were used to promote user interaction and foster exploration of alternative security practices.

Another component that was introduced into the security assessment toolbox was the use of 3D maps. The CRIMSON platform [12] was based on the then revolutionary idea that crisis managers could use a 3D map to visualize their threat environment. As mentioned, the technological "maturity" a decade ago did not allow for many ways of organising information, other than geographically related data. However, the work performed did provide the rudimentary means to build and run scenarios, allowing for media reports to be inserted into unfolding crisis scenarios.

An advancement of the above solution was the development and delivery of the INDIGO project [13], an innovative IT-system that integrates 3D-mapping, simulation tools and a highly effective method of information display made available to security professionals. The solution was developed to display a strategic representation of a crisis situation that is as complete and as easy as possible to understand. To succeed, this graphically displayed operational information was projected on a 3D map. VASCO will help complete the product line for security and crisis management developed by DIGI-NEXT and its partners in the frame of the CRIMSON[2] and INDIGO[3] EC projects.

3 Solution Framework

As the potential of CRIMSON and INDIGO platforms became evident, managers at the strategic level for government facility protection were involved. The challenge for a next generation security assessment solution will be to provide added value to the public safety and security agencies by enabling them to share security concepts and measures and promote their local or remote interaction. It is envisaged that the development of such a system will further promote the information sharing between security community members [14].

By introducing a method to quickly build a 3D reconstruction of a facility and its proximate environment, strategic and operational managers can work together to

---

[2] CRIMSON: The Crisis Simulation System, G.A. SEC4-PR-110500, PASR 2004.
[3] INDIGO: Innovative training and decision support for emergency operations, G.A. 242341, FP7-SEC.

understand and assess complex situations. The resulting 3D rendering of any building will illustrate the threats that manifest as a unique security incident. Additionally, it will allow security professionals to mobilize forces outside and inside a facility and interact with the facility's SMP. This 3D representation can be considered as the most accurate and intuitive tool for responding agents as it produces output that is readily used and eliminates the need for mental calculations, path-finding, etc. All locations, assets, actors, simultaneously occurring events and conditions can be represented and visually fed to security experts and expedite their introduction to the security challenges they will face.

3.1   User Requirements for 3D Reconstruction Use in Security

VASCO envisions to be of great assistance to security experts who have been tasked with protecting government and public buildings. VASCO's potential end users are (a) security teams responsible for the protection of government assets, (b) interdisciplinary first response teams (e.g. police, fire brigade, ambulance services, etc.) who most likely interact with the buildings and their occupants upon request and (c) security planners responsible for optimizing the security plans of government facilities. Additionally, the project inspires to promote and enhance the interaction and collaboration between all security stakeholders of a facility.

To facilitate and promote the interaction between security professionals and an innovative ICT platform, a fast learning curve should be offered to end users. The faster the end users learn to operate and exploit the advantages of a security suite, the sooner they will include the solution into their daily workflow of security tasks. The platform should enable both collocated and remote users with different security needs and interests to collaborate and cooperate, either around a multi-touch screen or interact remotely using an additional ICT platform and a secure network connection.

Initially the users should be introduced to security goals and objectives specific to the building and the threats they will be challenged to address. A scenario storyboard should provide a short narration of the mission: what to protect, against what, who shall be involved and in what way, which impacts to mitigate and how, what factors to consider and what data is available from the SMP. The aim of the storyboard is to offer security experts a concise but explanatory visualisation of their mission.

During the security assessment of a government building, any changes or annotations shall be stored and maintained for future reference. The inclusion of such a feature will allow the platform to be used also for after action debriefings, comparison of security methods and assessment, and as reference material for training sessions. The inclusion of a scenario database serves a dual purpose; first, as a knowledge transfer mechanism where the enhancements in existing security plans are documented and disseminated within the security community; second, as a benchmarking tool where different simulations for a number of security approaches will be compared against a selection of security parameters.

Documentation and plans related to the government building, memorandum of actions (MoA), and standard operating procedures (SOPs), should all be accessible from the platform. Stakeholders from both public and private sectors should be involved and collaborate on themes of pro-activeness and prevention, preparation, and response. Apart from cooperation between diverse national entities, users have indicated their preference to include attacker-defender functionality aiming to involve different security divisions either on national or international level. The initial VASCO user group members were 13 EU organisations (Ministries, universities, first responders, public authorities, and private organisations) from 4 EU countries.

3.2   3D Reconstruction Visualisation vs. Representation

A digital mock up (DMU) facility is the cornerstone of the SMP. It is an accurate 3D representation of the facility (building and perimeter) to be studied. The virtualised environment should include proximate urban elements (e.g. roads, other buildings in the area, transportation routes). Over the past decades, the 3D representation of buildings was a complex and time consuming process as is shown in Fig. 1, and the final output was a realistic, yet rigid representation of the building, without including the nearby urban environment.

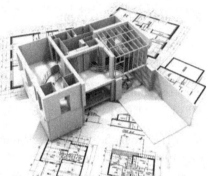

Fig. 1. Manual 3D building representation

To advance the 3D representation, different approaches were used for the outdoor and indoor areas. The VirtualGeo[4] technology, a 2D/3D Geographic Information System (GIS), is implemented to provide the visualization of the external view and the surroundings of the buildings. Additionally, the reconstructed environment should also provide the indoor view of a facility.

The benefits of the computerised 3D building reconstruction over that of the legacy reconstruction are shown in Fig. 2. The DMU includes a realistic representation of the 3D environment and it is optimised for modifications, changes, visualisation from different viewing angles, with varying environmental conditions. The works of [15–17] were used for constructing and representing the facility's interiors. Above all, users can insert security elements (any item that is part of their security toolbox) like cameras, entrance barriers, fences, alarm sensors in the DMU

---

[4] http://virtual-geo.com/en/.

and simulate the impact of their addition in the building's security. Moreover, the users using a multi-touch screen will be offered the option of focusing on certain areas of the virtual environment using different viewing angles, visualise the line of sight, and toggle between 2D and 3D representations.

Fig. 2. Legacy building representation and 3D representation with the surrounding environment

3.3 Solution Requirements

A solution for assessing the SMP for government buildings should facilitate the creation, simulation, and analysis of scenarios to explore effectiveness of tactics, technologies, and procedures in a range of environments, including the effectiveness of physical, cyber, and human behavior. The scenarios are a sequence of events used to validate the security mechanisms in place [18]. An example is a bomb threat followed by a fire within the perimeter of the facility. This scenario will trigger (i) the building evacuation plan, while (ii) a fire in the designated assembly point will disrupt the pre-determined evacuation route. Scenarios can be rehearsed with variations like changes in tactics, weather and daylight conditions, addition of threats, or changes on the locations and capabilities of security means.

The evaluation of scenarios via table top simulations, will support the development of policies and optimize the operational SMP for the facility. Furthermore, simulations can be used to document and justify relevant security decisions. Lessons learned from scenario rehearsals will provide value added knowledge to security planers for government buildings. Only the final plan needs real-life testing to verify the expected outcomes and validate the simulation results.

An ICT solution offers cost savings in the following manner: using DMUs, security experts can contribute to building security without visiting the site (or) with minimum site visits. Moreover, a virtual environment will promote the collaboration of experts from different agencies to contribute and validate the plans. Lastly, interactive scenarios with teams or individuals operating in "defender-attacker mode" will (i) test the SMP against a wider range of threats and (ii) provide competitive and valuable experience to security professionals.

4   The VASCO

A literature review on state of the art[5] crisis management systems and interviews of end users highlighted a need for sharing information, but also emphasized the need to have a system tailored for operational efficiency among every public facility stakeholder. Focus group interviews revealed that additional information should be shared among several organizations involved in a crisis, and above all parties should have access to the same and amended information sources and review identical security plans.

The VASCO project designed a tool to support the creation of a common operational picture that fits both training and operational purposes, as encouraged by [19]. The goal of the VASCO system is to support information exchange among members of the security community and promote the concept of the common operational picture.

4.1   Virtual Environment for Security Analysis

VASCO's relevance and interaction with an existing SMP for buildings is depicted in Fig. 3. This closed loop process, aside from a holistic optimization on security, will also allow security experts to study the impact from a potential failure of certain security elements or functions related to physical, human, and cyber-attacks or any combination of them for any security planning phase.

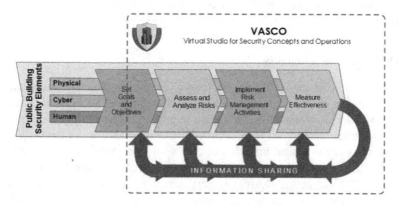

Fig. 3. VASCO application field in public buildings security

Starting from the defined security goals and objectives that should be listed in every government building SMP, security experts using the virtualization environment can:

1. Analyze and asses a range of risks
2. Implement different approaches for managing and controlling exposure to risks
3. Simulate the effectiveness of their actions using a variety of security measures.

---

[5] Internal deliverable of VASCO project (SEC-2013.2.1-1 - Evidence based and integral security concepts for government asset protection – Capability Project. G.A. 607737).

At any time during the facility's security assessment, the participants can assess the impact of their proposals and compare the effectiveness of their security plans throughout all the phases shown in Fig. 3. The resulting facility SMP will enhance the initial security goals and objectives.

Security professionals using the VASCO studio can accelerate and facilitate the threat assessment and placement of security equipment and surveillance means that will assist the preparedness plans and mitigation strategies for the building in question. Using 3D representation of a building, security reviewers can first visualise and then decide on the following:

- The selection of surveillance camera types (image sensor specifications and lens characteristics) that could provide broader supervision
- Place the surveillance cameras at optimal points around the building and its perimeter
- Identify surveillance vulnerabilities in the perimeter and indoor locations (where necessary) by using the line of sight functionality
- Map and then eliminate any blind surveillance zones around and within the building and its perimeter
- Plan alternative detection means like unattended sensor networks, passive infrared detectors (PIR) for the areas identified above, or enhance possible vulnerable areas by adding an additional security layer
- Proper placement of the security personnel and reaction forces within the facility
- Assessment of evacuation routes for combination of threats and various types of incidents.

4.2   3D Visualization Benefits

The reconstruction of any building, including its surrounding environment, using advanced computer graphics, can first of all provide a short but accurate introduction to security professionals of what they are meant to protect and what they should consider using actual parameters in a full scale approach. Interdependencies of the facility under study with parts of the critical infrastructure or with other buildings is visually represented. The passive use of the physical environment to reduce crime (or Crime Prevention Through Environmental Design) is very accurately represented if reconstructed using real world data. Furthermore, the concepts of natural surveillance, natural access control and territoriality are integrated and displayed using 3D representations.

Using the rendering capabilities of VASCO, security professionals can validate the performance of CCTV cameras placed anywhere in the virtually reconstructed environment, and view the surveillance security screenshots (Fig. 4). Moreover, security experts can move inside the digital mock up (DMU) of the building and focus on areas that will eventually be affected by a potential threat and extrapolate how this will affect the existing SMP. Security experts can relocate the threat to consider how changing the threats location will affect the required response actions. By providing the ability to virtually move around the facility safeguards that security personnel can assess their exposure to threats, and to identify the conditions and factors that might affect or jeopardise the security measures already in place (Fig. 5).

Fig. 4. Left: The visibility coverage of multiple security cameras enables end-users to acknowledge the hidden zones. Right: The virtual "operational control center" offers the possibility to see through all the virtual cameras

Fig. 5. Outdoor visibility representation

Aside from the description above, in which VASCO is used as a security planning tool, it can greatly benefit tactical security teams as a training or as an on-scene briefing tool. An accurate floorplan can be shared with responders via their smartphones while they are approaching a response scene. This enables them to know exactly how the building is laid out, where the personnel is usually located, while it ensures that all involved teams share identical information and have a common understanding of the threat. The blueprints of the facility can be annotated with the latest intelligence. Entry points can be marked, and the locations of existing forces can be shown, if desired. The assailants' location can be identified and marked as well.

As a training solution, virtualisation may promote knowledge transfer of successful security practices, disseminate lessons learned within the security community or highlight security compliance to international, national or industry operational security frameworks. The need for site visits is minimised and virtualisation ensures that all security stakeholders will have an accurate and updated understanding of the facility by virtually exploring the reconstructed environment.

4.3 Demonstrated Security Advancement

Four candidate user workshops were conducted in Greece, Netherlands and Sweden with agencies assigned to government building protection and crisis management tasks during the solution development phase, as part of VASCO's concept validation. Security experts were introduced to solution capabilities and then they were challenged to design a building's SMP and validate it afterwards. The security professionals valued having the option to create a digital replica of a building with the immediate urban environment which surrounds it.

The use of a building's virtual replica and of its proximate environment offers a safe setting in which security issues can be thoroughly assessed. Introducing numerous types of threats of varying impact in the virtual environment allows users to better grasp the potential consequences. Workshop participants confirmed that VASCO allows users to test actual approaches and pursue best practices by simulating diverse types of threats in a high-resolution, realistic environment. As such, it may provide an important leap from present-day security planning methodologies and tools, to new integral security concepts. Flexibility in choosing diverse viewpoints was well-received. Users welcomed the possibility of hiding or viewing any combination of building features to obtain unobstructed views of the areas of interest (Fig. 6).

Fig. 6. Left: Third floor exclusive view of property elements (furniture) Right: Second and Third floor combined view of stairs, inner walls, doors and windows

One feature unanimously seen as innovative, of high value and unique was the ability to identify the field of view and the areas covered from any vantage point, which the users recognized a useful tool for placing security personnel and relevant equipment (Fig. 5). Seeing from the perspective of, for example, a sniper, a security camera, a police car or a helicopter selectively placed in the environment was a very welcome capability, which is almost impossible to attain outside of a virtual environment.

4.4   Perspective of the VASCO Solution

Security practitioners and designers showed interest in using VASCO for a variety of purposes and at different levels of security planning. End users agreed that the added value resides in promoting interdisciplinary collaboration and allows professionals to visualize the environment they are asked to secure, enabling a more efficient and meaningful design and assessment of security measures. Furthermore, they have recommended two new functionalities that can elevate the performance of the developed solution.

First, a knowledge management repository and an associated functionality to promote training that will foster knowledge transfer within the VASCO security community. Best security practises for a range of government facilities can be narrated and stored as training material. Initially users can query the database using a subset of the fields shown in Fig. 7 while - as the number of scenarios in the database grow - the query shall support more complex searches. The use of VASCO is in full compliance with the EU legislative and regulatory framework for data protection based on the uniform approach of the EC Directive 95/46/EC[6], the recent 2016/679[7] and the national legislative and regulatory framework for data protection of each project member country.

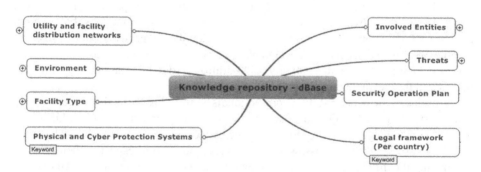

Fig. 7. VASCO knowledge repository concept

Second, by adding the functionality, which allows the injection of news and introduction of challenges, under certain criteria, the use of VASCO is elevated. Experienced security professionals can author a scenario using a timeline. They can plan a complex security situation in a detailed manner, involving members of security communities from different organisations and with different objectives (Fig. 8). Starting from a request to respond to a trivial security incident, a complicated situation will evolve in a controlled environment, where the efficiency of measures and security plans will be assessed. Thus beyond the facility's SMP assessment, a cross-functional collaboration exercise might highlight not only security weaknesses, but also possible interworking issues across different agencies, which require improvement.

---

[6] http://eur-lex.europa.eu/legal-content/EN/TXT/?uri=CELEX:31995L0046.
[7] http://eur-lex.europa.eu/legal-content/EN/TXT/?uri=OJ:JOL_2016_119_R_0001.

Fig. 8. Security scenario editor

A step further in VASCO's development could incorporate an analytics engine, allowing the system to search for weaknesses in the security design in an automated manner.

5   Conclusions

This paper has presented a cutting edge collaboration platform, which enables security professionals from both the public and private sector, and from different agencies and departments to jointly plan, design, formulate, test, adjust and optimise the SMP of public buildings and facilities in a virtual setting. Existing and planned[8] government buildings which are/will be used to host essential services and functions that are vital for our societal, economic, security and health functions are growing both in size and complexity. Since this expansion occurs within a security situation of growing security threats, supporting the interdisciplinary collaboration across different security communities is a highly recommended approach.

Multidiscipline security-related professionals with focus on facility security were enthusiastic about VASCO's novel solution capabilities, agreeing that digital mock up units offer advantages compared to current security design practices. It should be noted that the interviewed teams possess a diverse background with respect to their security culture and the different operational and legal frameworks they operate in. All of them recognized the versatility of the system, and shared thoughts on how they could use it in various ways, including: designing of security plans, risk assessment, mission planning, (on-site) briefings for tactical teams and after-action reports.

Throughout the state of preparation for a threat of variable impact, severity and urgency, VASCO would bring immense added value to the security forces, as it gives them the opportunity to examine and extensively test different security approaches for the same situation by varying specific influencing factors. In addition, VASCO would enable end users to store relevant information, reconstructing past cases and developing new test cases, establishing thus a large Knowledge Base for public building security design which may support comparative future studies. The envisaged platform allows the maximisation of the security protection level of any given public building, by running

---

[8] For the planned buildings, a detailed and finalized set of architectural drawings are required for the VASCO security editor to produce a virtual representation of indoor and outdoor environments.

a number of threat and risk scenarios while at the same time allowing security experts to gain knowledge and experience, optimizing the relative security management plan of the facility. The VASCO solution will be demonstrated in Athens during February 2017. Security professionals from both public and private domains and EU security officers will participate in two days' workshop assessing the end product.

Acknowledgements. VASCO project has received funding from the European Union's Seventh Framework Programme for research, technological development and demonstration under grant agreement no. 607737.

References

1. Freedonia (2016). http://www.freedoniagroup.com/, http://www.freedoniagroup.com/industry-study/2917/security-products.htm. Accessed 9 May 2016
2. Research and Markets (n.d). http://www.researchandmarkets.com, http://www.prnewswire.com/news-releases/global-electronic-security-systems-ess-market-2015-2020—surging-demand-for-cctv-and-video-surveillance-systems-300161080.html. Accessed 4 May 2016
3. Neuman, W.R.: The Demand for Security. IBM Global Business Services, Customs, Borders, and Revenue Management, Michigan (2008)
4. Federal Emergency Management Agency (FEMA): Site and urban design for security: guidance against potential terrorist attacks. CreateSpace Independent Publishing Platform (2007)
5. Interagency Security Committee: The Risk Management Process for Federal Facilities: An Interagency Security Committee Standard, 1st edn. Washington, D.C., Department of Homeland Security (2013)
6. Ahmad, A., et al.: Assessing the security of buildings: a virtual studio solution. In: 13th Annual Conference for Information Systems for Crisis Response and Management (ISCRAM), Rio de Janeiro, Brazil (2016)
7. Department of Housing and Public Works: Security management of government buildings (2012). http://www.hpw.qld.gov.au/SiteCollectionDocuments/SAMFSmgb.pdf. Accessed 27 Apr 2016
8. Rauschert, I., et al.: Designing a human-centered, multimodal GIS interface to support emergency management. In: Proceedings of the 10th ACM International Symposium on Advances in Geographic Information Systems (2002)
9. Bader, T., Meissner, A., Tscherney, R.: Digital map table with Fovea-Tablett®: smart furniture for emergency operation centers. In: Proceedings of the 5th International Conference on Information Systems for Crisis Response and Management (2008)
10. Qin, Y., et. al.: uEmergency: a collaborative system for emergency management on very large tabletop. In: Proceedings of the 2012 ACM International Conference on Interactive Tabletops and Surfaces, pp. 399–402 (2012)
11. Tena, S., et al.: TIPExtop: an exploratory design tool for emergency planning. In: Proceedings of the 11th International ISCRAM Conference, University Park, Pennsylvania, USA (2014)
12. Balet, O., et al.: The crimson project - simulating populations in massive urban environments. In: 8th World Congress on Computational Mechancs (WCCM 2008), Venice, Italy (2008)
13. Himmelstein, J., et al.: Interactive simulation technology for crisis management and training: the indigo project. In: 9th International Conference for Crisis Response and Management (ISCRAM), Vancouver, BC, Canada (2012)

14. Boin, A., et al.: Building an IT platform for strategic crisis management preparation. In: 2014 IEEE 10th International Conference on Wireless and Mobile Computing, Networking and Communications (WiMob), 8 October 2014, pp. 2–27 (2014)
15. Pintore, G., Agus, M., Gobbetti, E.: Interactive mapping of indoor building structures through mobile devices. In: Proceedings of the 3DV Workshop on 3D Computer Vision in the Built Environment, Tokyo, Japan (2014)
16. Pintore, G., et al.: Omnidirectional image capture on mobile devices for fast automatic generation of 2.5D indoor maps. In: Proceedings of the IEEE Winter Conference on Applications of Computer Vision (WACV), Lake Placid, USA (2016)
17. Pintore, G., Gobbetti, E.: Effective mobile mapping of multi-room indoor structures. Vis. Comput. **30**, 707–716 (2014)
18. Borglund, E., Öberg, L.-M.: Creation of an exercise scenario: a collaborative design effort. In: 11th International ISCRAM Conference, Pennsylvania, USA (2014)
19. Turoff, M., Chumer, M., Van de Walle, B., Yao, X.: The design of a dynamic emergency response management information system (DERMIS). J. Inf. Technol. Theor. Appl. (JITTA) **5**, 1–35 (2004)

Work Practice in Situation Rooms – An Ethnographic Study of Emergency Response Work in Governmental Organizations

Jonas Landgren[1](✉) and Fredrik Bergstrand[2](✉)

[1] Chalmers University of Technology, Gothenburg, Sweden
jonas.landgren@chalmers.se
[2] University of Gothenburg, Gothenburg, Sweden
fredrik.bergstrand@ait.gu.se

Abstract. This paper presents ethnographic accounts from multiple studies on situation room work in governmental organizations. The purpose of this paper is to make visible aspects of the work practice and provide triggers for future discussions regarding how such work practices could be supported with improved information technology. The findings show the collaborative nature of situation room work and how a variety of information technologies are embedded and intertwined in the practice. Assembling, monitoring, exploring, converging, and consolidating are key activities in a general work pattern in situation rooms.

Keywords: Situation rooms · Coordination · Collaboration · Work-practice · Ethnography · Crisis response

1 Introduction

Command centers [1], emergency operations centers [2–5], and national situation rooms [6] are all environments that have a strong focus on managing up-to-date information access, providing synthesized analysis, managing a "big picture" perspective, and the delivery of situation reports to decision makers. With an increased interest from government authorities in establishing these different types of specialized emergency and disaster response settings, there is also a need for an improved understanding of the work and practice conducted in these sociotechnical environments. Previous research regarding these environment is however extremely sparse, with researchers calling for more detailed studies of the actual work conducted within these environments [4, 7]. This paper is an attempt to make visible situation room work as an evolved practice from emergency operations work, having its own specific qualities. The situation room is a physical space where trained personnel with different expertise are assigned specific roles in order to temporary increase organizational analytic capacity and capability. The work is episodic and temporary [8] – as the

© Springer International Publishing AG 2016
P. Diaz et al. (Eds.): ISCRAM-med 2016, LNBIP 265, pp. 157–171, 2016.
DOI: 10.1007/978-3-319-47093-1_14

environment is assembled and staffed only when emergency events emerge, internally expanding established organizations abilities [7, 9]. At the same time, the work is continuously shaped and re-shaped in-order to adapt to the natural equivocality of emergency events [10].

In this paper, the focus is oriented towards a detailed description of a work practice where technologies and social arrangements are intertwined. The question this paper aims to answer is *what characterizes the work practice in situation room environments during emergency events?* The contributions of this paper consist of ethnographic accounts depicting this work practice, and a conceptualization of the work practice in terms of a five interconnected fundamental activities.

2   Coordination Environments

Control centers [11, 12], command centers [1], and emergency operations centers [2–5] are all designed to coordinate activities of actors working toward common goals. Situation rooms [6] have evolved from emergency operation practices, and have become an integrated part of these existing environments. The first modern control center, as we know and recognize them today, was NASA's Mercury Control Center (MCC). The MCC was designed in the mid 50ths to assist monitoring, planning, and to extend analytic capabilities of the astronaut's during NASA's first generation of manned space flights [13]. The design of the MCC offered operators, engineers and scientists a shared environment that allowed focused work as well as shared information areas, overview and awareness of ongoing activities. Control centers have since the late '80s received more attention in HCI and CSCW research. The seminal studies of control center operators in the London Underground conducted by Heath and Luff [11] was followed by additional studies of settings where operators have a critical role in monitoring complex events and performing coordinated actions to ensure the integrity of a specific socio-technical system. Suchman [12] later described these environments as centers of coordination, "characterizable in terms of participants' ongoing orientation to problems of space and time, involving the deployment of people and equipment across distances, according to a canonical timetable or the emergent requirements of rapid response to a time-critical situation."

Emergency operation centers (EOC) are presented in literature as large-scale locations for tightly integrated and co-located work, consisting of one physical environment for multiple agencies to jointly coordinate action during grand scale events [2–5]. EOCs either emerge from the in-situ need of multi-organizational coordination, or by the application of pre-existing response plans [2]. The main functions are to (1) coordinate response efforts between response organizations, (2) joint policy making, (3) oversee the management of response operations, (4) information gathering, (5) manage public relations, and (6) to host a range of different agencies, in times of critical emergencies and disasters, in order to enable time-critical coordination across sectorial and jurisdictional boundaries [14]. The EOC could be described as an arena where several authorities from different sectors work co-located in order to improve information sharing and coordination by the means of working in close proximity to each other. These facilities are technically sophisticated environments where personnel with extensive as well as limited experience [3] of crisis response work could collaborate in the response to ongoing disruptive events.

In contrast, command centers, as all as communication and coordination centers, are organization-specific environments that ensure rapid responses and efficient use of an organization's resources in order to immediately intervene to critical events [1, 11, 12]. Fire and rescue services, police authorities, paramedics and critical infrastructure operators are organizations with an extensive tradition of command center work [15]. The work in command centers relies heavily on pre-defined representations of the problem-domain as well as pre-defined response plans that cover a majority of possible situations [11]. Command centers are technically sophisticated environments designed to support the efficient and coordinated use of the organizations resources in relation to a number of ongoing incidents [11, 12]. Command centers also have dedicated operators to manage day-to-day operations, and in the event of a large-scale situation a command center has capacity to host visiting personnel from other agencies. Inappropriate and over-simplified models of military command and control are often used to explain or model command center and emergency response work [16], while models of continuity, coordination, collaboration, and support are often considered more appropriate [17].

Few studies are however oriented towards situations where professionals are engaged in activities that balance between ad-hoc situations and infrequent professional actions, and several researchers makes an emphasis on the lack of studies of real work, even of that in EOCs [4, 7, 14].

In contrast to the very ambitious and intriguing technology-driven studies [18–21] and analyses of EOC-work [2, 4, 5, 7, 14], this paper is an attempt to approach these environments with a focus on what people actually do as part of work [22] in the situation room. This shift of perspective allows us to look beyond specific technologies present in this environment and instead focus on the actual work that these technologies should aim to support. The findings presented here aim to add to the body of knowledge on work in command centers and emergency operation centers by outlining a situation rooms work practice that is not shaped according to strict protocols nor are the result of an immediate need for improvisation.

3 Research Approach

The study could be seen as an attempt to uncover a work practice visible in real work [22], and described in terms of its characteristics. The results presented in this paper are part of series of studies on crisis and emergency response work in governmental organizations during ongoing emergencies. Ethnographic fieldwork [23, 24], and particularly intense short-term ethnographic studies [25] conducted during emergency events, has been applied as the primary approach to gain deep insights about the investigated work settings. Approximately 200 h of participant observations has been conducted. The field studies have covered two large-scale and complex fires, one event of pollution of drinking water affecting 60.000 citizens, four events of extreme weather, two high-risk sports events, and finally one case of social unrest in suburbs. The field work has been conducted at two fire and rescue services, a regional health authority, the police authority, a regional administrative board, and a local municipality.

Fieldwork has been accomplished by negotiating access [23] with local and regional authorities involved in ongoing crisis events. When a specific crisis event or a soon-to-be expected societal disturbance has come to the research groups attention, contact has been established with the chief-in-command or a manager-in-charge in the organization in focus. When a formal decision to accept a researcher was reached, a researcher has then quickly traveled to the location of the specific organization and followed along key personnel in their ongoing work, as a participant observer. This approach has resulted in a rich empirical material that covers both commonly occurring critical events as well as infrequent events.

Data has been collected during formal meetings, phone-conferences, and collaborative work in situation room environments. The material collected consists of field-notes in paper-notebooks or laptops. Audio and visual material in terms of photo, recorded audio and video has been collected using smart phones. The data collection has focused on capturing aspects of the collaborative work in the situation rooms, such as whiteboard drawings, as well as on capturing illustrative examples of technology use as part of the collaborative work. In several of the events, additional material has been collected such as meeting protocols, extracts from computerized logs and personal notes. In addition to the above material, informal interviews have been conducted in order to revisit areas of interest as well as taking part of lessons-to-be-learnt sessions from events not covered by the aforementioned observations.

Analysis in ethnographic research is often not a distinct phase, but rather an integral part of the overall research process [23]. Early indications, ideas, or hunches, often shape the continuous work and data collection. Readings of the empirical data may later lay grounds for better developed concepts and categories. Our field observations, ongoing analytical process, and readings of the gathered data suggested re-occurring patterns in the work observed in situation room settings. These concepts implied specific structure to the organizing of work. A more rigorous analysis of these patterns followed a two-step process where the collected material from each event has been structured along an event timeline. Field notes, photos and videos have been mapped to its corresponding specific temporal location, supplemented by meta-data describing its specific context of origin such as phone-conference, meeting, dyadic interaction, and situated discussions. The analysis has focused on structural patterns, and not on specific instances of work. The analysis resulted in an observer-identified [23] tentative pattern of the studied work practices. The second part of the analysis focused on exploring these patterns across events. Important to note is that the pattern is not a representation of the formal and detailed routines of any the specific organizations but rather an illustration of a recurring pattern that characterizes this type of work.

4 Findings

This section presents the recurring patterns of situation room work practice. *Assembling, monitoring, exploring, converging*, and *consolidating* are key activities in a general pattern found in all settings and events studied. Ethnographic accounts from one of the severe weather events is used to present and to contextualize the findings.

The ethnographic accounts have been written as chronologically ordered episodes in the style of a realist tale [24]. The names used in the episodes have been replaced by invented names. The scene of the event is a situation room environment at one of the largest fire and rescue services in Sweden. The situation room setting is a physical location where senior commanders and assistants at the fire and rescue services together with specifically invited external authorities (such as the police and/or municipality) work and organize meetings in order to monitor and analyze the situation and coordinate actions in order to respond to the situation at hand. The work in the situation room runs under the leadership of the chief-of-staff. The chief-of-staff is reporting to the fire-chief-in-command who is the executive decision maker in the organization during incidents and crisis events. Figure 1 illustrates the open-room structure with a large meeting table at the center of the room.

Fig. 1. Overview of the situation room with the conference table in the middle of the room and work-stations along the whiteboard covered walls.

In contrast to work conducted in the emergency dispatch center during everyday emergency response to minor accidents, such as house-fire and traffic accidents, managed by the operative dispatch operators, this situation room is only activated when the organization expects complex events or face significant workload. Work is normally divided over specific functions, often including Human Resources, Logistics, Incident Response, Information, and Collaboration to increase the organizational capacity. The following sub-sections present the patterns of work in further detail.

4.1   Assembling

The work in a situation room is started through a series of activities focused on the activation and mobilization of necessary competencies. The situation room is not staffed in-between major emergencies, but as the need is evolving and shifting in relation to the emerging situation. These activities are categorized as *assembling*, since their objective is to ensure the initiation of work in the situation room as well as continuously ensure that necessary competences and capacities are available. Assembling is emergent, and shaped by the nature of the situation, being either a sudden onset, or part of a planned-for increase of capacity over time. The following ethnographic account depicts the assembling of the situation room during the onset of a severe autumn storm:

It is Friday afternoon. The chief-of-staff receives a phone-call informing about a planned inter-agency teleconference at 15:00 due to a warning for severe weather. Since the weather could have severe negative consequences at this time of the year, the chief-of-staff immediately calls the fire-chief-in-command to inform about the meeting. The teleconference at 15:00 includes a range of regional and local actors and is focused on the weather forecast. The meteorological services (SMHI) inform that in a few days from now, severe weather will develop, but at this point not extreme. Based on this information, the fire-chief-in-command and the chief-of-staff decide not to activate the situation room but instead continue with normal operations until the conditions might change.

On Sunday at 18:00, a new teleconference is organized where the meteorological services upgrade the weather-warning to a category 2 storm with a possibility developing into a category 3. Wind speeds will reach storm-level and the sea-water level is expected to rise significantly, starting Monday afternoon with a peak during Monday evening. The fire-chief-in-command and chief-of-staff decide to initiate the work in the situation room to closely monitor the developments. They also contact the County Administrative Board to discuss the need for meetings with local authorities in the region. During the evening, the initial work in the situation room results in preparations to ensure that all necessary functions in the situation room have dedicated personnel in place from lunch-time on Monday.

The episode illustrates that the *assembling* of the situation room is not necessarily an instrumental action prescribed by protocol, but rather, a deliberate and ongoing activity shaped by mutually and gradually-clarified insights. As is shown in the excerpt, assembling is not limited to competences and resources within the organization itself but is also addressing external relationships that are perceived as important.

4.2   Monitoring

A fundamental function for situation room work is to ensure a high level of awareness about of events with potential of posing significant risks to the society, either by loss of life or property, or by challenging social values. Work is in the initial phase emergent, but is over time transformed into a more rigid form as the event progresses and goes from nascent to existing. We categorize these activities that are accomplished in order to collect information regarding the emerging event as *monitoring*. Monitoring of a situation is more than just passively watching what is going on over time. The work includes active collection of information using online resources, such as news websites and road traffic information, making direct calls to specific authorities, as well as making use of information provided by other government agencies. Monitoring covers the delicate activity to collect and synthesize descriptions of specific aspects of the situation. The following excerpt is illustrating a conversation that the two analysts John and Martha are having with the chief-of-staff:

John: "I just got a new update from the meteorological services, and they say that their latest prognosis shows that the storm will be a category 2, and not category 3, wind speeds might still be very strong in the gusts. Landfall will be at 21:00, so an hour later than what was said previously. They also have a new update on the trajectory which is now more to the south."

Chief-of-staff: "Okay, add that info to the log so we can see how it might develop until the 16:00 met-report".

Martha: "I talked to the National Road Authority...they are preparing to stop the traffic across the cable-bridge when the wind-speed increases."

Chief of staff: "okay, do we have any estimations of when that might be?"

Martha: "somewhere around 18:00 or 18:30."

John: "I am worried about the water level in the harbor, you see here [pointing at the computer screen showing a water-level graph], the level is rising rapidly towards 140, we might get a lot of flooded places at the harbor-front."

Chief of staff: "okay, let's keep an eye on the hundred and forty mark."

What is shown here is how information regarding the expected storm is actively collected from different actors using a variety of means. The collected information is synthesized in order to make the situation tangible for continuous monitoring of the situation. Scale, impact, time, levels, geographical locations and trajectories become key descriptive properties when transforming the information into a synthesized form. In addition, affected infrastructures and identified risk areas are also used as a meaningful material in order to frame and shape the description of the specific conditions of the emerging situation. The *monitoring* activities produce a material that manifests the information environment upon which other situation room activities are both dependent upon, as well as shaped by.

4.3   Exploring

In times of uncertainties, there is an apparent risk that organizations passively await more detailed information instead of making use of the information available at hand. Making use of the collected information in situation room work could be described in terms of exploration. The focus in exploration is to look beyond the immediate information at hand and engage in activities that shape available information material into insights regarding the developing situation. Exploration involves a careful crafting of the material obtained in the monitoring activity. Crafting means a transformation of descriptive information into potential impact and possible consequences. The following episode illustrates the exploration of consequences of the expected storm:

The situation room is occupied with personnel involved in a range of preparations for the expected storm. The work is divided along several groups, each
with specific responsibilities and focuses. Martha and John at the
analysis-group have the responsibility to outline major impact and consequences of the storm. They are exploring potential consequences if the three
major bridges in the area will be closed for traffic. They are concerned about how
a closedown will affect the organization's general capability for rapid
responses. Martha and John are making hand-written notes on the analog whiteboard surface. The brief and barely readable notes materialize important
aspects based on the details received from the road-traffic authorities about the
planned restrictions in traffic.

A few minutes later, Martha transfer details from the analog whiteboard to
the interactive whiteboard (Fig. 2). This results in the creation of simplified
representations, superimposed on the geographical map-material, illustrating
the restrictions in road traffic across the bridges. She is also creating rough
visual reference points of the location of nearby fire stations. John is standing
next to Martha and is nodding as a signal that the representations distinctly
illustrate the important consequences.

Fig. 2. The interactive whiteboard with hand-written notes concerning the affected bridges.

This episode shows how the analysis-section is orienting their work towards key
objects, e.g. bridges, main roads and fire stations, that if they will be affected by the
storm will have negative consequences for the organization. The annotations on the
map serve the purpose of drawing attention to identified constraints that will shape the
range of options when it is time to craft necessary mitigating actions. One should note
that the materialization on the interactive whiteboard is not a 'consequence report' but
rather a carefully crafted material that is used in an iterative *exploration of possible
consequences.*

4.4   Converging

The perhaps most typical activity in situation room work are the round-table meetings that are scheduled at recurring points in time. These meetings are either run as a collocated meeting, a telephone conference call, or as a mix of them. The purpose of these meetings is to ensure that people and organizations involved in the response work have opportunities to provide and receive updates about the evolving situation. These meetings are the only formal occasion during the work where participants have the opportunity to learn about each other's work and insights. These meetings also serve as explicit instances to align and consolidate ongoing tasks. Round-table meetings are fundamental in situation room work since it is an activity that brings together insights from the various involved groups. These meetings are not just an opportunity to share and align insights, but also a forum for outlining major decisions, which in turn must be formally documented. The following episode illustrates the consolidation that takes place during a collocated round-table meeting run by the chief-of-staff:

The situation room is starting to get crowded when personnel from different groups join around the large rectangular table for the 'Chief-of-Staff meeting', that is just about to start. The chief-of-staff enters the room, talking on the cellphone. He finishes the call, click-open the meeting agenda on the computer attached to a video projector. He initiates the meeting with a short welcome and continues by asking the Fire-chief-in-command to give a brief overview of the current situation and expectations for the evening. The presentation by the Fire-chief is very brief and focused on informing that the local municipalities in the region seem to be well prepared for the storm. He also informs that the storm is expected to have its peak between 20:00-21:00 h, while pointing at simplified timeline representation (Fig. 3) of the 'peak' on an adjacent whiteboard.

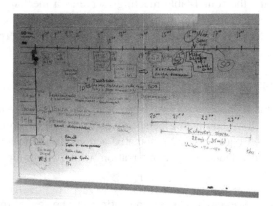

Fig. 3. Timelines with evolving activities and planned meetings sketched on a whiteboard. The lower right corner depicts the peak of the storm, including wind speeds and water levels.

This introduction is followed by a brief weather update indicating that the storm might take a more southern path than expected, which would result in less severe consequences in this area. The update is ended by a quick presentation of the current data from the sea-water-level diagram from the National Marine

Agency's website, indicating that the sea-level is high but not beyond the critical 140 mark.

The meeting then continues with a round-table style status report from each group. These verbal reports are condensed and followed by brief comments without lengthy discussions. Andrew and Steven from the logistics-group present the general principles in a minimum-resource plan developed in order to make sure that the general response preparedness is not affected too much. Martha at the analysis-group, informs that the cable-bridge will be closed at 18.30, and that they have assessed the needs in relation to the possibility and impact if the other two bridges also will be closed for traffic. Martha points at the interactive whiteboard and says: "as you can see, we will have few good options to reach H-island when they close the bridges". Her comment has made it clear that Andrews and Stevens minimum-resource plan has some weaknesses. The Chief-of-staff nods and the Fire-chief makes a brief comment that he would like to get a detailed update after this meeting, as input for a decision on reallocating rescue units.

At the end of the meeting, the Fire-chief underlines the importance for all groups to make notes on the whiteboard about the development in order to build a log that allow for a friction-free rotation of personnel when or if that will be needed. A new meeting is scheduled in three hours. The Fire-chief finishes by saying, "- we need to make a final decision about any reallocation of units before the bridges will be shut-down". During the entire meeting, Eve, the communications officer, has taken notes in a word-document that she saves in the event-log system as 'Protocol from chief-of-staff meeting 17:00'.

The episode illustrates how the round-table meeting is a key activity in situation room work where information is shared using brief reports in order to make visible an overview of insights rather than a detailed exploration of facts. Despite having verbal statements as the primary vehicle for conveying information, one should note that complex information material is made visible by making references to computer-generated diagrams, interactive maps as, well as figures crafted on whiteboards. As is shown in the episode, the round-table meetings serve as a mechanism to convey the general state of the situation to the many people involved in the work. This suggests that the underlying focus is to provide for planned points of convergence.

4.5   Consolidating

However, convergence is not always easy to achieve, since the different functions in the situation room might have conflicting perspectives caused by diverging interpretations about the potential consequences and associated actions. In the following episode, the fire-chief-in-command engage in a conversation with two groups of people with diverging perspectives:

The round-table meeting has ended and the Fire-chief is with Martha and John at the interactive whiteboard. Steven and Andrew at the logistics-group quickly joins the discussion and listen to Martha when she describes the consequences of having three of the bridges closed for traffic. Martha uses the geographical map projected on the interactive whiteboard as a reference in her argumentation. The tone of voice is neutral when she explains how she together with John has explored the likely impacts and the range of possible consequences.

The fire-chief turns to the logistics guys, asking them to describe their plan to meet the consequences (Fig. 4) presented by Martha. Steven points at the whiteboard on the right-hand side of the interactive whiteboard where they have outlined the minimum resource-plan. The minimum resource plan is represented as a detailed list of acronyms signifying fire-station areas followed by a set of acronyms describing the number of specific rescue units. An arrow indicates which area those units could be reallocated to.

Fig. 4. Fire-chief-in-command (center), facilitating the discussion between the analysis group and the logistics group to adjust the minimum resource plan

The discussion becomes suddenly intense when it becomes clear that there are differences in opinion about how specific rescue units should be reallocated. The fire-chief confronts the apparent differences in opinion between the parties and shifts the attention away from the specific details and asks the logistic-group to adjust their plan to meet a higher need of capacity by saying: "- I believe the minimum-plan is too lean, it would be great if you could slightly increase the capacity". The discussion ends and the logistic-group make a few changes and communicate the redesigned plan to the Chief-of-Staff. The updated minimum-resource plan is also added as an entry in the computerized event-log system.

The episode illustrates the sometimes-intense interplay between different perspectives among the groups in a situation room. Having divergent perspectives is not an uncommon phenomena of situation room work, since the work involves to continuously craft interpretations, plans and actions to what is perceived as being relevant in a situation that is evolving and where uncertainties provide constraints. The episode also illustrates how the fire-chief-in-command is actively participating in contributing to find a solution to the problem, without specifying what the exact solution might be. This suggests that striving for convergence of perspectives is a collaborative achievement dependent on both structures, such as round-table meetings, as well as having a capacity to facilitate ad-hoc consolidating activities.

5   Discussion

The empirical findings presented in this paper describe a work practice that we have labeled as situation room work. This work practice is found in a range of organizational environments, such as command centers, coordination centers and EOCs. These settings are specifically designed for responding to emergencies, crises and societal disruptions. Work in the situation room is designed in-situ, as a response to disruptive events that require additional analytic capabilities, continuous monitoring, analysis, and re-interpreting of fragmented and incomplete information in order to grasp the potential impact and consequences on societal functions. Situation room work practice differs from everyday work due to the inherently different properties of the disruptive phenomena which must be addressed in partly different ways of working. The findings indicate that situation room work seems to balance between design-oriented explorations of possible consequences and the protocol-based decision making found in EOCs.

Situation room work practice is episodic and temporary [8], and only becomes visible during serious situations. The practice as such might thus be difficult to both study and learn during every-day work or when the professionals in these settings are not confronted with the complexities of protecting a broad range of societal functions and values. Differentiating this practice from day-to-day operations is of importance since technology support for the everyday work practice and situation room work practice are fundamentally different.

Situation room work involves the time-critical collaborative activities of monitoring and transforming fragmented, conflicting, and equivocal information into a comprehensive materialization that covers key aspects of emerging or ongoing situations. Protocols, plans, and procedures may provide interaction mechanisms and the groundwork to get started, but the work will rather be shaped by the emerging situation. Control room work are designed according to pre-defined representations of the problem domain, for operators to act on pre-defined plans, and sudden contingencies requires improvisation [15]. As designers, we should acknowledge these differences and orient our designs away from pre-defined information consumption and direct it towards innovative means of co-production of information.

The contribution of this paper consists of the pattern of five interconnected activities manifesting the situation room work. These activities are general and have been observed during a series of ethnographic studies of response work during real emergencies. The activities are labeled *Assembling*, *Monitoring*, *Exploration* of possible consequences, planned points of *Convergence, and Consolidation of divergent interpretations*. A fundamental aspect of these activities is that they are accomplished with limited formal organizational support in terms of explicit process descriptions, methods or specifically designed technology. This does not mean that the participants engaged in situation room work are working without any underlying guiding principles, quite the opposite. Situation room work is characterized by a sensibility of the constraints presented by the situation at hand, which results in deliberate and careful crafting of actions. As illustrated in the findings, monitoring is oriented towards making important aspects of the situation tangible. Making the situation tangible opens up for insightful explorations of possible consequences. These interpretations are then negotiated towards a convergent view in carefully orchestrated roundtable meetings. These meetings both serve the function of giving a broad overview of the on-going situation as well as allowing detailed insights to be presented, allowing the participants in the meeting to co-create a comprehensive and converging view of the situation. Initial broad perspectives provide triggers to the participants allowing them to re-adjust or expand on new insights and perspectives. Reaching convergence also includes specific acts of managing divergence to facilitate and shape rather than explicitly decide which perspectives are valid.

6 Summary and Conclusions

This paper is written with the ambition to reduce the risk of having too much focus on technological capabilities and too little focus on the social aspects of the work practice. The ethnographic accounts illustrate that situation room work could be perceived as fragile collaborative achievements rather than time-critical decision-making. Ethnographic accounts from these environments could be a valuable material in future design-explorations. Previous research has to a large degree focused on the tasks, technologies and organizing as part of managing emergency response, but far too little attention has however been aimed at how actual work is achieved in regards to these aspects [4, 7, 14]. A motivation for this ethnographic research was the dissatisfaction with the available accounts of the work conducted in these environments, and the absence of detailed knowledge [23].

The aim of this paper was to address the question of what characterizes the work practice in situation room environments during emergency events. While attempting to answer this question this paper has presented ethnographic accounts of situation room work that is suggested to be understood as an evolved practice in contrast to traditional control room work [11]. The situation room work practice is manifested around five fundamental activities, characterized by the assembling of capacity, motivated by the need to make emerging events tangible, with a focus on exploring possible consequences of the emerging event, and work structured towards points of planned convergence, and consolidating divergent interpretations. This work is also fundamentally different from the work described by extent work on EOCs [2, 4, 5, 7, 14]. Making visible and differentiating this practice from day-to-day operations is of importance, since technology support for the everyday work practice and situation room work practice are fundamentally different.

References

1. Wybo, J.L., Kowalski, K.M.: Command centers and emergency management support. Saf. Sci. **30**, 131–138 (1998)
2. Quarantelli, E.L.: Uses and Problems of Local EOCs in Disasters (1978)
3. Kendra, J.M., Wachtendorf, T.: Elements of resilience after the world trade center disaster: reconstituting New York city's emergency operations centre. Disasters **27**, 37–53 (2003)

4. Lutz, L.D., Lindell, M.K.: Incident command system as a response model within emergency operation centers during Hurricane Rita. J. Contingencies Crisis Manag. **16**, 122–134 (2008)
5. Scanlon, T.J.: The role of EOCs in emergency management: a comparison of Canadian and American experience. Int. J. Mass Emerg. Disasters **12**, 51–75 (1994)
6. Bohn, M.K.: Nerve Center: Inside the White House Situation Room. Potomac Books Inc., Washington, DC (2003)
7. Johansson, R., Danielsson, E., Borglund, E.: Forskningsöversikt stabsarbete. Myndigheten för samhällsskydd och beredskap, Karlstad (2011)
8. Lee, C.P., Paine, D.: From the matrix to a model of coordinated action (MoCA): a conceptual framework of and for CSCW. In: Proceeding CSCW, pp. 179–194. ACM (2015)
9. McEntire, D.A.: Local emergency management organizations. In: McEntire, D.A. (ed.) Handbook of Disaster Research, pp. 168–182. Springer, New York (2007)
10. Weick, K.E.: Ambiguity as grasp: the reworking of sense. J. Contingencies Crisis Manag. **23**, 117–123 (2015)
11. Heath, C., Luff, P.: Collaboration and control - crisis management and multimedia technology in London underground line control rooms. Comput. Support. Coop. Work **1**, 69–94 (1992)
12. Suchman, L.: Centers of coordination: a case and some themes. In: Resnick, L.B., Säljö, R., Pontecorvo, C., Burge, B. (eds.) Discourse, Tools and Reasoning, pp. 41–62. Springer, Heidelberg (1997)
13. NASA, M.S.C.: Mercury project summary, including results of the fourth manned orbital flight. NASA SP-45 (1963)
14. Perry, R.W.: The structure and function of community emergency operations centres. Disaster Prev. Manag. **4**, 37–41 (1995)
15. Ley, B., Pipek, V., Reuter, C., Wiedenhoefer, T.: Supporting improvisation work in inter-organizational crisis management. In: Proceedings CHI, pp. 1529–1538. ACM (2012)
16. Stanton, N., Baber, C., Harris, D.: Modelling Command and Control: Event Analysis of Systemic Teamwork. Ashgate Publishing Ltd., Aldershot (2008)
17. Dynes, R.: Community emergency planning: false assumptions and inappropriate analogies. Int. J. Mass Emerg. Disasters **12**, 141–158 (1994)
18. Bergstrand, F., Landgren, J.: Visual reporting in time-critical work: exploring video use in emergency response. In: Proceedings of MobileHCI, pp. 415–424. ACM (2011) 2037436
19. Berndtsson, J., Normark, M.: The coordinative functions of flight strips: air traffic control work revisited. In: Proceedings GROUP, pp. 101–110. ACM (1999) 320308
20. Khalilbeigi, M., Bradler, D., Schweizer, I., Probst, F., Steimle, J.: Towards computer support of paper workflows in emergency management. In: Proceedings ISCRAM (2010)
21. Kunz, A., Alavi, A., Landgren, J., Yantaç, A.E., Woźniak, P., Sárosi, Z., Fjeld, M.: Tangible tabletops for emergency response: an exploratory study. In: Proceedings MIDI, pp. 10. ACM (2013)
22. Crabtree, A., Rouncefield, M., Tolmie, P.: Doing Design Ethnography. Springer, London (2012)
23. Hammersley, M., Atkinson, P.: Ethnography: Principles in Practice. Routledge, New York (2007)

24. Van Maanen, J.: Tales of the Field: On Writing Ethnography. University of Chicago Press, Chicago (2011)
25. Pink, S., Morgan, J.: Short-term ethnography: intense routes to knowing. Symb. Interact. **36**, 351–361 (2013)

Mediation Information System Engineering Applied to the Crisis Simulation

Aurélie Montarnal[1(✉)], Anne-Marie Barthe-Delanoë[2], Sébastien Truptil[1],
Frédérick Bénaben[1], and Audrey Fertier[1]

[1] Mines Albi, University of Toulouse, Campus Jarlard, 81000 Albi, France
{aurelie.montarnal,sebastien.truptil,frederick.benaben,
audrey.fertier}@mines-albi.fr
[2] INPT-ENSIACET, University of Toulouse, 4 allée Emile Monso, Toulouse, France
annemarie.barthe@ensiacet.fr

Abstract. Decision makers have to face an increasing number of disasters, natural or human-made, which complexity can be various (e.g. from a flood in a specific area to a CBRN accident), and across geographical and policy borders. To face the unexpected, practitioners commonly use simulation tools and train themselves on various situations. However, while simulation has become a cornerstone of the crisis management topic, plenty of simulation tools have been implemented for a lot of different applications and it is sometimes hard to choose the right set of tools to use together to better solve particular crisis situations. To avoid a waste of time and resources, and to foster the reuse of existing crisis simulation tools, this paper proposes a platform to (i) identify simulation tools, (ii) support interoperability among the tools by inferring simulation workflows that invoke the tools and (iii) execute those simulation workflows to improve crisis responses.

Keywords: Crisis simulation · Simulation tools · Semantics · Service composition · SOA

1 Introduction and Problem Statement

In recent years, the world has undergone many critical disasters, making always more human victims and material degradations. In [1], Pel et al. note that the intensity and the frequency have increased and raise the question of the importance for governments to be ready to react to such events. In line with them, Dugdale et al. [2] emphasize the importance of being able to simulate emergencies situations and particularly investigate on the computer-based simulations, which topic is currently booming. The need of simulation tools is actually dual: they are of the highest importance to attempt to forecast crisis behaviors and evaluate their impacts on the surrounding society and infrastructures, but they also are a necessity in preparing for future crisis (e.g. by allowing the setting up of realistic training scenarios to prepare the actors for such situations and for designing relevant contingency plans). Within the disaster operations management topic, the survey established by Altay and Green [3] shows that simulation is at one of

© Springer International Publishing AG 2016
P. Diaz et al. (Eds.): ISCRAM-med 2016, LNBIP 265, pp. 172–178, 2016.
DOI: 10.1007/978-3-319-47093-1_15

the top-priority concerns. Even though the literature in crisis management is very wide on the topic, the W3C Emergency Information Community Group raises the main current issue on this topic by [4] arguing that one of the main issues of crisis computer-based simulations tools is that they are now multiple, often dedicated to specific part of specific crisis (population evacuation, geographical behavior analysis, road traffic…) but they are not ready to work together, because they are not interoperable and unable to share and aggregate information relevantly. Such interoperability issue is also underlined by the required mutual aid when crises occur across the borders: geographical borders (at local, national and international levels) but also policy borders (organizations, public/private sectors, etc.). As a consequence, the crisis response phase could be enhanced and become more efficient: better reuse of existing software and information exchange flows for better coordination and forecasting and better decisions. Moreover, it would avoid governmental institutions from developing their own specific tools to fit their own information system, which is very expensive.

In this frame, this paper proposes to investigate a new kind of simulation platform, the goal of which is to provide a way to (i) define the articulation between already existing simulation tools, (ii) orchestrate them by enabling a unified interoperability that would not require any change on these tools and finally (iii) analyze and exploit their results in order to enhance the decision-making process both in response phases. This platform comes as a surrounding simulation layer to the IO-Suite software described in [5], which aims at supporting inter-organizational collaboration, especially in crisis situations. To tackle this challenge, the second part aims at introducing the IO-Suite software and its features, which are the foundation of these research works. Then the third part of this paper will focus on describing the proposed solution by explaining how to answer each of its challenges and positioning them within the literature. Finally perspectives will be given on the further use of such simulation platform.

2   IO-Suite as a Foundation

2.1   Introduction to IO-Suite

As expressed in the Introduction, the simulation platform proposed here is strongly based on previous research works that have been led within the IO-Suite software.

The IO-Suite provides a Mediation Information System (MIS) to support inter-organizational collaborations through three main modules:

The IO-DA (Design Assistant) concerns the business level of IO-Suite and aims at supporting crisis managers to gather relevant data, to formalize it as models and, then, to exploit this information to infer relevant collaborative business processes (i.e. which actors should execute which tasks, and when?). This step is based on three parts: (i) the modeling of the crisis situation, based on a specific core meta-model extended to a crisis layer, (ii) finding the business services that should be executed to resolve this crisis and (iii) automatically select the best set of partners to achieve them and order all these services into a business process.

The IO-WA (Worfklow Assistant) transforms the business processes into executable workflows, and orchestrates them by invoking each partner's service at the right time, in order to assist the coordination of the partners.

The IO-TA (Tracking Assistant) is dedicated to support an agility feature. Based on a Complex Event Processing (CEP), it gathers data on the field and detects any divergences between what the orchestrated collaborative process would expect and what really happens on the field. If divergences are detected, the collaborative process is adapted to better fit the reality, and then orchestrated in turn.

2.2   IO-Suite Simulation Layer to Improve the Preparation and Response Phases

Whereas the IO-Suite is able to provide decision makers with on-the-fly inferred business processes to support the crisis responses, simulation could be used in several ways to improve the system. On the one hand, it is very hard for men to predict the impacts of the process provided by IO-DA (those expected to solve the crisis -good- or the side effects -potentially bad), and that the process covers the entire situation. On the other hand, IO-TA is directly based on events that occur on the field: it can only notice "bad events" (i.e. signs of an aggravation of the crisis situation), but cannot prevent them. Hence, a simulation layer could provide IO-Suite with a way to forecast future situations, assess them (are they better or not that the current situation?) and adapt the current collaborative business process accordingly.

Beyond supporting the continuous improvement of collaborative processes during the response phase, such simulation layer could also be valuable to support the preparation phases. IO-Suite can indeed also be used to establish contingency plans or test scenarios, by entering realistic input models of crisis situations and obtaining the collaborative processes that could be considered to tackle them. Using simulation tools allows stimulating the system (i.e. by simulating events on the field) and, thus, obtaining a "projection" of the crisis situation (is it potentially going to be improved or not?). The input models can be refined in consequence, along with the collaborative processes inferred by IO-DA that can eventually be used as contingency plans.

Figure 1 depicts the steps of the three IO-DA's modules and sets the two main contributions expected from a surrounding simulation layer, both in preparation and response phases.

3   IO-Suite Simulation Layer

The proposed simulation layer is articulated along the three main IO-Suite's modules: (i) the selection of relevant simulation tools considering the crisis situation or the crisis scenario to be tested, (ii) the orchestration of these tools in a specific order and (iii) the feedback loops that allow exploiting the results of the simulation to adapt the collaborative process.

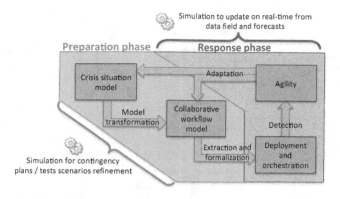

Fig. 1. Simulation workflow deduction through syntactico-semantic reconciliation

3.1 Deduction of Simulation Workflows

After that the collaborative process has been deduced by IO-DA, the actors of the crisis response, their activities to be executed and their order of execution are known. Selecting and articulating the relevant set of simulation tools to simulate the collaborative behavior of the actors during the response raises two main requirements: (i) having a knowledge base that lists the existing simulation tools and their functional features (i.e. what they are able to simulate) and (ii) being able to exploit this knowledge base in order to select the set of tools and order them into a simulation workflow (i.e. which simulation tools to execute when).

If the topic on the implementation of simulation tools has been widely studied as it is stated by [3, 6], establishing a formalized list of crisis simulation tools has not been explored so much. This is the reason why Barthe-Delanoë et al. [7] have decided to build the foundations of a taxonomy dedicated to collect and describe simulation tools according to their intrinsic features. Such taxonomy could be easily used as a knowledge base to know which are the potential simulation tools that could be selected.

It is proposed to consider the reconciliation from a business process to a simulation workflow as the one from a business process to a technical workflow (as proposed by IO-WA). On this topic [8] explains three kinds of possible syntactico-semantic (functional) reconciliations: from one business capability to one simulation tool (1-to-1), from one business capability to several complementary simulation tools (1-to-m) and from several business capabilities to several simulation tools (n-to-m). These kinds of reconciliations are depicted in Fig. 2. In addition, and to tackle the non-functional aspect of the reconciliation (e.g. finding appropriate tools on costs, software licenses... concerns), the works of [9] define a way to achieve an optimal selection of partners' services based on a framework of non-functional criteria.

3.2 Unification and Orchestration of Simulations Workflows

Once the simulation workflow has been deduced, it can be orchestrated. The two main challenges, here, lie on (i) the selection of the most adapted architecture to perform the

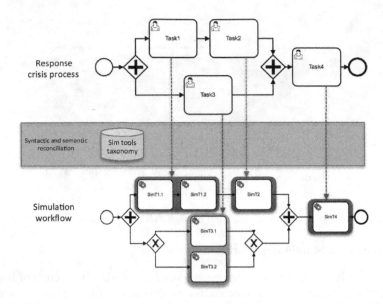

Fig. 2. Simulation workflow deduction through syntactico-semantic reconciliation

orchestration and (ii) the consequent lack of interoperability that prevent to use them homogeneously. These kinds of tools are indeed quite often developed for a specific use in specific situations, and, most of the time, they require specific configurations. Moreover, their input and output are rarely standardized.

To solve the first point, the idea is to still consider a simulation workflow as a technical workflow within a Service Oriented Architecture (SOA). A service bus (e.g. Enterprise Service Bus in the Service Oriented Architecture paradigm) can then be used to orchestrate the workflow. In such way, the MIS is able to invoke in time (i.e. following the simulation workflow order) each of the relevant simulation tools. However, this can only work if the data exchanged inside the bus follow the same format (both semantic and syntactic). This raises the need of a syntactico-semantic reconciliation (internal to the service bus, and independent of the simulation tools) among the tools.

To tackle the interoperability issue, the use of a unified approach is proposed, with a common metamodel allowing a semantic equivalence between the heterogeneous systems [10]. Thus, all input and output files of the tools should be converted to fit a unique format. That means that this unique format should be exhaustive enough to describe any of the objects that could be considered in crisis management. In this sense, a collaborative metamodel has been set up by [11] and provides a layered point of view: a core metamodel can be used to describe any collaboration whilst surrounding layers aims at refining objects relative to specific collaborations (e.g. a crisis layer that could itself be refined with a flooding layer and an earthquake layer).

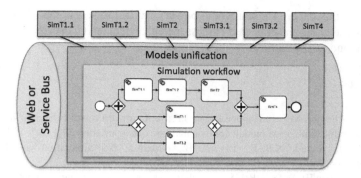

Fig. 3. Unification and orchestration of the simulation tools according to the simulation workflow

Figure 3 illustrates the orchestration architecture, with a model unification service, so that all the simulation tools could have homogeneous inputs and outputs, and therefore share and reuse information from one to another.

3.3 Simulation Feedbacks and Impacts Assessment

As exposed in [13] the purpose here is to detect the inaccuracy of the ongoing crisis response and to identify the most appropriate level of adaptation of the response to perform: (i) re-execute a disrupted activity, (ii) re-defining the collaborative network (as partners and/or their activities/resources have evolved in terms of availability, reliability, etc.), (iii) re-defining the collaborative situation and the pursued goals (as the crisis itself has evolved: new victims, new impacted areas, etc.). The simulation layer can support the decision-making by showing the effects of a decision on the whole system (the crisis itself, the collaborative network, the proper execution of the invoked activities) and, through the agility feature, underlines the pros and cons of such decision on the ongoing processes. Hence, the simulation layer can fruitfully combine the real-time data gathered by IO-TA's CEP and the forecasted data to refine the orchestrated resolution process.

4   Conclusion and Perspectives

We have presented an innovative simulation platform that comes as a layer surrounding a core software (IO-Suite) dedicated to support the collaborations among inter-organizational partners. This platform aims at reusing existing simulation tools and making them interoperable through three steps: (i) the deduction of simulation workflows, based on the crisis situation description and the crisis resolution collaborative platform deduced by IO-DA tool, (ii) the orchestration of these simulation workflows and its inherent interoperable issues resolution and (iii) the establishment and the exploitation of feedbacks resulting from the simulation forecasts, in response phase (for forecasting and preventing difficulties, before they actually arise). The further steps to these research works will be to benefit from all the previous implementations that have been made within the IO-Suite core, and to efficiently apply them to the simulation layer, as preconized in this paper. Then, it would be very fruitful to assess the whole proposed platform on use-cases and effectively assess the enhancement it can bring to real contingency plans and test scenarios.

References

1. Pel, A.J., Bliemer, M.C.J., Hoogendoorn, S.P.: A review on travel behaviour modelling in dynamic traffic simulation models for evacuations. Transportation **39**(1), 97–123 (2011)
2. Dugdale, J., Saoud, N.B.-B., Pavard, B., Pallamin, N.: Simulation and Emergency Management, vol. 16. M.E. Sharpe, Armonk (2010)
3. Altay, N., Green III, W.G.: OR/MS research in disaster operations management. Eur. J. Oper. Res. **175**(1), 475–493 (2006)
4. Emergency Information Community Group. https://www.w3.org/community/emergency/
5. Benaben, F., Truptil, S., Lauras, M., Salatge, N.: Management of collaborative behavior through a service-oriented mediation system: the case of crisis management. In: 2015 IEEE International Conference on Services Computing (SCC), pp. 554–561 (2015)
6. Galindo, G., Batta, R.: Review of recent developments in OR/MS research in disaster operations management. Eur. J. Oper. Res. **230**(2), 201–211 (2013)
7. Barthe-Delanoë, A.-M., Truptil, S., Bénaben, F.: Towards a taxonomy of crisis management simulation tools. In: ISCRAM 2015 Conference Proceedings – 12th International Conference on Information Systems for Crisis Response and Management, Kristiansand, Norway (2015)
8. Boissel-Dallier, N., Benaben, F., Lorré, J.-P., Pingaud, H.: Mediation information system engineering based on hybrid service composition mechanism. J. Syst. Softw. **108**, 39–59 (2015)
9. Montarnal, A., Barthe-Delanoë, A.-M., Bénaben, F., Lauras, M., Lamothe, J.: Towards automated business process deduction through a social and collaborative platform. In: Camarinha-Matos, L.M., Afsarmanesh, H. (eds.) Collaborative Systems for Smart Networked Environments. IFIP AICT, vol. 434, pp. 443–451. Springer, Heidelberg (2014)
10. ISO, ISO 14258:1998, Industrial automation systems and integration - Concepts and rules for enterprise models, ISO TC184/SC5/WG1 (1998)
11. Ramete, G.M., Lamothe, J., Lauras, M., Benaben, F.: A road crisis management metamodel for an information decision support system. In: 2012 6th IEEE International Conference on Digital Ecosystems Technologies (DEST), pp. 1–5 (2012)

Social Computing

Analyzing and Visualizing Emergency Information in a Multi Device Environment

Paloma Diaz, Teresa Onorati[✉], and Sergio del Olmo Pueblas

Universidad Carlos III de Madrid, Madrid, Spain
{pdp, tonorati}@inf.uc3m.es, solmo@inst.uc3m.es

Abstract. The information shared by people through social networks and ad-hoc collaborative applications can help emergency operation centers to understand better the situation and orchestrate a more efficient response. However, collecting and analyzing data generated by citizens is a challenging task due to the quantity and the heterogeneity of sources, not all of them equally reliable and precise. In this paper, we propose a multi device environment called emerCienMDE to allow emergency operators to gather, analyze and visualize these data interacting with different devices, such as tabletops, vertical displays, desktop computers or tablets. The environment is based on an ecology of participants that distinguish among different types of citizens, depending on their trustworthiness and skills. An exploratory focus group carried out with several emergency experts pointed out interesting findings about the integration of the citizen generated information into crisis centers being aware of the source and level of trust.

Keywords: Multi device environment · Information visualization · Social media · Emergency management

1 Introduction

The popularity of mobile technologies and social computing platforms such as social networks or blogs, has created a new kind of citizens always connected and sharing all kinds of data. This participation culture [1] is getting used to express their opinions and take an active part in many social and political issues, but also to post messages about emergencies and crises through different platforms. This information can be valuable for emergency operators both for the information provided, that can include not only texts but also pictures and videos, as well as for their geo-localization [2]. On the one hand, shared messages could contain useful and updated data about the situation, or pictures of damages and victims. On the other hand, the number of messages published from a particular area gives an idea about how many citizens could be involved in the event or if there is any problem with the communication infrastructures. For example, not having any activity in an affected area might suggest that communication networks are damaged. Citizen-generated data could be used to support the decision making process during different phases of the emergency management (EM so forth). Indeed, in US the Federal Emergency Management Agency (FEMA) considers citizens as *first responders* since they are the first ones in the affected area trying to react to the events [2–4].

© Springer International Publishing AG 2016
P. Diaz et al. (Eds.): ISCRAM-med 2016, LNBIP 265, pp. 181–194, 2016.
DOI: 10.1007/978-3-319-47093-1_16

However, this integration of information is not as simple and straightforward as it might be expected, and not only for technical reasons. There are at least two significant barriers that emergency managers argue to adopt technologies that make use of citizen generated information: dealing with huge quantities of data in real time and separating the wheat from the chaff [5]. User citizen generated data vary not only in their trust-worthiness but also in their relevance and quality [5, 6] to understand the problem at hand. In both cases, information technologies like visual analytics can help as far as the domain is modeled to provide meaning and relevance to each data item or collection. In [7] we described a theoretical approach to align the needs of emergency managers and the potential social capital provided by citizens that makes use of an ecology of participants where citizens are classified according to whether their information should be preprocessed (called *sensors*) or could be directly integrated into the system (called *trusted sensors*). Other categories include citizens who are prepared to process infor-mation and provide for example accurate evaluations or aid requests (*nodes*) and to act under supervision (*agents*).

Based on this framework, this paper explores potential interfaces that could help operators to integrate citizen generated information with other sources of information in a way that might facilitate decision making. With that purpose, emerCienMDE pro-vides a collaborative map-based tool that supports the execution of emergency plans, and the visualization of data collected from human and digital sensors during the response phase. Human sensors are citizens and experts whilst digital sensors are physical and electronic devices that can store automatically data like GPS locations, RFID tags, pressure or temperature. In order to be used in Emergency Operation Centers (EOC), emerCienMDE has been designed as a Multi Device Environment (MDE) so that different actors can cooperate at the same time on the same map interacting with different devices (i.e. tablets, desktop computers, tabletops or vertical displays). Each device offers the same functionalities, but the interface is adapted to the context of use to provide a better user experience. For instance, an operator can be collaborating from her EOCs desktop computer with first responders using mobile devices in the field or with other EOCs where large displays are used. Each one would require a different view of the information according to the device, the physical space and the task being performed.

The remaining of the paper is organized as follows. Section 2 reviews the state of the art about the use of tabletop applications for EM identifying most relevant features and current limitations. Section 3 describes the emerCienMDE environment, while Sect. 4 presents the exploratory focus group conducted with international experts in EM and Sect. 5 points out which are the main findings obtained from the focus group. Finally, some conclusions and some open issues to be further investigated are drawn.

2 Related Works

Several collaborative applications have been already proposed to support the different phases of the EM process that include preparedness, response, recovery and mitigation. In this context, we have analyzed some existing systems to identify common characteristics and limitations. As summarized in Table 1, our analysis focuses on six requirements related with the goals of our work: develop a system supporting a collaborative response phase (*R1. Real-time monitoring* of the emergency situation) that is carried out by professionals working in different physical contexts (*R2. MDE support* and *R3. MDE synchronization*), and integrates human and digital sensors information (*R4. Sensor tracking and Communication among participants*) in a way that can be interpreted by operators (*R5. Information visualization* and *R6. Information categorization*). Next paragraphs discuss these requirements before analyzing how they are addressed in some real systems.

(R1) Real-time monitoring of the emergency situation. During the emergency response, operators are in charge of executing a plan previously defined, assigning resources and coordinating specific courses of action. To be effective, this phase needs a real-time monitoring of updated and reliable data [6, 8] about the situation so that decision makers can develop a situational awareness that will inform their decisions [9].

(R2) MDE support and (R3) MDE synchronization. An efficient response usually requires an effective collaboration among emergency workers belonging to different units and corps and working in different physical environments: from crisis rooms, to control centers to the field. Tabletop tangible affordances can be exploited to improve collaboration in the emergency management since they help to improve awareness in co-located settings [10], but to support different needs of emergency workers multi device environments (MDE) are required so each professional can use the best device depending on the physical context and the task being performed. As Mark Weiser argued the value of ubiquitous computing does not reside in a unique device, but on the seamless integration of ecologies of devices to deal with all the interaction needs of a specific task [11]. Such seamless integration implies being able to synchronize the views of each participant in a collaborative task. Each operator should have the same knowledge about the crisis situation, as a first step to develop a Common Operational Picture (COP) that guarantees unity of response [12].

(R4) Sensor tracking and communication. Tracking information generated by citizens (called human sensors) as well as digital sensors can contribute to a better understanding of the situation. In this way, it is also possible to establish a bidirectional communication channel between operators and citizens to share useful information about the situation and the response activities [13].

(R5) Information visualization and (R6) Information categorization. One of the challenges in collecting large collections of data stands in generating meaningful representations [14]. This is particularly true in an EOC, where operators have to make quick decisions and they can not spend time filtering out information. With this purpose, effective visual analytics techniques and semantic categorization methods can be used in order to present collected data in a meaningful and easy to understand way as in [15].

We reviewed four systems to analyze relevant technological issues related with collaborative emergency response. This review does not intend to be comprehensive, among other reasons because most applications used in real OECs are not published for confidentiality and security reasons. The purpose of this study is to identify best practices and limitations.

CERMIT [16] is a multi-user interface to monitor emergency information for operators working in the EOC and field workers. Depending on the role, the system shows the same updated information through different interaction modes and devices. The operators in the EOC use light points and lasers over a vertical or horizontal display, while field units interact with mobile devices. The interaction ecology does not include desktop computers that are generally very common in the EOCs. No analysis is performed over collected data and no communication is supported among the users of the system.

CoTracker [17] supports decision making in crisis situations showing related information on a map. Users can choose a time lapse for accessing information or just navigate real-time data generated during the emergency response. One innovative characteristic of this system is the possibility of interacting with the surface using tangible elements, like pens, blocks or frames, but any other device is not considered. Moreover, the system does not include any information collection mechanism nor a communication channel among the users of the application.

Differently from CERMIT and CoTracker, ePlan [18] provides a multi device environment for training exercises in emergency response. It includes an iPad for individual activities, a tabletop for showing general views of the situation, and a vertical display for visualizing information about an event or a training session. Information is collected from both social platforms, like Twitter, blogs or news channels, and digital sensors, like traffic cameras. However, ePlan does not provide any mechanism to analyze and make sense of collected data or to establish a bidirectional communication with users.

Similar to ePlan, Bader et al. in [19] proposed a digital map table with Fovea-Tabletts as a tabletop with a vertical display and a mechanism to track tablets placed on it. Interacting with these multiple devices, users can move information from their personal workspace to the digital map for collaborative purposes. The tabletop and the vertical display are used to visualize information about the situation and facilitate the discussion among operators in the EOC. Sensor tracking and the communication with users as well as the analysis of available data are not considered.

As summarized in Table 1, the four applications offer real-time monitoring and information visualization mechanisms (R1 and R5). Except for CoTracker, the other three also support different interaction modes in a synchronized multi device environment (R2 and R3). However, about the requirement R4 just ePlan provides a geo-localized visualization of data available from different sensors (i.e. social platforms and digital sensors), but no communication is established with users. Finally, considering the volume of managed information during an emergency, there is a lack in mechanisms to categorize and analyze collected data (R6) for helping operators in making sense of them and better understanding the situation.

Table 1. Met and unmet requirements for considered tabletop applications

Requirement	Cermit	CoTracker	ePlan	Bader et al.
R1	Yes	Yes	Yes	Yes
R2	Yes	No	Yes	Yes
R3	Yes	No	Yes	Yes
R4	No	No	Partially	No
R5	Yes	Yes	Yes	Yes
R6	No	No	No	No

3   The EmerCienMDE Environment

When an emergency occurs, the EOC is in charge of making decisions about actions to perform and resources to reach an effective solution. To improve the efficiency of the response phase, it is crucial to have a clear understanding of the current situation collecting updated information from both digital and human sensors. Receiving data about temperature, GPS coordinates, light or pressure, just to name few examples of digital sensors, could help to figure out the real magnitude of the event or any other exceptional circumstances. In the same way, people act like human sensors sharing on social networks or mobile applications details about the emergency that might be unknown to the authorities. During large scale disasters, like the Japan tsunami in 2011 or the hurricane Sandy in 2012, people shared a great amount of textual and multimedia data hard to analyze and take advantage from [4, 20]. We propose a solution where the emergency plans and the information collected from digital and human sensors are integrated to facilitate their interpretability and the interaction with both the data and the information sources.

EmerCienMDE is a real-time MDE application that offers synchronized and adapted views for multiple devices, including tabletops, vertical displays, desktops and tablets. The operators can collaborate actively from any work context (i.e. same EOC, different EOC or field units) sharing the same common operational picture of the emergency situation and the same set of functionalities. Changes can be made from any device and at any time with an automatic update in all devices guaranteeing a real-time monitoring of the situation. As shown in Fig. 1, the horizontal display is used to support co-located collaboration and the vertical display is mainly for visualization

Fig. 1. The multi device environment of emerCienMDE

purposes. Other devices, including desktop computers, laptops and tablets support geographically distributed collaboration.

The system interaction is focused on a map-based representation where the information collected from digital and human sensors is integrated into the emergency plan (see Fig. 2a). Each resource and information is geo-localized and is represented by an icon. Users can interact directly with the map or choose one of the options available in the circular menu that include showing tweets, taking notes, creating geo-localized emergency alerts, and exit. Alerts have a description, a type of risk (i.e. human or material) and a level of severity (i.e. high, medium or low). Another menu is available on the left side of the tabletop to select an emergency plan to apply and to filter the type of sensors that have to be displayed in the map. As digital sensors, we consider the geographical location of useful resources, such as ambulances, containers, fences or shelters, already defined in the emergency plan. As human sensors, we collect tweets about the event organized taking into account two issues: the author's reliability and the tweet relevance. About the first point, five types of citizens are considered [6]: *citizens*, who receive information from authorities; *sensors* who can receive and send information to the authorities; *trusted sensors*, like sensors with a high reliability (e.g. VOST teams); *nodes*, who can provide more detailed and accurate information; and *agents* who can make decisions and execute actions under the supervision of the EOCs. Each one of them is associated to a color to facilitate their identification in the map (see Fig. 2b).

About the relevance, once the tweets have been collected a semantic method is applied to get the most relevant topics. The result is a semantic categorization based on domain ontologies and ad-hoc data mining techniques, already presented in [15]. The categories used to organize tweets in collaboration were identified with an emergency expert and they include emergency, place, description, time and general. The display is divided into four areas (Fig. 2b): the upper left corner shows a heat map where tweets are distributed per location and volume according to a heat color code; the upper central part there is a tree map where terms are represented as boxes, which size and opacity depend on their relevance respect to the tweet set and the color is related to the category; the right part contains a list of tweets related to the current event; finally, the lower part shows the map in the horizontal display with resources and information from both the emergency plan and the sensors deployed in the area.

-a-   -b-

Fig. 2. The horizontal (a) and the vertical (b) displays of the emerCienMDE environment

4 Exploratory Focus Group with Experts

The main goal of emerCienMDE is to provide a collaborative map where operators can manage activities to perform, available resources and information collected from social platforms. Since this kind of systems that are expected to be used in critical situations cannot be deployed in real settings easily, so to evaluate its potential utility we applied an approach were prototypes are discussed and evaluated with experts in focus groups as suggested in [21]. The focus group involved six experts from different countries with an extensive experience in the area of emergency management. Considering that their daily activities take up most of their time and they couldn't participate in long sessions, we split the focus group into two parts: synchronous and asynchronous sessions. During the synchronous session, we invited them to join a video conference to foster the discussion about the utility of emerCienMDE. After that, they could follow up the discussion in an asynchronous way posting comments on a website where all the information used in the synchronous session was available.

Based on the requirements identified in the state of the art, the focus group aimed at exploring experts' opinions and suggestions about the following issues:

- Real time usage of the collaborative map (R1 – real-time monitoring of the emergency situation)
- Utility of a MDE, including smartphones, tablets, laptops and tabletops and adaptability of available functionalities (R2 – MDE support and R3 – MDE synchronization)
- Potential utility of information generated by human and digital sensors for experts (R4 – sensor tracking and communication)
- Potential utility of visualization techniques for representing collected data from human and digital sensors (R5 – information visualization and R6 – information categorization)
- Perception of the system utility.

4.1 Participants

We involved six international experts who had also taken part in an online course organized by the Spanish Civil Protection about citizen participation in emergencies. All of them had more than five years of experience in EM activities working for different Latin American and Spanish organizations. In particular, five of them have spent between eighteen and thirty years working in emergency response and preparedness. Their expertise is mostly related to managing specific type of crisis (e.g. natural disasters, massive evacuations or fires). More details about them are listed in Table 2.

Table 2. Participants at the exploratory focus group

ID	Experience (#years)	Country	Expertise area
#1	18	Argentina	Massive events for sports
#2	25	Spain	Natural disasters
#3	30	Argentina	Natural disasters
#4	23	Colombia	Risk management
#5	24	Peru	Natural disasters & evacuations
#6	>5	Colombia	Mitigation & risk management

4.2 Set up

In order to concentrate the participant's focus on the functionalities of the system, we used four videos about how emerCienMDE works. Videos were made available, along with a text description before the synchronous sessions so that participants could have a look at them. For the asynchronous session, videos were posted on a blog that was used to collect related opinions and suggestions. In the next paragraphs we describe each video goal according to the requirements introduced in Sect. 2 and the topics that were raised to promote discussion among the focus group participants.

First Video: Monitoring Sensors. The first video is about the real-time monitoring of data collected from sensors (R1 – real-time monitoring of the emergency situation). The main screen of the tool is shown with the collaborative map where different kinds of sensors are localized, including operators (e.g. firemen, policemen, ...) and resources (e.g. ambulances, roadblocks, drones, ...). For each sensor, we can change the position or delete it if not needed. Moreover, we can create alerts as emergency situations occurred in a specific place. The alerts have a color representing their severity (i.e. yellow for low, orange for medium and red for high). A color code is also used for the ecology of participants: yellow for citizens, light blue for sensors, dark blue for trusted sensors, green for nodes and purple for agents. It is also possible to communicate with the human sensors localized in the map through an ad-hoc message service. After the video, we involved the participants in a discussion about the utility of emerCienMDE in a real emergency scenario (question Q1 in Table 3). We were also interested in their opinions about the ecology of participants and the possibility to monitor citizens playing different roles (question Q2 in Table 3).

Table 3. Discussion topics for the first video

ID	Questions
Q1	Do you think emerCienMDE could be used in a real emergency scenario?
Q2	Do you think it is useful to monitor citizens playing different roles in an emergency scenario?

Second Video: Visualizing Information. In the second video, we moved the attention of the evaluators from the horizontal surface to the vertical one. They had the possibility to see how information is collected from citizens through different channels

(R4 – sensor tracking and communication), analyzed and visualized (R5 – information visualization and R6 – information categorization). Considering that participants did not have a strong background in information systems and technologies, it was particularly interesting for us evaluating the understandability and learnability of proposed visualizations (i.e. heat-map and tree-map), and communication channels (i.e. tweet stream and message service). Experts were asked to give their opinions about two main issues: the meaningfulness of the visualizations (questions Q1 and Q2 in Table 4), and how citizens' participation can improve the emergency response (question Q3 in Table 4). During the discussion, we also asked for any improvement, suggestion or potential weaknesses (question Q4 in Table 4).

Table 4. Discussion topics for the second video

ID	Questions
Q1	What idea do you get from looking at data represented in the visualizations?
Q2	Do you think that the visualizations could be useful for managing information in emergency response?
Q3	Do you think that involving citizens with different levels of reliability could improve emergency response?
Q4	Can you identify any weakness in the visualizations and communication channels?

Third Video: Multi Device Environment. The third video focuses on setting up a multi device environment to interact with emerCienMDE in multiple ways (R2 – MDE support and R3 – MDE synchronization). The main views of the application are given by two large surfaces: a tabletop and a vertical display. The tabletop allows emergency operators to collaborate over the same map and make decisions about needed activities and resources for the response phase. The vertical display is primarily used for visualization purposes. In this case, the discussion among the participants was aimed at gathering their opinions about the perceived utility of a multi device environment to manage great volumes of information (questions Q1 and Q3 in Table 5) and to enhance the collaboration among different actors. In this last case, the operators could use a different device depending on their specific needs and consequently available features and interface design have to be adapted (questions Q2, Q3 and Q4 in Table 5).

Table 5. Discussion topics for the third video

ID	Questions
Q1	Do you think it is useful to have two screens in the same environment (a vertical one for information visualization for everyone in the center and a horizontal one for executing specific tasks and collaborate with others)?
Q2	Do you think it is useful to have the information screen and the table-top available for everyone in the EOC?
Q3	Would you use it in real emergency operations? (If negative response, why?)
Q4	Do you think this application improves the collaboration among operators in the EOC and among operators and citizens?

Fourth Video: MDE with Smart Devices. The aim of the fourth video was to collect suggestions about the use of smart devices. Experts were asked to think about the utility of a tablet in an EOC as well as in an emergency scenario (R3 – MDE synchronization). In the first case, the tablet is mainly used for communicating with other devices in the same space to support the collaboration among a group of operators (questions Q2 and Q4 in Table 6). In the second case, the operators are working in the emergency scenario and the tablet can be an effective communication channel with the EOC (questions Q1 and Q3 in Table 6).

Table 6. Discussion topics for the fourth video

ID	Questions
Q1	Do you think you would use smart devices (e.g. tablets) working in an emergency scenario?
Q2	Do you think you would use smart devices (e.g. tablets) working in an EOC?
Q3	What functionality do you think should or should not be supported in the tablet version of emerCienMDE to be used in an emergency scenario?
Q4	What functionality do you think should or should not be supported in the tablet version of emerCienMDE to be used in an EOC?

5   Results from the Exploratory Focus Group

The questionnaires in Tables 3, 4, 5, and 6 were used as scripts for encouraging the discussion among the experts. Analyzing topics and suggestions outlined during the focus group, we have found out some interesting results about how to improve the utility and applicability of an approach like emerCienMDE that are summarized in the following sections using the requirements identified in Sect. 2.

5.1   R1 – Real-Time Monitoring of the Emergency

EmerCienMDE allows both citizens and emergency operators to create alerts about any kind of critical events, including also small or domestic accidents. Even if experts consider that this solution is easier than traditional channels (e.g. 112 or 911 phone calls), they are concerned about possible false information or misunderstandings. This risk affects also citizens playing as *trusted sensors* unless they rely on an official source. Experts agreed to keep these alerts separated from the ones created in the EOC or received from official channels. Once citizens' alerts have been received, the EOC should be in charge of checking them before starting any response activity, as they do currently. They found that visualizing the source of the alert in the map using the ecology of participants can help to discriminate among information sources.

5.2   R2 – MDE Support and R3 – MDE Synchronization

The MDE was considered an efficient and effective solution for improving the collaboration in an EOC, in particular considering that large surfaces as tabletops are already used in many organizations. Nowadays large displays in EOC are mainly used for showing maps, statistics, videos or other general details about the current scenario. From their perspective, the innovative value of emerCienMDE relies upon the possibility of collecting data from both digital and human sensors and giving operators a common and integrated space to collaborate actively, despite their geographical location. About tablets and other smartphones, experts discussed extensively on how to adapt the tool and which features could be considered. These devices are very popular due to their characteristics portability and connectivity. To exploit their usage, instead of a full screen map it could be better to show a short summary of what is going on with most critical data: an image of the situation, a detail of the map, the nearest resources or the most important messages. Evaluators also pointed out that in case of emergency the communication infrastructures could be damaged affecting also the Internet connection. For this reason, the information deployed in such devices should be minimal to facilitate access even under low connectivity.

5.3   R4 – Sensor Tracking and Communication

Monitoring both digital and human sensors gives a detailed picture of the current situation. While digital sensors are already considered in several EOC, human sensors represent an innovative way to improve the citizens' participation. The experts liked the idea to give a more active role to citizens for both sending information about an emergency and performing some actions depending on their profile. The ecology of participants as a categorization based on the expertise and the reliability of each one of them was considered as a good way to approach this challenge. A consequence can be to fasten up the crisis detection and the information updates. Moreover, knowing exactly the position of each affected citizen in the map can help operators to see where a critical event is happening and which are the most vulnerable points as well as the human resources that are available.

5.4   R5 – Information Visualization and R6 – Information Categorization

The volume of collected information can grow exponentially depending on the scale of the emergency. Moreover, shared messages could contain different kinds of data, like photos, videos and texts. Among such a huge quantity and variety of data, operators can easily miss some important details or receive false or irrelevant ones. To cope with this problem, emerCienMDE proposes two different semantic based visualization techniques for information collected from twitter: a tree-map and a heat-map. Initially, participants expressed their concern about the overflow of information and the necessity to categorize and represent all data in an effective and efficient way. After the videos, they found the heat-map easy to understand and navigate: the color code for distinguishing and interpreting data. Moreover, it is common to find this kind of visualization in different applications and people are becoming to get used to it. About the tree-map, experts had some difficulties in reading the terms and recognizing their organization in semantic categories, something that can be expected since it was the first time they interacted with this visualization technique. Anyway, they were able to identify that the visualization was about a bus accident in a South region of Spain (i.e. Murcia). Both visualizations might be useful for representing the geographical distribution and the semantic meaning of collected messages. While the heat-map was considered easier to learn and interpret, the tree-map needs to be improved either changing the categorization, the representation of the terms or providing helpful clues in the user interface.

6   Conclusions and Future Works

When an emergency occurs, it is crucial to guarantee an efficient cooperation among operators in the EOC, field units and affected citizens. All of them have a relevant role to play for guaranteeing an effective response and to deal safely and quickly with the situation. From the analysis of existent applications in literature, we identified a lack in gathering and visualizing information maintaining a synchronized view in different devices, which was the goal that inspired the development of emerCienMDE. We also identified six requirements to guide the analysis of the literature and the next design phase: real-time monitoring of the emergency situation (R1); MDE support (R2) and MDE synchronization (R3); sensor tracking and communication (R4); information visualization (R5) and information categorization (R6).

The prototype emerCienMDE makes it possible to integrate information from heterogeneous sources, digital and human, using several complementary views (from a map representation of the situation to semantic visualizations of social networks). The goal of MDE is to explore the alternative visualizations that operators need to make sense of the situation and orchestrate an action. Thus the proposed visualization techniques aim at giving a general view of represented data but also support a detailed navigation if required. In this way, operators can build a common understanding of the situation and get a clear image about what is happening in the emergency field observing data generated by the sensors, whose trustworthiness is also made explicit and visual through the ecology of participants.

The prototype was evaluated during an exploratory focus group with international emergency experts. The focus group used videos to promote both synchronous and asynchronous discussion. The questions explored the six identified requirements and as a result, we found out that the experts agreed about them and their relevance for designing this kind of applications. We also verified that emerCienMDE effectively implements them and, finally, we collected suggestions about how to improve it focusing in particular on the interpretability of the tree-map.

More information sources and tools are required before such kind of technology can be deployed in and adopted by real EOCs, but the findings of the focus group suggest that the combination of an MDE platform with multiple visualizations based on a categorization of information sources might be a step further into integrating citizens in active emergency management. To start with, it would be necessary to integrate other social networks as well as specific mobile applications for notifying emergencies and alerts. Additionally, more research on how to motivate citizen participation and how to cope with privacy issues is required before deploying technologies for citizens.

Acknowledgments. This work is supported by the project emerCien grant funded by the Spanish Ministry of Economy and Competitiveness (TIN2012-09687).

References

1. Jenkins, H., Purushotma, R., Weigel, M., Clinton, K., Robinson, A.J.: Confronting the challenges of participatory culture: media education for the 21st century. John D. and Catherine T. MacArthur Foundation Reports on Digital Media and Learning. MIT Press (2009)
2. Jaeger, P.T., Shneiderman, B., Fleischmann, K.R., Preece, J., Qu, Y., Wu, P.F.: Community response grids: e-government, social networks, and effective emergency management. Telecommun. Policy **31**(10), 592–604 (2007)
3. Stallings, R., Quarantelli, E.L.: Emergent citizen groups and emergency management. Public Adm. Rev. **45**, 93–100 (1985)
4. Goodchild, M.F.: Citizens as sensors: the world of volunteered geography. GeoJournal **69** (4), 211–221 (2007)
5. Díaz, P., Aedo, I., Herranz, S.: Citizen participation and social technologies: exploring the perspective of emergency organizations. In: Hanachi, C., Bénaben, F., Charoy, F. (eds.) ISCRAM-med 2014. LNBIP, vol. 196, pp. 85–97. Springer, Heidelberg (2014)
6. Ludwig, T., Reuter, C., Pipek, V.: Social haystack: dynamic quality assessment of citizen-generated content during emergencies. ACM Trans. Comput. Hum. Interact. (TOCHI) **22**(4), 17 (2015)
7. Diaz, P., Aedo, I., Romano, M., Onorati, T.: Supporting citizens 2.0 in disasters response. In: Proceedings of MeTTeG 2013, pp. 79–88 (2013)
8. Turoff, M., Chumer, M., Van de Walle, B., Yao, X.: The design of a dynamic emergency response management information system (DERMIS). JITTA J. Inf. Technol. Theory Appl. **5**(4), 1 (2004)
9. Endsley, M., Bolté, B., Jones, D.G.: Designing for Situational Awareness: An Approach to User-Centered Design. CRC Press, Boca Raton (2003)
10. Hornecker, E., Marshall, P., Dalton, N.S., Rogers, Y.: Collaboration and interference: awareness with mice or touch input. In: ACM Conference on Computer Supported Cooperative Work, pp. 167–176. ACM (2008)
11. Weiser, M.: The computer for the 21st century. Sci. Am. **265**, 94–104 (1991)
12. Copeland, J.: Emergency response: unity of effort through a common operational picture. Strategy Research Project, U.S. Army War College (2008)
13. Mergel, I.: Social media adoption: toward a representative, responsive or interactive government? Proceedings of the 15th Annual International Conference on Digital Government Research, pp. 163–170 (2014)
14. Keim, D.A., Mansmann, F., Schneidewind, J., Ziegler, H.: Challenges in visual data analysis. In: Tenth International Conference on Information Visualization (IV 2006), pp. 2–7 (2006)

15. Onorati, T., Díaz, P.: Semantic visualization of twitter usage in emergency and crisis situations. In: Bellamine Ben Saoud, N., et al. (eds.) ISCRAM-med 2015. LNBIP, vol. 233, pp. 3–14. Springer, Heidelberg (2015). doi:10.1007/978-3-319-24399-3_1
16. Piazza, T., Heller, H., Fjeld, M.: Cermit: co-located and remote collaborative system for emergency response management. In: International Conference of SIGRAD, pp. 12–20 (2009)
17. Kunz, A., Alavi, A., Landgren, J., Yantaç, A.E., Woźniak, P., Sárosi, Z., Fjeld, M.: Tangible tabletops for emergency response: an exploratory study. In: International Conference on Multimedia, Interaction, Design and Innovation, p. 10. ACM (2013)
18. Chokshi, A., Seyed, T., Marinho Rodrigues, F., Maurer, F.: ePlan multi-surface: a multi-surface environment for emergency response planning exercises. In: 9th ACM International Conference on Interactive Tabletops and Surfaces (ITS 2014), pp. 219–228. ACM (2014)
19. Bader, T., Meissner, A., Tscherney, R.: Digital map table with Fovea-Tablett®: smart furniture for emergency operation centers. In: 5th International ISCRAM Conference, pp. 679–688 (2008)
20. Ichiguchi, T.: Robust and usable media for communication in a disaster. Sci. Technol. Trends Q. Rev. 4, 44–55 (2011)
21. Hevner, A., Chatterjee, S.: Design Science Research in Information Systems, pp. 9–22. Springer, New York (2010)

Which Centrality Metric for Which Terrorist Network Topology?

Imen Hamed[1]([✉]), Malika Charrad[1,2], and Narjès Bellamine Ben Saoud[1]

[1] Univ. Manouba, ENSI, RIADI LR99ES26,
Campus Universitaire Manouba, 2010 Manouba, Tunisia
hamedimen@gmail.com, malika.charrad@riadi.rnu.tn,
narjes.bellamine@ensi.rnu.tn
[2] ISIMed, Université de Gabes, Gabès, Tunisia

Abstract. Recently, an exponential growth in the use of social network analysis (SNA) tools has been witnessed. SNA offers quantitative measures known as centralities which allow the identification of important nodes in a given network. In fact, determining such nodes in terrorist networks is a way to destabilize these cells and prevent their criminal activities. Identifying key players is highly dependent on structural characteristics of nodes. Therefore, many approaches rely on centrality metrics to propose various disruption strategies. Indeed, knowledge of these measures helps in revealing vulnerabilities of terrorist networks and may have important implications for investigations. It is debatable how to choose the suitable centrality measure that helps effectively to destabilize the terrorist network. In this paper, we aim to answer this question. We first provide an analytical study where we identify 6 topologies of terrorist networks and discuss the appropriate metrics per topology. Secondly, we provide the performed experimental analysis on five data sets (with 5 different topologies) to prove our analytical conclusions.

Keywords: Terrorism · Network topology · Centrality metric

1 Introduction

Terror is the calculated use of violence or the threat of violence to attain political or religious ideological goals through intimidation, coercion, or instilling fear [21]. This strategic and tactic crime is considered as a very complex phenomenon due to its secretive nature. Different strategies have been proposed to reveal the secrecy of terrorist networks. Social Network Analysis (SNA) is prominent among them. This latter consists in transforming the set of terrorists into network structures where the nodes represent attackers and the links are the connections between them. SNA provides deeper insights about the nodes and their interactions. Different works applying SNA on terrorist attacks were proposed such as modeling dynamic covert networks [14], analyzing links between individuals [19], subgroup detection and key players identification [14]. In this paper, we focus mainly on key players identification. In fact, the disruption of terrorist cells requires the isolation of important nodes. To do so, it is fundamental to measure centrality metrics.

© Springer International Publishing AG 2016
P. Diaz et al. (Eds.): ISCRAM-med 2016, LNBIP 265, pp. 195–208, 2016.
DOI: 10.1007/978-3-319-47093-1_17

These latter characterize a node's position in the graph. Centrality metrics have been successfully involved in terrorist networks destabilization methods. Thus, there is certainly a need for an accurate choice of centrality indices to effectively identify influential nodes in networks. The goal of this paper is not to perform a traditional social network analysis but rather to evaluate the validity of different centrality measures according to the topology of the network by conducting an empirical study on real-world terrorist data sets. Throughout this paper, we first present background about terrorist networks properties and their different topologies (Sect. 2). Then we discuss proposed destabilization approaches using centrality metrics (Sect. 3) and we review consequently the measures used in this purpose (Sect. 4). Then, we provide a matching between different terrorist networks topology and different centrality metrics (Sect. 5). To prove our theoretical analysis, we distinguish five different terrorist data sets (Sect. 5) where we apply commonly used centralities on them and compare the results (Sect. 6). This is followed by conclusion and future work section.

2   Terrorist Networks

Terrorist networks are described as amorphous, invisible, resilient, dispersed... [6]. So, it is difficult to visualize them. The problem with such networks is that it is highly covert and most of the time it is incomplete. Three main problems encounter the terrorist cells analysis [7]:

- Incompleteness: Some nodes or links may be missing in the investigated network.
- Fuzzy boundaries: The relationship between criminals is always unclear.
- Dynamic: These networks are changing continuously.

  Regarding these problems, modeling terrorist networks becomes a hard task. In fact, gathering data is challenging if the terrorists are not arrested. And even if the information exists, mapping ties between individuals is difficult. Indeed, secrecy is a prime concern in these cells. Covert networks often do not behave like normal social networks [6]. Ties between individuals are invisible. Besides, it is not possible to cluster nodes based on these ties because they are not their real connections but rather intermediaries between them and the other actors. The authors in [11] claim that these networks are separated by larger than normal degrees of distance between their participants which adds the possibility of mapping them as distributed networks. Another important property of terrorist networks is that they are purposive [11], they differ from each other by their formal properties. Thus, modeling terrorist cells becomes of great interest. In fact, the authors in [12] distinguished different models of terrorist organizations based on many factors. Structural properties of these dark cells differ according to their needs to be hidden, to get protected and to maximize their profit. Basically, there are 6 categories of terrorist networks structures. The following table summarizes these different topologies providing the correspondent shape of each category and its properties also proposing the best destabilization strategy (Table 1).

Table 1. Terrorist networks topologies, related properties and suggested disruption strategies

Topology	Shape	Properties	Disruption strategy
Corporate based network E.g. Irish Republican Army (IRA)		The network is composed of subgroups with different goals (propaganda subgroup, finance subgroup...)	Detecting the leaders of the subgroups as important nodes in the network
Politburo based network E.g. Red Army Faction (RAF)		Central committee which decides all the strategy of the network	Detecting the members of the central committee as key players in the network
Shura based network E.g. Turkish Al Qaida November 2003		members are of equal importance	Detecting the leader who has more connections
Multi-cell based network E.g. 9/11 attack data set		Cells are connected with key players	Detecting the nodes connecting the cells
Brokerage based network E.g. Ergenekon data set		The brokerage members are fully trusted by the leaders of the cells	Detecting the brokerage members as important nodes
Lonely wolf based network		The wolf plans, supplies and attacks in the hand of one terrorist	Detecting the wolf member as important node

3   Related Work

A branch of centrality metrics has been proposed to study the terrorist networks. The most used centrality indices are: degree, betweenness, closeness and eigenvector centralities [8–10]. The degree centrality is the number of connections a node holds. Betweenness of a node measures the number of shortest paths passing through this node while the closeness is its inverse. The eigenvector retrieves the node that allows the maximum of flow to pass through it. These traditional measures have been incorporated in various terrorist networks disruption strategies. Once these nodes are recognized and removed, it becomes easier to destabilize the network. The authors in [8] propose an algorithm that relies on three centrality measures: degree centrality, closeness centrality and betweenness centrality to retrieve the financial manager who is considered as the most important node in the network to be isolated. The same metrics were used in addition to the eigenvector centrality in [9,10] to deduce the hierarchy of the network and recognize then the most influential nodes. The researchers in [5] introduce a new metric "influence index" to detect influential nodes in the terrorist network. This measure relies basically on the shortest paths between nodes and the rule of influence which consists in three degree of influence. i.e. a node is influenced by other nodes that lie at three degree of separation but not by those beyond. Detecting the nodes with highest importance in the studied network has been the goal of different destabilization approaches. The works proposed in [1] address the issue of node's global importance in the network retrieved by traditional betweenness centrality. The authors aim to find the important nodes to a given node. The dependency of a node on other nodes is measured by the importance of these nodes and the trust between these nodes. So, the authors propose the reliance measure as a new metric to measure the importance and the trust and identify then the important nodes to a given node. The authors in [15] propose to use a recently developed metric to identify influential nodes namely the percolation centrality. It has been developed in the past to identify important nodes in the flow of information, spreading rumors or contagious diseases in a network. The authors apply this measure to the scenario of terrorist networks to retrieve the information spreaders.

All these works are considered as qualitative approaches and do not provide any quantitative analysis of terrorist networks. Furthermore, these approaches assess the importance of a node by focusing on the role played by this node but fails to capture any positive or negative synergy between different groups. Considering these limits, the authors in [2] propose to consider the terrorist network as a coalition and to adopt centralities proposed in game theory such as Meyrson value and Shapely value based centralities [3,4]. These latter are a weighted average quantifying a node's marginal contribution to the coalition. Hence, it becomes possible to quantitatively identify important nodes and the synergy between them. (e.g. the bomb expert, the funding terrorists).

Several approaches were proposed to defeat terrorist cells using a branch of centrality metrics. However, it still lacks a methodology or an approach that guides the choice of the correspondent centrality metric to effectively disrupt the terrorist cells. Nevertheless, the works in [12] may be considered as a first step towards this approach. The authors present a classification of terrorist networks according to their ideology and characteristics that affect their shape. Accordingly, six categories of terrorist network topologies with different characteristics have emerged. The authors also give an example of real world data set for each category. In this paper, we aim to pursue the works in [12] and propose for each category the correspondent centrality metric in the disruption strategy. We provide experiments to justify our choices.

4   Centrality Metrics

4.1   Preliminaries

We design the terrorist graph as G. G consists of a pair (N,E) where N is the set of nodes and E is the set of edges that connect different nodes.

An edge e_{ij} represents opportunities for flow between vertices i and j. A path between two nodes is the set of edges connecting those two nodes. Once this set is minimized, the path is called the shortest path. This latter may also be called the geodesic distance between given nodes. The Adjacency matrix, $A \in M_{nn}(\Re)$, of network G is defined such that each matrix element, a_{ij}, indicates if G contains an edge e_{ij} connecting vertex v_j to v_i [19].

$$a_{ij} = \begin{cases} 1 & \text{if there is an edge connecting } v_i \text{ to } v_j \\ 0 & \text{otherwise.} \end{cases} \tag{1}$$

4.2   Centrality Metrics in Terrorist Network Destabilization

As it is presented in related work section, terrorist networks destabilization rely on different centrality metrics mainly degree, betweenness, closeness and eigenvector centrality.

The degree centrality [13] is used to measure the number of connections each node holds in the network.i.e. the number of neighbors for a given node. For an oriented graph, the degree centrality is composed of indegree and outdegree. Accordingly, indegree is a count of the number of ties directed to the node and outdegree is the number of ties that the node directs to others. The number of these connections may be considered as an indicator of the importance of a node in a given network. Formally the degree centrality is:

$$CD(v) = \sum_{j \in G} \frac{(e_v j)}{n - 1} \tag{2}$$

Although this centrality is simple to compute, it is a local measure which ignores the global structure of the network.

The betweenness centrality [13] is prominent among centrality indices. In fact, it provides an insight of the intermediary important nodes in a graph. So the node's importance is proportional to the number of shortest paths which pass the node among all node pairs. Mathematically, this measure is defined as follows:

$$BC(v) = \frac{1}{(N-1)(N-2)} \times \sum_{s \neq v \neq t} \frac{\sigma(s,t)(v)}{\sigma(s,t)}. \tag{3}$$

So, it is expressed as the fraction of shortest paths between source node s and target node t that pass through a given node v: $\sigma_{s,t}$ (v), averaged over all pairs of node in a network $\sigma_{s,t}$. N is the number of nodes in the network.

Unlike the degree centrality, this metric considers the whole network. It is applicable to networks with disconnected components. It is also efficient in case of information flow. However, for some nodes which do not lie on shortest paths between any two other nodes, the betweenness centrality turns to 0 while those nodes may be important.

The closeness centrality [13] measures the average shortest path length between the node and all other nodes in the graph. Therefore the node's importance is inverse-proportional to the sum of all shortest-paths (denoted here as $dist(v,t)$) to other nodes. Formally, the closeness centrality is defined as follows:

$$Cc(v) = \sum \frac{1}{dist(v,t)} \tag{4}$$

The main limit of this metric is its inapplicability to networks with disconnected components.

The eigenvector centrality [19] uses the adjacency matrix A to retrieve the node that allows the maximum flow to pass within. Its mathematical presentation is as following where α is a parameter.

$$\alpha \times v = A \times v \tag{5}$$

This metric is suitable for studying spreading phenomena. However it may not scale well in case of networks with homogenous communities.

The group centrality [16] is the combination of all these metrics. It identifies the most central group in the network rather than nodes. This metric is useful in detecting communities or groups of nodes in a given graph.

5   Which Centrality Metric for Which Terrorist Network?

The main aim of this paper is to match each terrorist network topology with the correspondent centrality metric. Starting with the first category, the corporate based networks consist in different subgroups in the network: financial subgroup, propaganda subgroup, armed subgroup etc. These subgroups are led by important nodes which are the leaders. To destabilize this network, it is crucial to detect these leaders. The destabilization approach starts by identifying different subgroups in the network then to recognize the leaders of these groups. Therefore, traditional centrality metrics are not able to detect hidden groups of terrorists in the dark cell. So, we propose to use the group centrality to identify different groups. Once the groups are retrieved, we propose to use the degree centrality to identify the most central node in each group. So the destabilization approach here is two steps process.

The second category is the Politburo based terrorist network. This type of terrorist cells consists in one central committee which decides all the strategy of the network. Thus, it is important to retrieve this committee. We propose thereafter to use the group centrality mainly the kpset function [17] which identifies the most central group of players in a network. The destabilization approach here is a single step process. Retrieving the central committee is the target. No other processing is needed.

The third category is the shura based networks. "Shura" means "consultation"; the potential leader is the terrorist with more consultations: the node with more connections. So, the most important node is the most central node. Therefore, to identify key players in such networks, it is sufficient to use traditional centrality metrics: closeness, betweenness and degree.

The fourth category is the Multi-cell based network. Terrorist networks are formed of different cells. The key players are the nodes connecting these cells. To disrupt this kind of networks, it is crucial to retrieve the cells composing the network. We opt for the use of group centrality to identify different groups then we compute the betweenness centrality for the nodes connecting these cells. So, the disruption strategy is two step process using two centrality metrics: group centrality and betweenness centrality.

The fifth category is the brokerage based network. The important key players are the brokerage members. These latter are fully trusted by other members of the network. They are also considered as influential nodes. However, they are not the most central nodes in the network. So, traditional centrality measures are not able to detect these members since these nodes are characterized as "trusted" and "influential". It is possible, thereafter to use the newly introduced metrics "the reliance measure" and/or the "influence index". The reliance measure combines two essential aspects to detect this kind of nodes mainly "importance" and "trust". Also, the influence index measure may be helpful in revealing these nodes. So, to detect brokerage members we propose to use the reliance measure and the influence index.

The last category is the wolf based terrorist network. A principal actor "The wolf" acts secretly in the hand of one terrorist who is the important node This node is peripheral and is connected to only one node. This latter is an important node holding many connections. We are looking for the node connected to important neighbors. Consequently, we may use the eigenvector centrality to retrieve this node. Other centralities such as: degree, betweenness and closeness are not able to find it because they reveal the most central node. The eigenvector centrality is able to find the node which is not central but connected to central ones.

6   Experimental Results

We experiment on five different real world data sets (detailed next) representing five categories: corporate based networks, politburo based networks, shura based networks, multi-cell based networks and brokerage based networks. For the last category: Lonely wolf based network, we do not have any real world data set so we may not conduct any experimental analysis. For each data set, we constructed its adjacency matrix to build the graph and process our experiments on it in R [20]. Due to space limitation, we omit the data sets representations. We present in the following sections the experimental results of the five data sets.

6.1   Corporate Based Terrorist Network: IRA Case Study

The IRA (Irish Republican Army) is a network of terrorists consisting of 55 individuals [18]. We use [18] to build our adjacency matrix and visualize the network in R. This cell is formed of different subgroups: financial, propaganda. . . According to Fig. 1, there are only two important key players to be isolated which are node 28 and 37. However, the network consists of more than two subgroups. Therefore, we propose to identify different subgroups in the network then to retrieve the central nodes inside these groups. So, we start by applying group centrality to this data set.

According to the group centrality, this network consists in five different subgroups which are: $g1 = V4, V5, V6, V7, V8$, $g2 = V12, V13, V14, V15, V16, V17, V18, V19$, $g3 = V20, V22, V23, V24, V25, V26, V27$, $g4 = V28, V29, V30, V31, V32, V54, V55$ and $g5 = V37, V38, V39, V40, V41, V42, V43, V44, V45, V46, V47, V48$. Once the groups are known, we apply the degree centrality to recognize the leaders of these groups. These latter are respectively: V7, V14, V22, V28 and V37. So to effectively disrupt this network, it is necessary to isolate these nodes.

6.2   Politburo Based Terrorist Network: RAF Case Study

The RAF (Red Army Faction) is a German terrorist network composed of 29 individuals [7]. We took the data from [7] and represent it in R. The topology of this data set is based on a central committee that decides all the strategy of the network. The key players in the network to be isolated are the members

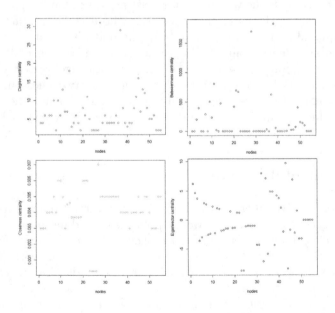

Fig. 1. IRA traditional centralities

of this central committee. This committee is close to front end members [7]. The following figure represents the corresponding values of the four traditional centrality metrics for each node.

According to Fig. 2, we may notice that important nodes with high degree centrality, have also high betweenness values and closeness ones. These nodes are most central in the network. However these nodes do not form a committee and some of them does not have any relationship with other nodes. Therefore, these metrics are not able to detect key players in this network. We propose to use the group centrality based on degree centrality. This metric identifies the most central group in a given network. Using this centrality we may identify the central committee. As we can see, the network is composed of three dense subgroups $g1 = V4, V5, V6, V7, V8, V9$, $g2 = V10, V11, V14, V15, V16$ and $g3 = V21, V22, V23, V24, V25, V26, V27$. The group of nodes that have the higher group centrality is the group $g2 = V10, V11, V14, V15, V16$ as it is indicated in Fig. 3. So, the central committee in the RAF terrorist network to be isolated is the group of nodes $V10, V11, V14, V15, V16$.

6.3   Shura Based Terrorist Network: Turkish Al Qaida, November 2003

The data set studied here represent the terrorists of the November 2003 attack in Turkey [7]. The adjacency matrix is constructed using the data in [7] to

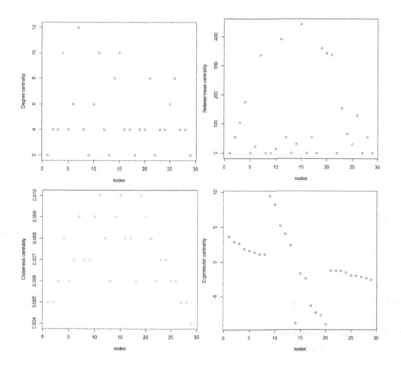

Fig. 2. Traditional centrality metrics of RAF data set

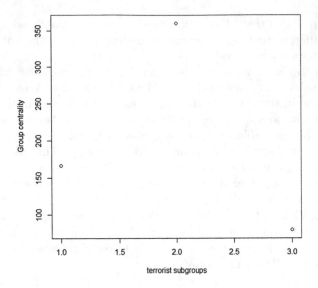

Fig. 3. Most central group in RAF

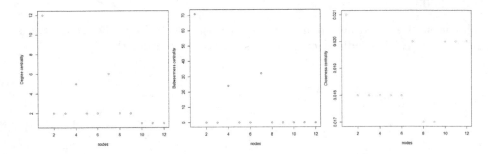

Fig. 4. Centrality metrics of Turkish Al Qaida November 2003 data set

obtain the graphic representation of the terrorist network which is composed of 12 members. The potential leader is the node with more "consultations" which is the most central node. Traditional centrality metrics in this case may retrieve the key players in this cell. So, we present in Fig. 4 the values of the degree, betweenness and closeness centrality metrics.

As it is shown in Fig. 4, the node with the highest centralities values is the node V1. To destabilize this network, it is necessary to isolate the leader which is node V1.

6.4 Multi-cell Based Terrorist Network: 9/11 Attack Case Study

This well known data set represents the 9/11 attack terrorists [2]. To obtain the terrorist network representation, we used the data in [2]. There are 19 members who participated in the attack. The topology of the network is composed of different cells. The key players are the nodes connecting these cells also characterized as intermediary nodes. In this case, the betweenness centrality may be used to retrieve these nodes after identifying the composing cells. These latter according to the group centrality are: $C1 = V1, V2, V3$, $C2 = V5, V7, V9, V11, V12$, $C3 = V13, V14, V16, V17, V18$. The intermediary nodes are: $V4, V16, V8$ and $V15$. The following figure illustrates the different values of different centralities in the network. We may notice that degree centrality and eigenvector do not retrieve the desired results. The nodes retrieved by the closeness are $V5, V7, V9$ and $V16$. However, these nodes are not the intermediary nodes. The nodes $V4$ and $V16$ are considered of high betweenness centrality. So these nodes are connecting cells and they are the key players in the network (Fig. 5).

6.5   Brokerage Based Terrorist Network: Ergenekon Network Case Study

The Ergenekon turkish terrorist organization is composed of 33 members [7]. We use data in [7] to visualize our network in R. The key players in this network are the brokerage members who are considered as influencers and fully trusted by other members. Figure 6 represents the correspondent values of traditional centrality metrics. As it is indicated in [7] the brokerage members in the Ergenekon

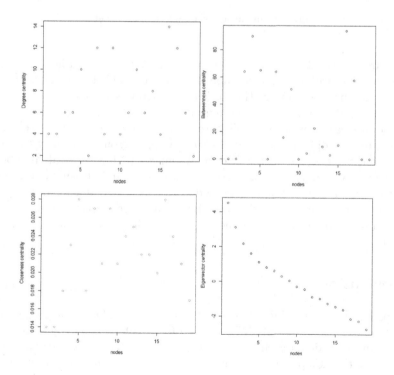

Fig. 5. Centralities of 9/11 data set

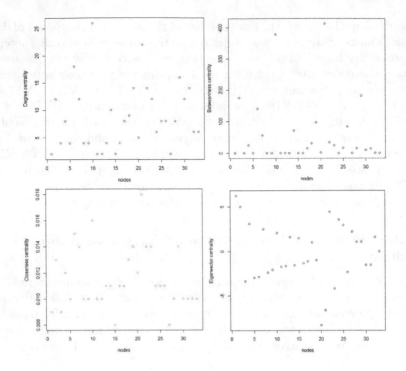

Fig. 6. Centralities of Ergenekon data set

network are nodes V2 and V30. However, as we may notice in Fig. 6 none of the four measures above identify those nodes as "important". Hence we have to opt for other measures to identify the brokerage members in this network such as the influence index and the reliance measure.

Corporate based networks, politburo and multi-cell based ones rely on an active group of people in the network. So, we apply group centrality to retrieve them. Then, we opt for degree and betweenness to find central members in these groups. A combination of degree, betweenness and closeness is necessary to identify central terrorist in Shura based networks. The definition of key players changes for the last category: the most important node is not the most central node but rather the most trusted one. So none of these metrics would reveal the key node.

7   Conclusion

In this paper, we studied different centrality metrics widely used especially in the terrorist organizations analysis. We focused on the different topologies of terrorist networks and provide for each topology the correspondent centrality metric that may identify the key players therein. This paper contributes by providing first steps towards the matching between centrality metrics and the correspondent network topology. The experiments conducted on five different data sets prove our theoretical analysis and lay the ground for further investigations.

As a future work, we aim first to measure the reliance measure and the influence index of the last category so we can confirm our theoretical results. Besides in order to complete our work, we will look to a data set of the lonely wolf category. The scope of this paper is on terrorist networks, a further analysis and experimentation on other data sets category and large scale graphs is needed as future work.

References

1. Magalingam, P., Davis, S.: Ranking the importance level of intermediaries to a criminal using a reliance measure. arXiv preprint arXiv:1506.06221 (2016)
2. Michalak, T.P., Rahwan, T., Skibski, O., Wooldridge, M.: Defeating terrorist networks with game theory. IEEE Intell. Syst. **1**, 53–61 (2015)
3. Michalak, T.P., Aadithya, K.V., Szczepanski, P.L., Ravindran, B., Jennings, N.R.: Efficient computation of the Shapley value for game-theoretic network centrality. J. Artif. Intell. Res. **46**, 607–650 (2013)
4. Skibski, O., Michalak, T.P., Rahwan, T., Wooldridge, M.: Algorithms for the Shapley and Myerson values in graph-restricted games. In: Proceedings of the 2014 International Conference on Autonomous Agents and Multi-agent Systems, pp. 197–204. International Foundation for Autonomous Agents and Multiagent Systems, May 2014
5. Xuan, D., Yu, H., Wang, J.: A novel method of centrality in terrorist network. In: Seventh International Symposium on Computational Intelligence and Design (ISCID), December 2014, vol. 2, pp. 144–149. IEEE (2014)
6. Krebs, V.E.: Mapping networks of terrorist cells. Connections **24**(3), 43–52 (2002)
7. Sparrow, M.K.: The application of network analysis to criminal intelligence: an assessment of the prospects. Soc. Netw. **13**(3), 251–274 (1991)
8. Berzinji, A., Kaati, L., Rezine, A.: Detecting key players in terrorist networks. In: 2012 European Intelligence and Security Informatics Conference (EISIC), pp. 297–302. IEEE, August 2012
9. Azad, S., Gupta, A.: A quantitative assessment on 26/11 Mumbai attack using social network analysis. J. Terrorism Res. **2**(2), 1–10 (2011)
10. Nasrullah, M., Larsen, H.L.: Structural analysis and mathematical methods for destabilizing terrorist networks. In: Proceedings of the International Conference on Advanced Data Mining Applications, pp. 1037–1048 (2006)
11. Fellman, P.V., Clemens, J.P., Wright, R., Post, J.V., Dadmun, M.: Disrupting terrorist networks: a dynamic fitness landscape approach. In: Minai, A.A., Braha, D., Bar-Yam, Y. (eds.) Conflict and Complexity, pp. 165–178. Springer, New York (2015)
12. Ozgul, F., Bowerman, C.: Characteristics of terrorists networks based on ideology and practices. In: 2014 European Network Intelligence Conference (ENIC), pp. 95–99. IEEE (2014)
13. Bonacich, P.: Factoring and weighting approaches to status scores and clique identification. J. Math. Soc. **2**(1), 113–120 (1972)
14. Karthika, S., Bose, S.: A comparative study of social networking approaches in identifying the covert nodes. Int. J. Web Serv. Comput. **2**(3), 65 (2011)

15. Hamed, I., Charrad, M.: Recognizing information spreaders in terrorist networks: 26/11 attack case study. In: Bellamine Ben Saoud, N., Adam, C., Hanachi, C. (eds.) ISCRAM-med 2015. LNBIP, vol. 233, pp. 27–38. Springer, Heidelberg (2015). doi:10.1007/978-3-319-24399-3_3
16. Everett, M.G., Borgatti, S.P.: The centrality of groups and classes. J. Math. Sociol. **23**(3), 181–201 (1999)
17. http://rpackages.ianhowson.com/cran/keyplayer/
18. http://news.psu.edu/story/264519/2013/02/18/research/international-center-study-terrorism-focuses-latest-research
19. Everton, S.F.: Network topography, key players and terrorist networks (2009)
20. https://www.r-project.org/
21. http://www.inf.fu-berlin.de/lehre/WS06/pmo/eng/audio/Chomsky.pdf

Issues in Humanitarian Crisis

Towards an Agent-Based Humanitarian Relief Inventory Management System

Maroua Kessentini[1,2(✉)], Narjès Bellamine Ben Saoud[1], and Sami Sboui[2]

[1] Univ. Manouba, ENSI, RIADI LR99ES26,
Campus Universitaire, Manouba 2010, Tunisie
maroua.kessentini@gmail.com,
narjes.bellamine@yahoo.fr
[2] SQLI Services, Technopole Manouba, Manouba, Tunisia
sbouis@yahoo.fr

Abstract. Natural disasters have reached unpredictable intensity around the world during the last two decades. Therefore, rapid response to the urgent relief in an efficient way is necessary for alleviation of disaster impact in the affected areas. Humanitarian Supply Chain Management plays a crucial role for disaster response management. Warehouse and inventory management is a key activity. Its effectiveness and efficiency are challenging issues during emergency response. In fact, by ensuring appropriate fast and well organized distribution of emergency relief supplies, damages would be mitigated and more lives saved. This paper draws first a literature review to better define humanitarian supply chain management and highlight inventory management characteristics and needs in a post-disasters context. An agent-based model and a simulator are developed in order to enable decision makers find efficient scenarios to respond effectively to urgent requests following a disaster. First simulation results are discussed.

Keywords: Humanitarian supply chain management · Inventory management · Rapid response · Urgent requests · Agent based modeling and simulation

1 Introduction

The impacts of disasters have attracted research and policy makers' attention in the recent years. In this context, disaster response focuses on the following functional areas: assessment, procurement, transportation, warehousing, and distribution [9]. Such functions encompass a range of activities, including the establishment of a rescue command center, collection of information about the disaster area, identification of appropriate sites for shelters, determination of the best evacuation routes, transportation for evacuation and delivery of relief material, installation of medical and fire-prevention and emergency construction facilities [10]. Hence, a vast range of problems arise in supply chain management during humanitarian emergency response.

In the general business field, supply chain (SC) links the point of origin of supply (suppliers) to the point of consumption (end customers). The supply chain management

© Springer International Publishing AG 2016
P. Diaz et al. (Eds.): ISCRAM-med 2016, LNBIP 265, pp. 211–225, 2016.
DOI: 10.1007/978-3-319-47093-1_18

(SCM) concept refers to the integration of all activities and processes associated with the transformations and flows of material, information, and finance from the raw material stage through the end user. Hence, the ultimate goal of any SCM is to deliver the right supplies in the right quantities to the right locations at the right time [1].

In disaster management field, the concept of SCM, also known as humanitarian supply chain (HSC), refers to the flows of goods and information between humanitarian organizations, donors (i.e. suppliers) and beneficiaries (e.g. victims) in order to minimize the impact of a crisis [3]. In fact, HSC is a complex socio-technical system that operates in a dynamically evolving context. Due to the potential disruption of information and communication systems, it is often difficult to collect and share knowledge covering all types of flows and processes about a given HSC. The complexity is introduced by the politically volatile climate, the local infrastructures damages, the multiplicity of stakeholders having various incentives, the dynamics of the emergency operations and the information uncertainty about demand, transportation network (infrastructures) and available resources [3–5].

In this context, humanitarian supply chain management (HSCM) can be defined as "The process of planning, implementing and controlling the efficient, cost-effective flow and storage of goods and materials, as well as related information, from the point of origin to the point of consumption for the purpose of alleviating the suffering of vulnerable people" [2]. HSC operations challenge is to rapidly provide relief supplies and rescue personnel to a large number of destination nodes geographically scattered over the disaster region so as to minimize human suffering and death [2]. Due to the sudden occurrence of disasters, SCM in humanitarian organizations have to evolve towards increased effectiveness and efficiency in terms of responsiveness [6].

In humanitarian operations the time benefit is more important than economic benefits. Time is essential in aiding affected people due to a large number of problems including damaged transportation infrastructure, limited communication, and coordination of multiple agents [7]. Consequently, HSCM is one of the most crucial functions of an effective disaster response that it is required to procure, store and distribute relief supplies for the assistance of beneficiaries affected by disasters [8]. In addition, inventory management plays a critical role in emergency situations, including storing and managing essential items and providing them to disaster victims [11].

The goal of this research is to propose an emergency inventory management model of response to urgent requests following a disaster. The increasing complexity of global emergency relief operations create a critical need for effective and efficient humanitarian inventory management processes. Therefore, the question discussed in this paper is how to respond rapidly and effectively during a disruptive event, specifically natural disasters, to the urgent request of customer? i.e. how to minimize the amount of unsatisfied demands over time and reduce the response time assisting disaster victims.

The paper structure is as follows. In Sect. 2, we draw a literature review of humanitarian supply chain and humanitarian inventory management, and identify the main research issues. In Sect. 3, we introduce the emergency inventory management model we developed and the related agent-based simulator we implemented. In Sect. 3.4, we present the first obtained simulation results by analyzing different combinations of scenarios. Section 4 provides conclusions and directions for further research.

2 Literature Review: Humanitarian Supply Chain Management and Inventory Management

Research in humanitarian supply chain management, particularly in the area of humanitarian inventory management, can be considered as a new area that requires the understanding and application of tools and knowledge from multiple disciplines.

While research and practice is usually applied in the context of commercial logistics, humanitarian supply chain and inventory management has recently gained attention because it is uniquely different from commercial supply chain.

Below, we first review studies that address various humanitarian supply chain management problems after the presentation of the main difference between humanitarian supply chain management and commercial supply chain management. Then we briefly review the difference between humanitarian inventory management and commercial inventory management and the relevant literature on humanitarian inventory management.

2.1 Commercial vs. Humanitarian SCM

While humanitarian supply chain is similar to commercial supply chains in the flow of supplies via a series of components, they differ in their motives and the realms at which they operate.

Table 1. Main differences between commercial and humanitarian supply chain management

Topics	Commercial supply chain management	Humanitarian supply chain management
Objective of system	Maximize profit	Save lives and help beneficiaries
Supply chain design	From supplier's supplier to customer's customer	From donors and suppliers to beneficiaries
Customer	End user = buyer	End user (beneficiaries) $\neq$ Buyer (donors)
Actors supplier	Known Supplier generally known in advance	Multiplicity in nature but scarcity in numbers Supplier and/or donor uncertain
Demand	Fairly stable Usually forecast/Known	Irregular Uncertainties
Shelf life	Some years but trends to shorten	Some weeks to some months in total
Material flow	Commercial products	Resources like vehicles, shelters, food, drugs
Information flow	Generally well-structured	High importance of the media Means of communication often reduced

(Continued)

Table 1. (*Continued*)

Topics	Commercial supply chain management	Humanitarian supply chain management
Financial flows	Bilateral and known	Unilateral and uncertain
Human flows	Limited usually	People flows Knowledge transfer
Lead time	Mostly predetermined	Approximately zero lead time
Inventory control	Safety stocks	Challenging inventory control
Delivery network	Location of warehouses and distribution centers	Ad hoc distribution facilities
Technology	Highly developed technology	Less technology is used
Performance measurement	Based on standard supply chain metric	Time to respond the disaster, percentage of demand supplied

Based on the strategic goal of humanitarian supply chains on saving lives and relieving human suffering, decisions are taken in a very short time and are often based on limited and incomplete information. Table 1 summarizes the main differences between commercial and humanitarian supply chain management. In fact, HSCs are characterized by highly responsive (effective) instead of efficient (cost effective) processes for commercial ones. Their demands are relatively unstable, uncertain and unpredictable. Donors play the role of buyers and beneficiaries of end users. A great importance is given to speed (effectiveness). The environment is highly volatile and unstable. The supply chain design is partly temporary and unknown given additional flows of personnel as well as knowledge and skills [6, 9].

2.2   Humanitarian Supply Chain Problems

Traditionally, disaster management can be divided into four phases: mitigation, preparedness, response and recovery. These phases are known collectively as the disaster operations life cycle [33]. Mitigation refers to the performance of activities that either reduce the long-term risk of a disaster or diminish its potential consequences. The preparedness stage relates to the community's ability to respond when a disaster occurs and involves all those activities performed in order to accomplish a more efficient response. Response stage refers to the deployment of vital resources and emergency procedures as guided by plans to preserve life, property, and the governing structure of the community. And finally, recovery involves actions taken in order to restitute the normal functioning of the community [33]. Considering the disaster as a temporal event, these four phases can be reduced in two stages: before phase (pre-event) and after (post-event) disaster [34].

Much research can be found in the literature about humanitarian supply chain in each phase of disaster management with different objectives and using diverse methodologies. Based on the literature, we identify the main humanitarian supply chain studied problems and the related modeling techniques: A specific problem is the *relief chain distribution design.* The design of the relief distribution systems aims to determine the number and location of the distribution centers and the amount of relief inventory to stock therein [30]. Authors in [10] develop a relief-distribution model using the multi-objective programming method for designing relief delivery systems in a real case in order to minimize the total cost and the total travel time, and maximize the minimal satisfaction during the planning period. Researchers in [30] consider facility location decisions for a humanitarian relief chain responding to quick-onset disasters and implement a model that determines the number and locations of distribution centers in a relief network and the amount of relief supplies to be stocked at each distribution center to meet the needs of people affected by the disasters.

Effective supply allocation among demand locations is vital in humanitarian supply chain. Effective supply allocation refers to develop an effective distribution plan in order to equitably allocate and deliver relief supplies from distribution centers to beneficiaries affected by disasters. [18] proposes a mixed integer programming model that determines delivery schedules for vehicles and equitably allocates resources, based on supply, vehicle capacity, and delivery time restrictions, with the objectives of minimizing transportation costs and maximizing benefits to aid recipients. [19] presents a dynamic allocation model that optimizes pre-event planning for meeting short-term demands for emergency supplies at shelter locations under uncertainty about what demands will have to be met and where those demands will occur. [28] proposes a stochastic optimization approach for the storage and distribution problem of medical supplies to be used for disaster management under a wide variety of possible disaster types and magnitudes.

Humanitarian relief operations in both the preparedness and response phases is one of the most important elements of humanitarian supply chain management. [26] gives a multi-objective robust stochastic programming approach for disaster relief logistics under uncertainty. [27] focuses on the problem of minimizing the level of casualties after a major earthquake from a multi-agent, multi-phase point of view and presents the main advantages of quantitatively captures the efficiency of coordination. Renovation of deteriorated and low quality buildings and developments, strengthening the existing transportation infrastructures, and locating/allocating emergency aid levels are three main activities involved in this problem.

2.3   Inventory Management in Emergency Situations

Inventory management is the main part of any supply chain of a firm that plays an important role in the supply chain decisions. Furthermore, inventory management, as defined by [12], refers to the accurate tracking of the flow of goods and the managing of its movement from raw materials to the ultimate consumer. The process of inventory management has to cope with many challenges given the complex environment caused by unpredictable and turbulent demand, requirements on product variety, delivery lead-time and quality of product [13].

In the case of disasters, environment becomes more and more complex while the availability of supplies becomes an extremely difficult task for inventory managers with a limited capacity of storage and distribution, poor information feedback and a multiplicity of decision-makers [14]. With these requirements, stocking of emergency supplies becomes a necessity in order to facilitate the rapid mobilization of available resources during emergency operations [5].

When competing in such complex and critical environment, emergency inventory management is an extremely difficult task for managers that has attracted the attention of several researchers and policymakers and pushed them to better deal with this problematic and to design an effective system of an emergency inventory management when a disaster occurs [14, 15].

Disasters trigger the need for relief items. The flows of such items in the disaster area are determined by humanitarian inventory management system [16].

Similarly to supply chain management, there are critical issues that differentiate the commercial and humanitarian inventory management. While the aim of humanitarian inventory management is to meet the needs of disaster survivors in a timely fashion, it is faced a high degree of uncertainty, unknown and multiple suppliers, hardly predictable demand and minimal lead times [17]. Table 2 clarifies this difference.

Table 2. Properties of commercial and humanitarian inventory management

Topics	Commercial inventory management	Humanitarian inventory management
Objective of system	Higher service level	Saving human lives
Inventory system design	Predetermined	Dynamic
Demand	Based on historical data	Based on quick assessment
Supply	Strategic inventory	Social inventory
Delivery network	Low-cost source	Nearest source
Inventory control	Scheduled arrival	Finding the responsive supplier

2.4 Humanitarian Inventory Management Problems

A sub-problem of the general humanitarian supply chain problem is efficient and *quick response humanitarian inventory management.* The aim of the humanitarian supply chain will be to support the affected communities as effectively as possible, i.e., the minimization of unsatisfied demand, the minimization of the overall cost and minimization of the lead-time.

Table 3 summarizes the literature review and give a classification of humanitarian inventory management methods we identified. [22] presents a stochastic programming model minimizing costs, to support the decision process of inventory policy which best satisfies the demand for food in shelters when hurricane winds are about to impact a town. [17] presents a stochastic humanitarian logistics inventory management approach in a two-stage relief supply chain that assumes a uniformly distributed function for the two stochastic variables (i.e. lead-time and demand) to support decision-making during the relief response phase. [11] presents a new approach for modeling logistics and inventory operations after a natural disaster using probabilistic cellular automata. [29] focuses on developing an inventory management strategy for a warehouse supporting a complex emergency relief operation and presents a stochastic inventory control model

Table 3. Humanitarian inventory management methods classifications

		Goals			Phases	
		Unsatisfied demand minimization	Overall cost minimization	Lead-time minimization	Post-disaster	Pre-disaster
Pre-positioning	Pystem dynamics modeling [22]		+	+	+	
Inventory relocation	Optimization model with a rolling horizon solution method [19]	+	+		+	
	A mixed-integer programming model with a rolling horizon solution method [21]	+	+		+	
	Optimal and a heuristic approach [23]	+	+		+	
Minimal safety stock level	Time-dependent stochastic model using the p-level efficient points algorithm [18]		+		+	+
	Case study–based approach [5]		+		+	+
Order quantities and reorder points	Stochastic inventory control model [24]		+		+	
	Inventory management models using mathematical model, heuristic model and naive model [25]	+	+	+	+	
Inventory operations	A stochastic programming model [20]		+		+	
	Probabilistic cellular automata approach [11]		+		+	
	A two-stage stochastic approach [17]			+	+	

that determines optimal order quantities and reorder points for a long-term emergency relief response. [31] addresses the problem of determining order quantities and reorder points for an inventory system operating within a warehouse responding to the complex emergency and analyses different inventory management policies using a performance measurement system, which accounted for resource, output and flexibility.

Another sub-problem of humanitarian inventory management is *inventory relocation problem*. When an overlapping of disasters occurs causing an increase in local demand, goods must be relocated to existing depots in a way which enables rapid supply to regions with new and urgent demand. This situation is known as inventory relocation. [21] study an inventory relocation problem which can occur in such overlapping disaster settings. An optimization model for such situations is developed based on penalty costs for non-satisfied demand. [23] presents a mixed-integer programming model for inventory relocation and distribution in humanitarian operations, which can be applied after the occurrence of an increase in local demand and which take into account two objectives: The minimization of unsatisfied demand and overall cost minimization. [25] develops an optimal and a heuristic approach for optimal stock relocation under uncertainty in the context of post-disaster humanitarian operations.

Pre-positioning inventory problem can be considered as one of the most important problems of humanitarian inventory management. The pre-positioning of relief supplies in countries prone to disasters improves the delivery of relief supplies during the immediate disaster response. [24] evaluates the effects of pre-positioning of inventory and investing in disaster management capabilities through system dynamics modeling during the immediate response phase of a disaster.

3   Humanitarian Relief Inventory Management Model

3.1   General Description

Once a disaster occurs, humanitarian operations are carried out in order to support the affected disaster areas and organizations are called to assess the type and amount of relief supplies. A number of *relief centers* must be erected to meet the needs of beneficiaries. These relief centers are served from a *local warehouse* within the area. During an ongoing humanitarian operation, the distribution of the relief items can be planned using the existing infrastructure and demand forecasts. Based on this information, *relief supplies* begin to be *shipped* from the local warehouse to the relief centers.

In our work, we assume that the local warehouse location, the number and location of the relief centers are known. However, we should notice that the selection of relief center locations is itself an important issue. It must be selected considering various factors, such as security and safety, transportation infrastructure, and available transportation modes.

Therefore, the supply relief chain considered in this paper consists of a local warehouse and a number of relief centers, as depicted in Fig. 1: A local warehouse, which is located in a central or capital city of the disaster-affected region, supplies relief centers which are located directly in the disaster-affected areas. At each relief center, a known and limited amount of the relevant relief item is in stock, as it is needed for the ongoing humanitarian operation. The local warehouse, however, is assumed to have unlimited inventory to serve relief centers.

Unplanned incidents can occur during an ongoing humanitarian action and cause a sudden increase of demand. The obvious reaction, when the demand increases in one of the relief centers, would be to deliver from neighboring relief centers. This intuitive behavior seems to be a good solution since delivery from the local warehouse may take longer than delivery from neighboring relief centers. Therefore, we define two modes in our model: Transshipment relations between relief centers can exist (mixed strategy: scenario A) or not (centralized strategy: scenario B) (see Fig. 1). In fact, even in scenario A, relief center can be served either from another relief center (If there is sufficient supply at this center) or from the local warehouse.

In our model, we consider two kinds of demands at the relief centers: (1) *regular demands* occurring from regular daily operations and which can be forecasted for every center and period and (2) *urgent demands* resulting from the additional sudden increases of demand for multiple types of relief items.

Moreover, the transportation times for transshipments between relief centers as well as between the local warehouse and each relief center are taken as parameters. They must be adjusted in the beginning of simulation to model different situations.

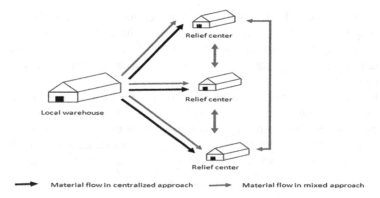

Fig. 1. Structure of the relief chain

3.2 The Emergency Inventory Management Model

Our aim is to study how to satisfy the maximum number of demands coming from the different relief centers and reduce the response time. Therefore, our model consists of two types of actors and the interaction between them as follows: (1) Local warehouse, which stores and distributes emergency relief supplies to a number of relief centers. (2) Relief centers, which consist in serving affected people. Each relief center has a limited capacity for each resource consumed by affected people. (3) Requests (or demands): a request occurs for multiple types of relief items at each relief center.

In order to keep the model simple, at this stage of development, we made the following assumptions:

- The current inventories of all relief centers are limited and known.
- Inventory of the local warehouse is assumed to be unlimited. This may be realistic if we consider restocking from other sources—i.e., buying the goods from local, global and regional suppliers as well as donations from individual people or donor organizations—is possible.
- A network of relief centers has been established, i.e. center locations are assumed to be given and their distances and average travel times are assumed to be known.
- The regular demand of relief items needed is known.
- A sudden change in demand during the ongoing humanitarian operation (demand increase) can occurs in one region, which triggers the re-planning of the allocation and distribution of the relief item.
- The planning horizon for the intervention is limited and known

3.3   The Developed Agent-Based Model and Simulator

To implement our model, we define a system based on the coordination of different kinds of software agents.

- Relief-Center-Agent: Each relief center is represented by an agent responsible of providing forecast of future needs of the center, the current stock levels and the quantity of supplies consumed by affected people every day. This agent is also responsible for updating the current stock levels after sending, reception and consuming of supplies.
- Local-Warehouse-Agent: this agent has to receive data of regular and urgent requests from each relief center in order to provide the global distribution of existing supplies. In case of urgent demand, this agent is asked to determine the nearest centers that can meet this urgent request based on data received from each relief centers (current stock level) in order to minimize delivery time.

The processing flow of this agent-based system is as follows (see Fig. 2):

Once a crisis occurs, local warehouse and relief centers are generated. After creating the relief centers, the Local-Warehouse-Agent is notified with the relief centers' information and on goods needed. After receiving requested supplies or after their consumption, relief-center- agent update current stock level. The relief-center- agent informs Local-Warehouse-Agent about items consumed and current stock level each period. The Local-Warehouse-Agent treats the requests received from relief-center-agent according to the relief centers information.

In addition, and for the mixed approach, once the Local-Warehouse-Agent receives an urgent request, this agent determines near centers of relief center asking for urgent supplies including itself. After that, this agent determines the quantity that will be delivered from each center selected based on current stock level of this center. So, the

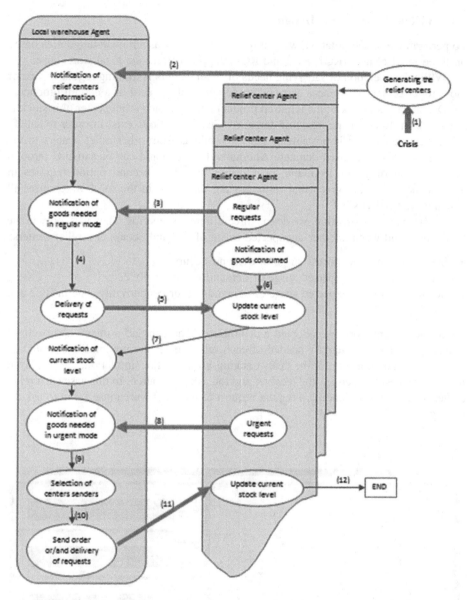

Fig. 2. Overview of the agent-based emergency inventory management simulator

Local-Warehouse-Agent sends an order to the selected centers to deliver the quantity of supply to the requested relief center.

We used the Jade platform [32] to develop the simulator. The whole simulator is under development and testing.

3.4 Virtual Experiments Design

To perform the first simulation, we configure our settings as a humanitarian area based on three relief centers (RC1, RC2 and RC3) supplied from one local warehouse.

While the operation of satisfying needs of relief centers is running regularly, one or more relief center experiences an unexpected surge of demand of a certain product.

Despite a base stock of the required product exists at each relief center, this stock is not sufficient to cover the surge of demands. Several options exist in order to satisfy this urgent demand. It is possible to deliver products from other relief centers to the relief center with increased demand. Alternatively, a demand can be satisfied through transportation of goods from the local warehouse. This second option requires in general more time but given that resources are unlimited in the local warehouse; all demands can be satisfied.

To simulate this situation, we define three different scenarios. They vary only in the way where and when another unexpected surge of demand occurs at a relief centers:

- Scenario 1: no unexpected surge of demand occurs
- Scenario 2: one unexpected surge of demand occurs in RC2
- Scenario 3: two unexpected surge of demands occur concurrently: one in RC2 and one in RC3

In the current work, we adopted a centralized approach and a mixed approach. In both approaches, the quantity needed of each relief center are randomly generated.

As it is shown in Fig. 3, the tasks tracking all along the simulation, are displayed for each request: the sender, the receiver and the asked resource. In this case each relief center agent starts by sending a regular request to the local warehouse agent to ask for supply.

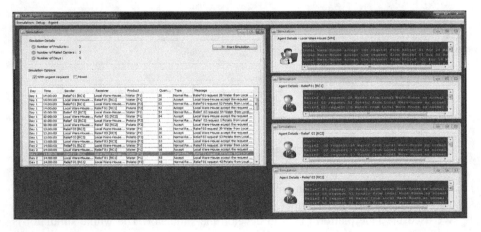

Fig. 3. Tracking of request during simulation

4 Conclusion

Motivated by the criticality and complexity of the problem of emergency inventory management in cases of disaster, we proposed a multi-agent system for improving coordination between the various relief centers in order to respond rapidly and effectively to urgent requests.

Our system aims to answer the following question: how to respond rapidly and effectively to urgent requests following a disaster. For this, we studied the emergency supply chain by comparing it with the commercial supply chain. We then focused our reflection on inventory management in both normal and emergency situations and proposed an agent based system to keep track of details of large scale disaster response operations in order to minimize loss of life and human sufferings.

As a future work, applying the proposed approach on a series of scenarios to study its capabilities to handle large scale problems is our ultimate goal. We also consider studying the impact of limited capacity of local warehouse in customer demand satisfaction.

References

1. Chandraprakaikul, W.: Humanitarian supply chain management: literature review and future research. In: The 2nd International Conference on Logistics and Transport, Queenstown, vol. 18 (2010)
2. John, L., Ramesh, A.: Humanitarian supply chain management in India: a SAP-LAP framework. J. Adv. Manag. Res. 9(2), 217–235 (2012)
3. Charles, A., Lauras, M.: An enterprise modelling approach for better optimisation modelling: application to the humanitarian relief chain coordination problem. OR Spectr. 33(3), 815–841 (2011)
4. Charles, A., Lauras, M., Tomasini, R.: Learning from previous humanitarian operations, a business process reengineering approach. In: Proceedings of the 6th International ISCRAM Conference, p. 40 (2009)
5. Ozguven, E., Ozbay, K.: Case study-based evaluation of stochastic multi commodity emergency inventory management model. Transp. Res. Rec. J. Transp. Res. Board 2283, 12–24 (2012)
6. Widera, A., Dietrich, H.A., Hellingrath, B., Becker, J.: Understanding humanitarian supply chains–developing an integrated process analysis toolkit. In: 10th International ISCRAM Conference, Germany (2013)
7. Luis, E., Dolinskaya, I.S., Smilowitz, K.R.: Disaster relief routing: integrating research and practice. Socio-Econ. Plann. Sci. 46(1), 88–97 (2012)
8. Howden, M.: How humanitarian logistics information systems can improve humanitarian supply chains: a view from the field. In: Proceedings of the 6th International ISCRAM Conference, Gothenburg, Sweden (2009)
9. Hellingrath, B., Widera, A.: Survey on major challenges in humanitarian logistics. In: Proceedings of the 8th International ISCRAM Conference–Lisbon, vol. 1 (2011)
10. Tzeng, G.H., Cheng, H.J., Huang, T.D.: Multi-objective optimal planning for designing relief delivery systems. Transp. Res. E Logistics Transp. Rev. 43(6), 673–686 (2007)

11. Mulyono, N.B., Ishida, Y.: Humanitarian logistics and inventory model based on probabilistic cellular automata. Int. J. Innovative Comput. Inf. Control 10(1), 357–372 (2014)
12. Mitra, S., Reddy, M.S., Prince, K.: Inventory control using FSN analysis–a case study on a manufacturing industry. Int. J. Innovative Sci. Eng. Technol. 4(2), 49–55 (2015)
13. Verwater-Lukszo, Z., Christina, T.S.: SystemDynamics modeling to improve complex inventory management in a batch-wise plant. In: Proceedings of the 15th European Symposium on Computer-Aided Process Engineering, Barcelona, Spain, 29 May–1 June 2005, pp. 1357–1362 (2005)
14. Alem, D., Clark, A.: Insights from two-stage stochastic programming in emergency logistics. In: Proceedings of the ISCRAM 2015 Conference, Kristiansand (2015)
15. Ozguven, E., Ozbay, K.: A secure and efficient inventory management system for disasters. Transp. Res. C Emerg. Technol. 29, 171–196 (2013)
16. Gösling, H., Geldermann, J.: Methodological tool kit for humanitarian logistics. In: Proceedings of the 11th International ISCRAM Conference, pp. 190–194 (2014)
17. Das, R., Hanaoka, S.: Relief inventory modeling with stochastic lead-time and demand. Eur. J. Oper. Res. 235(3), 616–623 (2014)
18. Balcik, B., Beamon, B.M., Smilowitz, K.: Last mile distribution in humanitarian relief. J. Intell. Transp. Syst. 12(2), 51–63 (2008)
19. Rawls, C.G., Turnquist, M.A.: Pre-positioning and dynamic delivery planning for short-term response following a natural disaster. Socio-Econ. Plann. Sci. 46(1), 46–54 (2012)
20. Ozbay, K., Ozguven, E.: Stochastic humanitarian inventory control model for disaster planning. Transp. Res. Rec. J. Transp. Res. Board 2022, 63–75 (2007)
21. Rottkemper, B., Fischer, K., Blecken, A., Danne, C.: Inventory relocation for overlapping disaster settings in humanitarian operations. OR Spectr. 33(3), 721–749 (2011)
22. Salas, L.C., Cárdenas, M.R., Zhang, M.: Inventory policies for humanitarian aid during hurricanes. Socio-Econ. Plann. Sci. 46(4), 272–280 (2012)
23. Rottkemper, B., Fischer, K., Blecken, A.: A transshipment model for distribution and inventory relocation under uncertainty in humanitarian operations. Socio-Econ. Plann. Sci. 46(1), 98–109 (2012)
24. Kunz, N., Reiner, G., Gold, S.: Investing in disaster management capabilities versus pre-positioning inventory: a new approach to disaster preparedness. Int. J. Prod. Econ. 157, 261–272 (2014)
25. Blecken, A., Danne, C., Dangelmaier, W., Rottkemper, B., Hellingrath, B.: Optimal stock relocation under uncertainty in post-disaster humanitarian operations. In: 2010 43rd Hawaii International Conference on System Sciences (HICSS), pp. 1–10. IEEE (2010)
26. Bozorgi-Amiri, A., Jabalameli, M.S., Al-e-Hashem, S.M.: A multi-objective robust stochastic programming model for disaster relief logistics under uncertainty. OR Spectr. 35(4), 905–933 (2013)
27. Edrissi, A., Poorzahedy, H., Nassiri, H., Nourinejad, M.: A multi-agent optimization formulation of earthquake disaster prevention and management. Eur. J. Oper. Res. 229(1), 261–275 (2013)
28. Mete, H.O., Zabinsky, Z.B.: Stochastic optimization of medical supply location and distribution in disaster management. Int. J. Prod. Econ. 126(1), 76–84 (2010)
29. Beamon, B.M., Kotleba, S.A.: Inventory modelling for complex emergencies in humanitarian relief operations. Int. J. Logistics Res. Appl. 9(1), 1–18 (2006)
30. Balcik, B., Beamon, B.M.: Facility location in humanitarian relief. Int. J. Logistics 11(2), 101–121 (2008)

31. Beamon, B.M., Kotleba, S.A.: Inventory management support systems for emergency humanitarian relief operations in South Sudan. Int. J. Logistics Manag. **17**(2), 187–212 (2006)
32. Jade.tilab.com, Jade Site—Java Agent DEvelopment Framework. http://jade.tilab.com/. Accessed 05 Juin 2016
33. Galindo, G., Batta, R.: Review of recent developments in OR/MS research in disaster operations management. Eur. J. Oper. Res. **230**(2), 201–211 (2013)
34. Douglas, A., Alistair, C.: Insights from two-stage stochastic programming in emergency logistics. In: Analytical Modelling and Simulation Proceedings of the ISCRAM 2015 Conference, Kristiansand, 24–27 May (2015)

Knowledge Management for the Support of Logistics During Humanitarian Assistance and Disaster Relief (HADR)

Francesca Fallucchi[1]([✉]), Massimiliano Tarquini[2],
and Ernesto William De Luca[1,3]

[1] University Guglielmo Marconi, Rome, Italy
{f.fallucchi,ew.deluca}@unimarconi.it
[2] Consorzio S3log, Rome, Italy
massimiliano.tarquini@s3log.it
[3] Georg Eckert Institute, Braunschweig, Germany
deluca@gei.de

Abstract. Knowledge Management can be essential for handling disaster information, creating knowledge bases that can cover very complex events and can vary in size and type. The challenge is to establish mechanisms for the correlation of data coming from various sources to support the Humanitarian Assistance and Disaster Relief (HADR). We propose a method for multi-source information correlation using an approach based on the sudoku principles to determine which record pairs have to be considered, for comparison. This paper presents a system which can aid in early warning and provide decision support for disaster response and recovery management through the integration of heterogeneous data sources form different organizations.

Keywords: Data linkage · Disaster information · Knowledge base system

1 Introduction

The humanitarian response in disaster relief is today strongly supported by the digital technology and is connected to the big challenge of handling a huge amount of available data. The main investors in this challenge are companies like Facebook, Google, Twitter, Yahoo, and Microsoft, who routinely deal with petabytes of data on a daily basis. Epidemic that began in 2010 in Haiti exemplifies how big data could have been used to better support agencies, organizations, and institution in the humanitarian response. An analysis on news media reports through HealthMap, Twitter postings, and government-reported cases was performed of the first 100 days of the outbreak. Data scientists found that the number of officially reported cases varied in correlation with the amount of tweets and news reports. In fact, the informal sources (Twitter and HealthMap) were able to make the trend in volume available two weeks earlier. Using informal big data provides earlier insight into the evolution of an epidemic, with important implications on the disease control measures, which is improved, can ultimately save more

© Springer International Publishing AG 2016
P. Diaz et al. (Eds.): ISCRAM-med 2016, LNBIP 265, pp. 226–233, 2016.
DOI: 10.1007/978-3-319-47093-1_19

lives. Humanitarian organizations have acquired an exemplary know-how with their numerous former experiences, but a number of stakeholders poses a problem of coordination, considering that the different actors, often widely different in nature, size and specialization, are also compartmentalized in their operating modes [2]. Helping the survivors becomes an absolute priority and requires the implementation of highly complex logistical operations. All the processes of planning, implementing and controlling the efficient, cost-effective flow and storage of goods and materials as well as related information, from the point of origin to the point of consumption for the purpose of meeting the end beneficiary requirements and alleviate the suffering of vulnerable people is called humanitarian logistics, as defined in the Humanitarian Logistics Conference (HLC) [15]. Managing past knowledge for reuse can expedite the process of disaster response and recovery management. KM in HADR is referred to the entire process of acquisition, management, and utilization of disaster information and knowledge for the support of HADR operations [18]. Humanitarian logistics in emergency relief consists in managing supplies from source to the beneficiaries efficiently and effectively. The management of logistical operations, has been, for many years, the weak link in the relief chain.

The aim of this paper is to present a knowledge management system for supporting the humanitarian logistic response to a natural or man-made disaster. We propose a framework that can be used to effectively and efficiently predict emergency related problems, whose knowledge can improve the response in future disasters. The rest of the paper is organized as in the following: after the related work (Sect. 2), we describe the HL-KMS framework (Sect. 3) with its system architecture and its functionalities. Furthermore, we report a case of study that illustrates how the knowledge base of Geo-Political and Economical map of Italy can be used for future mapping and understanding of other HADR related domains (Sect. 4). Finally, we draw conclusions and future work (Sect. 5).

2 Related Work

In order to improve the monitoring of humanitarian aid, actors will have to learn how to co-elaborate and co-manage relief chains. Then, it is necessary to better define the logistical coordination difficulties throughout the complexity of humanitarian operations [7]. Saving lives will not be possible without developing a knowledge management system, which learns from previous disasters by capturing, codifying, and transferring knowledge about logistics operations [12]. There are systems like SUMA(Supply Management Project) [3], a management tool for post-disaster relief supplies, that use a simple software on laptop computers to track and sort incoming donations and their destinations, allowing disaster managers to see what they have at disposal and send it where it is needed. Related work done on humanitarian logistics shows that research focusing on transportation optimization issues helps, especially looking at the monitoring of all relief chains. These works model the use of transport resources in disaster relief, by referring, for example, to models imported from the military context [13,16]. Although transport management remains a major concern in the literature on humanitarian logistics, it is no longer the only one.

Managing past knowledge plays an important role in the process of disaster response and recovery management. KMS is vital for disaster detection, response planning, and efficient and effective disaster response and management [11]. KMS plays an important role in gathering and disseminating the natural disaster related information. Murphy and Jennex [10] explore the use of KMS with an emergency information system, concluding that KMS should be included in more crisis response. Mistilis and Sheldon [8] report that knowledge is a powerful resource to help governments and organizations in order to plan and manage disasters and crises. Some groups have proposed and created KMSs that allow for more efficient use of data and faster response. One example that has been proposed is the Information Management System for Hurricane disasters (IMASH) [6], an information management system based on an object-oriented database design, able to provide data for response to hurricanes. Wolz and Park [17] present another example of knowledge-based system, which serves as an electronic central repository to meet the information needs of the humanitarian relief community. There are other several KMS for the support of specific disaster such as in India [9], in Hurricane Katrina [11], and in Malaysia [5]. These systems have resulted in a step change in the efficiency and effectiveness of HADR chains; such improvements have the potential to achieve similar advances in humanitarian logistics.

A first step towards the development of a broad humanitarian logistics KMS is described in [14] where a conceptual model and an associated taxonomy is given to support the development of a body of knowledge in support of the logistic response to a natural or man-made disaster. Few relief organizations or agencies, however, use situation reports for relief planning or post-disaster studies because they are not well structured for the reuse and analysis. In these cases a huge human effort and long time are needed to locate and process those relevant documents.

A system able to acquire and link heterogeneous natural or man-made disaster related information coming from different sources could positively help the humanitarian logistic organization response.

3   Knowledge Management for Big Data HADR

With the advent of big data the humanitarian field has been changed. In order to use big data in humanitarian logistic organization response, there are multiple steps in the process that must be undertaken before being able to make decisions based on the information. Each company owns one or more information sources built according to specific requirements, however this does not allow to have an overview of the data. This problem become even worse if there is an integration plan of these data with external sources, such as external companies' data sources or open data. The purpose of our approach is to identify the correct correlations between the data contained in the database. Assuming that sources are able to provide their information in a table, we need algorithms that is able to join the lines of the various tables of sources, taking count of errors and inconsistencies that may occur. The classical approach is a process of record pairing that select the only pairs belonging to the same logical object. The search in not cross-linked data is through two-dimensional entities. The relevant data are recognized with natural language processing. Different questions have to be addressed like: are two logical objects the same entity? Which are the relevant relationships between two entities? It will thus be necessary to create algorithms capable to perform the linkage record operation between the data of the various possible correlated sources. It should be noted that, being in a multi source environment, the problem doesn't deal only with the comparison of two tables, but with the comparison of n tables from m different sources. Moreover, sources may also detected in different moments and then it's necessary to manage the execution of the transaction between the current state of knowledge base and the new source. To realize a diachronic multi source RL we propose to correlate only more certain candidates records of each source produced by sudoku method heuristics. The innovation of this reconciliation is also for the return entity and the associated knowledge. There is better accuracy of research. Furthermore there are more reliable results because the knowledge base is more rich and multidimensional.

Our proposal is to develop a software capable of collecting, harmonizing, reconciling data coming from heterogeneous sources. Produced data can, be integrated with external business intelligence systems or used to produce reports and synoptics to monitor, in real time, the trend of the monitored phenomenon. In our method, we first aggregate certain records and store aggregated data into the KMS, than we use aggregated data into the KMS to aggregate a smaller number of certain records. We propose a Humanitarian Logistics Knowledge Management System (HL-KMS) able to acquire information coming from different sources. Our framework performs linkage operation between heterogeneous data from different information sources using a sudoku approach and performs data analysis generating new knowledge. In this way we guarantee validity of the information content by keeping a constant trade-off between data quality and the need of human help.

Figure 1 presents the HL-KMS framework and the related 5 modules. Each of these modules populate the Knowledge Base. The framework provides a layered architecture for data management. The different modules can operate sequentially or independently one from each other. Each module can have one or more components. The first phase of the process consists in the acquisition of the data to solve, given heterogeneity problems, misalignment problems and inconsistency problems all due to the multiplicity of data sources (Data Preparation module). Once the sources have been suitably normalized, it is possible to understand if two observations refer to the same entity by proceeding with an operation of linkage between certain candidate records with the sudoku heuristic (RL-Sudoku module). To discovery new knowledge, the reasoner module browses the relationship between the cross-linked data (Reasoner Relationship module). The search engine indexes the cross-linked data to allow the later research (Knowledge Base Engine module). Validity of the information content is guaranteed by keeping a constant trade-off between data quality and the need for human help (Data

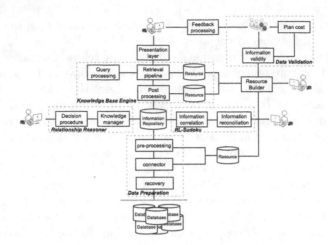

Fig. 1. HL-KMS framework Functional Architecture

Validation module). Quality control is a process governed by predictable costs, in accord to [1]. The HL-KMS framework has a series of dashboards that provide analysis of the data for decision support.

4   A Case Study: Mapping of Geo-political and Infrastructural Situation in Italy

In this section, we explain how we incorporated and collected Big Data into a HADR framework. We describe a real use case, which has been started in 2007. The main goal of the project was to create a Geo-Political and Economical map of Italy, using Big Data as a knowledge base, for future mapping and understanding of other HADR related knowledge domains. Approaching the problem with a software platform would be restrictive because of multiple related issues (known or unknown). In the following, some examples of questions having impact on logistics are reported.

– Where are the impacted populations?
– What does the effected population need?
– Which are the missing gaps to be addressed?

To answer these questions we decided to use a preventive approach that consists in creating a knowledge base capable of providing an information substrate to be used when necessary. Such knowledge base can be used to extract HADR relevant information and decision support. The generated knowledge can be used also to implement strategies to approach a real scenario in terms of supporting decision and consequent enhancement of the knowledge base (knowledge can be used to generate knowledge). The following table presents a list of data sources that have been used respectively in Public Administration Open Data, in Italian Companies Data, and in other relevant big data data-sources (see Table 1). Sources in

Table 1. Public Administration Open Data, Italian Companies Data, and other relevant big data data-sources

—Public Administration Open Data—		
Name	Type	Contents
IPA	Structured	Index of public administration covering PA, Public Security, Defense
Ancitel/Ancitada	Structured	Containing data about municipalities in terms of resident population, extension of the territory
LineAmica	Structured	Index of public administration covering PA, Public Security, Defense
MinSanita	Structured	Covering health
MISE	Structured	Index of communication and internet service providers
MIUR	Structured	Covering education
—Italian Companies Data—		
Name	Type	Contents
Guidamonaci	Unstructured	Italian Companies grouped by industry sector
EPO (European Patent Office)	REST services	Information about filed patents per company and market product classification
—Other relevant big data data-sources—		
Name	Type	Contents
Google	Unstructured	An entry point to navigate the internet for specific contents
World Wide Web	Unstructured	Information space where web resources are identified by URLs
Open Street Map	Structured	Open Geo Data
ICANN	Text-Unstructured	Index of ISP, domains, ip owners

the table have been linked using our sudoku approach. They have been used to create and, then, populate the Geo-Political and Economical Italian knowledge base. This knowledge base can be positively used to provide decision support for disaster response and recovery management.

5   Conclusion and Future Work

In this paper we presented our framework used to generate a KMS. We created a Geo-Political and Economical map of Italy as a knowledge base for future mapping and understanding of other HADR related domains. We described how we used our framework for collecting and integrating information resources from different public and private organizations, in order to support decision makers. We also discussed the provision of data analysis for a wide range of HADR scenarios. We will work on integrate our system with our ontology-driven system that automates the processes of data collection, knowledge extraction, and representation from the web [4] to reconcile disaster information with web sources and to improve our knowledge base.

References

1. Bianchi, M., Draoli, M., Fallucchi, F., Ligi, A.: Service level agreement constraints into processes for document classification. In: Proceedings of the 16th ICEIS 2014, pp. 545–550 (2014)
2. Chandes, J., Pache, G.: La coordination des chaines logistiques multi-acteurs dans un context humanitaire: quels cadres conceptuels pour améliorer l'action? Logistique Manag. **14**(1), 33–42 (2006)
3. de Goyet, C.V., Acosta, E., Sabbat, P., Pluut, E.: Supply management project, a management tool for post-disaster relief supplies. World Health Stat. Q. **49**, 189–194 (1996)
4. Fallucchi, F., Alfonsi, E., Ligi, A., Tarquini, M.:. Ontology-driven public administration web hosting monitoring system. In: Proceedings OTM - Workshops OnToContent 2014, pp. 618–625 (2014)
5. Hassan, N.A., Hatiyusuh, N., Rasha, K.: The implementation of knowledge management system (kms) for the support of humanitarian assistance/disaster relief (ha/dr) in malaysia. Int. J. Hum. Soc. Sci. **1**(4), 89–112 (2011)
6. Iakovou, E., Douligeris, C.: An information management system for the emergency management of hurricane disasters. Int. J. Risk Assess. Manag. **2**(3–4), 243–262 (2001)
7. Chandes, J., Pache, G.: Strategizing humanitarian logistics: the challenge of collective action (2010)
8. Mistilis, N., Sheldon, P.: Knowledge management for tourism crises and disasters. Tourism Rev. Int. **10**(1–2), 39–46 (2006)
9. Sujit, M., Biswajit, P., Hermang, K., Rajeev, I.: Knowledge management in disaster risk reduction. The Indian approach. Ministry of Home Affairs, National Disaster Management Division, Government of India (2005)
10. Murphy, T., Jennex, M.E.: Knowledge management, emergency response, and hurricane katrina. Int. J. Intell. Control Syst. **11**(4), 199–208 (2006)
11. Otim, S.: A case-based knowledge management system for disaster management: fundamental concepts. In: Proceedings of the 3rd International ISCRAM Conference, Newark, NJ (USA), pp. 598–604 (2006)
12. Rolando, T., van Wassenhove, L.N.: Humanitarian Logistics (Vol. INSEAD Business Press). Palgrave Macmillan, Basingstoke (2009)
13. Pettit, S.J., Beresford, A.K.C.: Emergency relief logistics: an evaluation of military, non-military and composite response models. Int. J. Logistics Res. Appl. **8**(4), 313–331 (2005)
14. Tatham, P., Spens, K.: Towards a humanitarian logistics knowledge management system. Disaster Prev. Manag. Int. J. **20**(1), 6–26 (2011)
15. Thomas, A., Mizushima, M.: Logistics training: necessity or luxury. Forced Migr. Rev. **22**(22), 60–61 (2005)

16. Weeks, M.R.: Organizing for disaster: lessons from the military. Bus. Horiz. **50**(6), 479–489 (2007)
17. Wolz, C., Park, N.-H.: Evaluation of reliefweb. In Office for the Coordination of Humanitarian Affairs, UN, Forum One Communications (2006)
18. Zhang, D., Zhou, L., Nunamaker, J.F.: A knowledge management framework for the support of decision making in humanitarian assistance/disaster relief. Knowl. Inf. Syst. **4**(3), 370–385 (2002)

Sentiment Analysis of Media in German on the Refugee Crisis in Europe

Gerhard Backfried$^{(\boxtimes)}$ and Gayane Shalunts

SAIL LABS Technology GmbH, Vienna, Austria
{gerhard.backfried,gayane.shalunts}@sail-labs.com

Abstract. Since the summer of 2015, the refugee crisis in Europe has grown to be one of the biggest challenges Europe has faced since WW2. The development of this humanitarian crisis are the topic of discussions throughout Europe and covered by media on a daily basis. Germany in particular has been the focus of migration. Over time, in Germany and the neighboring German speaking countries a shift could be observed, from the initial hospitable *Willkommenskultur* (welcome culture), to more reserved and skeptical points of view. These factors - Germany as the prime-destination for migrants, as well as a shift in public perception and media coverage - are the motivation for our analysis. The current article investigates the coverage of this crisis on traditional and social media, employing sentiment analysis to detect tendencies and relates these to real-world events. To this end, sentiment analysis was applied to textual documents of a data-set collected from relevant and highly circulated German, Austrian and Swiss traditional media sources and from social media in the course of six months from October 2015 to March of 2016.

Keywords: Sentiment analysis · Media analysis · Refugee crisis

1 Introduction

Sentiment Analysis (SA) tackles the problem of determining the objectivity or polarity of the input. The main parameters defining the scope of an SA method are the target language, domain and media type (traditional or social media). The most common application is the monitoring of public opinions in marketing (product reviews) and politics (election campaigns). Whereas the research field is active, most publications are limited to the domains of movie and product reviews in English. SA-approaches can be divided into two broad categories: machine learning and lexicon-based ones. Machine learning methods are implemented as supervised binary (positive/negative) classification approaches, in which classifiers are trained on labeled data [1,2]. The dependency on a labeled dataset is considered a major drawback, as labeling is usually costly and impossible in some cases. In contrast, lexicon-based methods [3] use a predefined set of patterns (*sentiment dictionary* or *lexicon*) associating each entry with a specific sentiment and score and do not require any labeled training data. Here the challenge lies in designing an appropriate lexicon for the target domain.

© Springer International Publishing AG 2016
P. Diaz et al. (Eds.): ISCRAM-med 2016, LNBIP 265, pp. 234–241, 2016.
DOI: 10.1007/978-3-319-47093-1_20

A comparison of eight state-of-the-art SA methods (SentiWordNet [4], SASA [5], PANAS-t [6], Emoticons, SentiStrength [7], LIWC [8], SenticNet [9] and Happiness Index [10]) is performed in [1]. All experiments are carried out using two English datasets of Online Social Networks messages. The authors report that the examined methods have different levels of applicability on real-world events and vary widely in their agreement on the predicted polarity. The authors in [11] also limit their work to English, but target the domain of news. SA is applied in the context of the refugee crisis to tweets in English by [12]. In general, the number of SA approaches for languages other than English is limited. SentimentWS [13,14] analyze textual data in German. In the present paper, the state-of-the-art SA tool SentiSAIL [15] is employed as it supports the processing of content in German and has been adapted to the domain of news articles, specifically to news on disasters and crises [16].

The analysis of sources in German is motivated by the fact that Germany and Austria are affected by the refugee crises to a great extent. Swiss sources in German were also included due to their proximity, even though the situation in Switzerland is different. The period of time covered by this paper corresponds to an important period, when the initial, enthusiastic welcome-culture was slowly fading and being replaced by more concerned opinions as to whether the affected countries would be able to cope with the massive influx of refugees. The sources covered reflect traditional and social media and include the leading news outlets of the three countries, as well as a variety of accounts from Twitter and Facebook (only publicly available information was processed!).

The current article makes the following contributions: (i) presents an automatically compiled corpus of texts from traditional and social media in German, covering the refugee crisis over a period of six months from October 2015 to March 2016, (ii) investigates the temporal development of sentiment across the different sources and types of media, (iii) identifies the most prominent sources and differences in their behavior across the period. The remainder of the paper is organized as follows: Sect. 2 clarifies the methodology of SentiSAIL. Section 3 presents the corpora, empirical setup and findings. Section 4 concludes the work and proposes alleys for further research.

2   SentiSAIL Lexicon-Based Approach

SentiSAIL is a multilingual SA tool addressing the domain of general news and particularly the coverage of disasters/crises [15,17]. It is based on one of the state-of-the-art SA methods, SentiStrength [7] and integrated into the SAIL LABS Media Mining System (MMS) for Open Source Intelligence (OSINT) [18]. SentiSAIL addresses content from traditional and social media in a variety of languages (English, German, Russian, Spanish, French and Arabic). Performance of SentiSAIL on a trilingual traditional media corpus is reported in [15]. SentiSAIL was also used to analyze social media data in German concerning the European floods 2013 [17]. Like [3], it employs a lexicon-based approach, using lexicons of words associated with scores of positive or negative orientation.

Features such as stemming, boosting (intensification or weakening), negation as well as the scoring of phrases and idioms aim to model the structure and semantics of the language. Whereas SentiStrength is optimized for and evaluated on social media content, SentiSAIL targets both social and traditional media data. Social media features are parameterized and may be disabled during traditional media processing. SentiStrength and SentiSAIL features are compared in [15] on a proprietary traditional media corpus, reporting SentiSAIL's performance improvement to be moderate for English and considerable for German and Russian. SentiSAIL, like [19], solves a dual classification task by assigning a text into one of the following 4 classes: *positive, negative, mixed* (both positive and negative) or *neutral* (neither positive, nor negative). The dual classification scheme is motivated by the ability of humans to experience positive and negative emotions simultaneously [20]. The classification of input text is performed in a 3-step process as outlined in [15].

3   Experimental Setup and Results

The corpus of documents in German covering the humanitarian crisis of refugees in Europe was compiled using the SAIL LABS MMS, a system for the collection and processing of data from open sources [18]. It spans documents from traditional media (Web-Feeds and -pages) and from social media (Twitter, Facebook) covering the period from October 2015 to March 2016. Documents from traditional media comprise 48733 articles from 68 of the most circulated traditional media sources in Germany, Austria and Switzerland. The social media corpus contains 16593 tweets, posts and comments from Twitter and Facebook from a total of 5996 accounts. All documents were selected by using keywords based on the German word *Flüchtling* (refugee). The same words were subsequently excluded from SA to avoid negative bias.

Figures 1 and 2 present a break-down of the percentages of documents of three sentiment classes for traditional and social media. All texts pertaining to the *mixed* class are considered as half-*positive* and half-*negative* for all evaluations and visualizations. They clearly display the higher percentage of sentiment-laden content on social media, where the neutral class only accounts for 21 % compared to 67 % on the traditional media. Figure 3 displays the percentage of positive, negative and neutral articles compared to the overall volume of traditional media articles per day. Over time, a slight upward trend can be observed for both, the negative and positive classes, with a more pronounced rise of negative documents possibly indicating more polarized reporting. The percentage of neutral documents decreases accordingly. Figure 4 is the equivalent chart of Fig. 3 for social media. A slight rise in negative posts can be observed over time, while positive posts decline and neutral ones stay on approximately the same level. The percentages of positive and negative posts are both constantly higher than on traditional media, confirming that sentiment is generally expressed more actively on social media (a *comments* section of traditional news typically behaves like social media in this respect). Overall, the dominating temporal sentiment in traditional

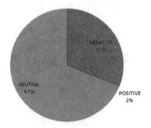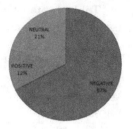

Fig. 1. Sentiment distribution in traditional media

Fig. 2. Sentiment distribution in social media

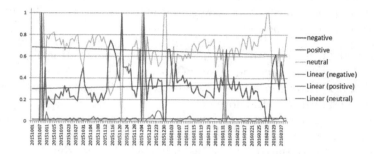

Fig. 3. Relative sentiment of traditional media

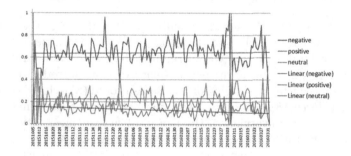

Fig. 4. Relative sentiment social media

media is *neutral* whereas social media are dominated by *negative* sentiment. This trend persists throughout the observed period and may be explained by the tendency of traditional media to provide rather unbiased coverage, whereas content on social media tends to be sentiment-laden. This tendency is in line with the findings of [21], who report on social media reactions to news on traditional media.

Table 1. Statistics for top-5 active sources per country

	Germany	Austria	Switzerland
Number of articles top-5 sources	13280	7737	3966
Avg ratio negative/positive	120.08	24.31	58.29
Avg % neutral	65 %	69 %	70 %
Avg % negative	34 %	30 %	29 %
Avg % positive	1 %	2 %	1 %

It is difficult to precisely relate all positive and negative peaks in sentiment for traditional and social media to real-world events; however, the following events may be related to those peaks[1].

- October 29 2015: (negative) Pegida[2] demonstrations attacking Germany politicians Angela Merkel and Sigmar Gabriel.
- November 21 2015: (negative) cancelation of the soccer-match between Germany and France in Hannover
- December 15 2015: (negative) left-extremist demonstrations and clashes between demonstrators and police in Leipzig
- January 1 2016: (negative) sexual assaults by migrants during New Year's celebrations in Cologne
- February 7 2016: (negative) Pegida Aktionstag (day of action)
- March 22 2016: (negative) terror attacks at Brussels Airport.

Of the above events, the sexual assaults committed during the New Year's celebrations in Cologne likely had the greatest impact on media coverage and also resulted in legal action by the German state. However, several other key events which happened during the period - e.g. Austria's introduction of upper-limits (Feb 19), the effective closing of the Balkan route (March 10) or a summit with Turkey (March 18) - do not seem to have left direct traces on sentiment.

Table 1 displays an overview of the five most active (most articles) sources per country[3]. The ratio of negative to positive articles is most pronounced for Germany with Swiss and Austrian newspapers exhibiting a much lower ratio. The percentage of neutral articles is similar for all three countries, indicating that objectiveness is approximately the same for the most active sources. The percentage of positive articles is approximately the same for the three countries;

---

[1] Information about these events has been taken from http://zeitstrahl-flüchtlingskrise.org, providing excellent coverage and history of events concerning the refugee crisis, accessed on 2016/06/08.

[2] Pegida: Patriotische Europäer gegen Islamisierung des Abendlandes (Patriotic Europeans Against the Islamisation of the West), www.pegida.de.

[3] Germany: Passauer Neue Presse, Frankfurter Allgemeine, Focus, Welt, Spiegel; Austria: Der Standard, Kleine Zeitung, Salzburger Nachrichten, Die Presse, Wiener Zeitung; Switzerland: Neue Zürcher Zeitung, Aargauer Zeitung, Tagesanzeiger, Basler Zeitung, 20 Minuten.

the percentage of negative articles slightly higher for Germany. Passau, at the border of Germany and Austria became a hot-spot for migrants crossing into Germany, which may explain the unusually high number of articles produced by the *Passauer Neue Presse*. Based in the Austrian province bordering Germany, the *Oberösterreiche Nachrichten* is the Austrian paper with the highest percentage of positive articles. The *General-Anzeiger Bonn* and 20 *Minuten* are the most positive papers for Germany and Switzerland respectively. The three papers with the highest circulation - *Bild* (Germany), *Kronenzeitung* (Austria) and *Tagesanzeiger* (Switzerland) - dominate news distribution and are known to have a large impact on public opinion. Bild and Kronenzeitung exhibit a slightly more positive tendency than the top-5 most active papers in the respective countries, whereas *Tagesanzeiger* is slightly more negative than the average Swiss papers.

4   Conclusion and Future Work

The paper presented the results of applying SA to a corpus of textual data covering the European refugee crisis during the period of October 2015 to March 2016. The distribution of sentiment in traditional media was substantially different from that of social media, with more neutral content being published in traditional media. Both types of media show a tendency for negative content to increase over time. On social media, a decline of positive posts could be observed. These changes may be related to the general shift of attitudes towards refugees over the observed period. The percentages of positive, negative and neutral sentiment for the five most active news sources in Germany, Austria and Switzerland are similar, with German sources exhibiting slightly more negative articles. Several real-world events could be connected to the local maxima in sentiment values. Other notable events were not directly reflected in the sentiment of articles and posts. Future work will include the analysis of actors and voices on social media to gain further insights on how these are linked to traditional media and on differences detected between actors from the different countries.

References

1. Gonçalves, P., Araújo, M., Benevenuto, F., Cha, M.: Comparing and combining sentiment analysis methods. In: Proceedings of the 1st ACM Conference on Online Social Networks (COSN 2013), Boston, USA, pp. 27–38. ACM (2013)
2. Pang, B., Lee, L., Vaithyanathan, S.: Thumbs up? Sentiment classification using machine learning techniques. In: Proceedings of the ACL Conference on Empirical Methods in Natural Language Processing (EMNLP 2002), pp. 79–86, Philadelphia, PA, USA (2002)
3. Taboada, M., Brooke, J., Tofiloski, M., Voll, K., Stede, M.: Lexicon-based methods for sentiment analysis. Comput. Linguist. **37**(2), 267–307 (2011)

4. Esuli, A., Sebastiani, F.: SENTIWORDNET: a publicly available lexical resource for opinion mining. In: Proceedings of the 5th Conference on Language Resources and Evaluation (LREC 06), pp. 417–422 (2006)
5. Wang, H., Can, D., Kazemzadeh, A., Bar, F., Narayanan, S.: A system for real-time twitter sentiment analysis of 2012 U.S. presidential election cycle. In: ACL (System Demonstrations). pp. 115–120 (2012)
6. Gonçalves, P., Benevenuto, F., Cha, M.: PANAS-t: A Pychometric Scale for Measuring Sentiments on Twitter. CoRR abs/1308.1857 (2013)
7. Thelwall, M., Buckley, K., Paltoglou, G., Cai, D., Kappas, A.: Sentiment strength detection in short informal text. J. Am. Soc. Inf. Sci. Technol. **61**(12), 2544–2558 (2010)
8. Tausczik, Y.R., Pennebaker, J.W.: The psychological meaning of words: LIWC and computerized text analysis methods. J. Lang. Soc. Psychol. **29**(1), 25–54 (2010)
9. Cambria, E., Speer, R., Havasi, C., Hussain, A.: SenticNet: a publicly available semantic resource for opinion mining. In: AAAI Fall Symposium: Commonsense Knowledge, pp. 14–18 (2010)
10. Dodds, P.S., Danforth, C.M.: Measuring the happiness of large-scale written expression: songs, blogs, and presidents. J. Happiness Stud. **11**(4), 441–456 (2009)
11. Balahur, A., Steinberger, R., Kabadjov, M., Zavarella, V., van der Goot, E., Halkia, M., Pouliquen, B., Belyaeva, J.: Sentiment analysis in the news. In: Proceedings of the 7th International Conference on Language Resources and Evaluation (LREC 2010), Valletta, Malta, ELRA (2010)
12. Coletto, M., Esuli, A., Lucchese, C., Muntean, C.I., Nardini, F.M., Perego, R., Renso, C.: Sentiment-enhanced multidimensional analysis of online social networks: perception of the mediterranean refugees crisis. In: Workshop on Social Network Analysis Surveillance Technologies (SNAST 16), San Francisco, USA (2016)
13. Remus, R., Quasthoff, U., Heyer, G.: SentiWS - a German-language resource for sentiment analysis. In: Proceedings of the 7th International Conference on Language Resources and Evaluation (LREC), Valletta, Malta, pp. 1168–1171 (2010)
14. Momtazi, S.: Fine-grained German sentiment analysis on social media. In: Proceedings of the 8th International Conference on Language Resources and Evaluation (LREC 2012), Istanbul, Turkey, ELRA, pp. 1215–1220 (2012)
15. Shalunts, G., Backfried, G.: SentiSAIL: sentiment analysis in English, German and Russian. In: Perner, P. (ed.) MLDM 2015. LNCS (LNAI), vol. 9166, pp. 87–97. Springer, Heidelberg (2015). doi:10.1007/978-3-319-21024-7_6
16. Backfried, G., Göllner, J., Quirchmayr, G., Rainer, K., Kienast, G., Thallinger, G., Schmidt, C., Peer, A.: Integration of Media sources for situation analysis in the different phases of disaster management: the QuOIMA project. In: Proceedings of European Intelligence and Security Informatics Conference (EISIC 2013), Uppsala, Sweden, pp. 143–146 (2013)
17. Shalunts, G., Backfried, G., Prinz, K.: Sentiment analysis of German social media data for natural disasters. In: Proceedings of the 11th International Conference on Information Systems for Crisis Response and Management (ISCRAM), University Park, Pennsylvania, USA, pp. 752–756 (2014)
18. Backfried, G., Schmidt, C., Pfeiffer, M., Quirchmayr, G., Glanzer, M., Rainer, K.: Open source intelligence in disaster management. In: Proceedings of the European Intelligence and Security Informatics Conference (EISIC), pp. 254–258, Odense, Denmark. IEEE (2012)
19. Wilson, T., Wiebe, J., Hoffmann, P.: Recognizing contextual polarity: an exploration of features for phrase-level sentiment analysis. Comput. Linguist. **35**(8), 399–433 (2009)

20. Norman, G.J., Norris, C.J., Gollan, J., Ito, T.A., Hawkley, L.C., Larsen, J.T., Cacioppo, J.T., Berntson, G.G.: Current emotion research in psychophysiology: the neurobiology of evaluative bivalence. Emot. Rev. **3**(3), 349–359 (2011)
21. Tan, C., Friggeri, A., Adamic, L.A.: Lost in propagation? Unfolding news cycles from the source. In: Proceedings of the 10th International AAAI Conference Web and Social Media (ICWSM 2016), Cologne, Germany (2016)

Author Index

Printed in the United States
By Bookmasters